Feminism, Sexuality, and Politics

Feminism | Sexuality

and Politics

ESSAYS BY ESTELLE B. FREEDMAN

The University of North Carolina Press | Chapel Hill

Manufactured in the United States of America

Designed by April Leidig-Higgins

Set in Minion by Copperline Book Services, Inc.

The paper in this book meets the guide-lines for perma-
nence and durability of the Committee on Production
Guidelines for Book Longevity of the Council on Library
Resources.

This volume was published with the generous assistance
of the Greensboro Women's Fund of the University of
North Carolina Press.

Founding Contributors: Linda Arnold Carlisle, Sally
Schindel Cone, Anne Faircloth, Bonnie McElveen Hunter,
Linda Bullard Jennings, Janice J. Kerley (in honor of
Margaret Supplee Smith), Nancy Rouzer May, and Betty
Hughes Nichols.

Library of Congress Cataloging-in-Publication Data
Freedman, Estelle B., 1947 –
Feminism, sexuality, and politics: essays /
   by Estelle B. Freedman.
p. cm — (Gender and American culture)
Includes bibliographical references and index.
ISBN-13: 978-0-8078-3031-4 (cloth: alk. paper)
ISBN-10: 0-8078-3031-3 (cloth: alk. paper)
ISBN-13: 978-0-8078-5694-9 (pbk.: alk. paper)
ISBN-10: 0-8078-5694-0 (pbk.: alk. paper)
1. Feminism — United States — History.   2. Women's
studies — United States.   3. Homosexuality — United
States — History.   4. Sex — Political aspects — United
States.   I. Title.   II. Gender & American culture.
HQ1419.F74 2006
306.7082 — dc22   2005034982

cloth   10 09 08 07 06   5 4 3 2 1
paper   10 09 08 07 06   5 4 3 2 1

For Susan

OTHER BOOKS BY ESTELLE B. FREEDMAN

No Turning Back: The History of Feminism and the Future of Women (2002)

Maternal Justice: Miriam Van Waters and the Female Reform Tradition (1996)

Intimate Matters: A History of Sexuality in America (with John D'Emilio) (1988)

The Lesbian Issue: Essays from Signs (coedited) (1985)

Their Sisters' Keepers: Women's Prison Reform in America, 1830–1930 (1981)

Victorian Women: A Documentary Account of Women's Lives in Nineteenth-Century England, France, and the United States (coedited) (1981)

Contents

Part Two | Sexual Boundaries

Preface

FOR THE PAST thirty-five years, I have participated in a movement to create a usable history of women, one that challenges conventional versions of the past and also speaks to the world around us. The essays in this book document this larger historical enterprise and explore connections between the intellectual task and the political practice of feminism. Compiling this volume has given me new perspectives on the historical questions I have explored, the historical contexts for them, and the personal paths that brought me to both feminism and the study of women's history.

A decade ago, when someone first suggested that I publish my major articles, the project seemed premature to me, but the idea took root. When I later mentioned it to Kate Torrey at the University of North Carolina Press, she and Linda Kerber convinced me to pursue it. I am deeply grateful to both of them for helping me shape this volume. In addition to eight reprinted articles, I have included three new essays: a personal introduction; an overview of my book on feminism, *No Turning Back* (chapter 5); and a revised version of earlier articles about historical contributions to legal cases (chapter 10). Although the reprinted articles have not been substantially revised, I have made minor corrections and deleted some repetitive passages. For this collection, I have added headnotes to provide context for each essay.

In addition to the colleagues and friends I acknowledge in the reprinted articles, I want to thank those who responded to drafts of the original essays. Barbara Allen Babcock, Ricki Boden, Nancy Cott, John D'Emilio, Linda Gordon, Linda Kerber, Susan Krieger, Ilene Levitt, Sue Lynn, Elaine Tyler May, Joanne Meyerowitz, James Mohr, Peggy Pascoe, Renee Romano, Esther Rothblum, and Nancy Stoller each improved the quality of my thinking and writing, as did the extremely thorough and helpful anonymous reviewers for the University of North Carolina Press. Paula Wald provided expert copyediting. I am also thankful to Mary Rothschild for the oral history she conducted about my career and to Kathryn Kish Sklar, who made a digital transcript of that interview available to me. The graduate students I have advised have taught me much of what I know about women's history; one of them, Andrea Davies Henderson, furnished outstanding editorial assistance as I prepared this book. The fellows and staff at the Stanford Humanities

Center during the 2004–5 academic year created an ideal setting for completing this project.

My mother, Martha Freedman, did not live to see this volume, but her spirit continues to infuse my work. I am grateful for her wisdom and wit and for the support of my sister Mickey Zemon and my niece Jenna Moskowitz, who help sustain her legacy. Above all, I thank my partner, Susan Krieger, who for the past twenty-five years has both enabled my best work and encouraged all of my other passions.

Feminism, Sexuality, and Politics

Introduction | Identities, Values, and Inquiries | A Personal History

FEMINIST HISTORY calls on us to imagine the world in new ways. It has the power to alter social relations by exposing the undeserved privileges that perpetuate long-standing social inequities. *Feminism, Sexuality, and Politics* presents my major contributions to rethinking history through the lens of feminist analysis. It explores the origins and strategies of women's activism, ranging from prison reform to feminism, and argues for the importance of valuing women in a society that has long devalued women's contributions. It highlights the regulation of sexual boundaries, with an emphasis on the malleability of both sexual identities and sexual politics.

The ten essays that follow include synthetic overviews, monographic research, and applications of feminist scholarship within classrooms and courtrooms. Readers may discern in these chapters the evolution of my thinking, which reflects in part the maturation of women's history and the politics of American feminism. From an initial focus on white middle-class women reformers, my scholarship has expanded to explore sexuality and race as well as gender, men as well as women, and cultural meanings as well as social experience. Central to my approach is the development of a social constructionist analysis of inequalities.

As I reflect back on the scholarship, teaching, and politics that have informed my writing for over three decades, I detect several underlying currents: questioning hierarchy, valuing women, and retaining an outsider's perspective. In my efforts, I have long been inspired by Virginia Woolf's dictum in her 1938 work *Three Guineas* that newly educated women must "in no way hinder any other human being, whether man or woman, white or black," from gaining access to privilege.[1] To introduce this collection, I would like to discuss the personal influences that brought me to appreciate Woolf's words and to place my work in a broader feminist and intellectual context.

The Politics and Scholarship of Women's History

I began my graduate training as a historian at a particularly auspicious moment for educated American women. The revival of feminism in the late 1960s stimulated both a curiosity about women's past and a commitment to advancing sexual equality. By 1970, the year I enrolled in a doctoral program at Columbia University, feminism had percolated into American popular consciousness. The publicity surrounding the women's liberation movement was shaking the foundations of educational and cultural institutions. That year, Kate Millett's revised dissertation on sexism in literature, *Sexual Politics*, helped revolutionize academic inquiry on gender, while Robin Morgan's popular anthology of writings on women's liberation, *Sisterhood Is Powerful*, inspired a generation to engage in consciousness raising. It was also the year that the American Historical Association formally acknowledged that women had suffered professionally because of sex discrimination. Just as I decided to become a scholar, a sea change in academia permitted my generation to create a "new women's history." In Linda Kerber's apt summary, "The generic 'he' that had been alleged to encompass women's experience as well as men's turned out to be a fraud."[2] The challenge of documenting women's lives and understanding both past inequality and resistance to it engaged this generation of scholars. Our goal was to correct the record by excavating women's historical experiences as complex agents of social change, not only to empower women but ultimately to transform all of American culture.

More than a profession, then, women's history resembled a mission to proselytize what we learned. Building on the idealism of the 1960s and propelled by the feminist politics of the 1970s, we set out to restore women to history in part to achieve gender equity at large. Over the next quarter century, we did in fact infiltrate classrooms and beyond. Students from elementary schools to universities learned about elite heroines, housewives, female wage laborers, and feminist organizers. Beyond the classroom, too, women's history spilled into public life. The National Women's History Project, historical museums and national parks, urban women's history walking tours, documentary films, and even U.S. postage stamps transmitted the message broadly. In public policy debates and legal battles, women's historians weighed in during the 1980s on workplace discrimination and abortion rights, as they have more recently on welfare policy and lesbian and gay rights.

The legal gains of feminism, including the demise of sex quotas in graduate admissions, made entry into academic life possible for many of my generation. These opportunities in turn fueled our desire to reshape the profession. We felt compelled not only to expand the curriculum by adding women's lives to the classes we taught but also to redress continuing sex and race discrimination in hiring and promotion. For those of us forging a feminist path in the university, scholarship and politics have never been mutually exclusive. Accused by skeptics of being only political, and thus by definition unqualified to be objective scholars, we resisted the charge on multiple grounds. We acknowledged that all academic inquiry is, on some level, political, whether it serves to sustain existing power relations or to challenge them. At the same time, we insisted on creating an engaged scholarship that met the highest professional standards, and we tried to train the next generation of historians to do so.

Academic scholarship that dissents from the prevailing wisdom about what is historically important may be labeled political even when it meets those high standards, for to acknowledge any contemporary concerns raises the specter of a "presentism" that presumably biases one's conclusions. A first-year graduate student brought home to me the dilemma of integrating the political and the scholarly during a class I taught in the 1980s. He had just read my essay "Separatism as Strategy" (chapter 1) and asked me respectfully, "How did you get away with being so political?" My politics, I explained, motivated the historical questions I asked but not the answers I reached. I had been intrigued by feminist strategies in the past because of the revival of feminism around me; my historical inquiry had revealed both positive and negative legacies of that past. The process of writing that article, I added, helped shape my views about feminism as much as my political questions affected my scholarship. Moreover, both my politics and my historical interpretations have altered further over the course of my career (as the essays in chapters 2 and 5 illustrate).

At the time, I might also have told this student, but did not, that I did *not* entirely get away with it. Many of us paid steep costs for our admittedly feminist politics. As I explain in chapter 3, I had to fight to keep my job at Stanford University in large part because of perceptions that women's history was "mere" politics. Having to defend my work and the project of feminist history during the two years of my tenure review deepened my commitment to an engaged scholarship and a more equitable academy. It also reinforced my belief in the power of women's communities.

Identity and Community: Forging a Personal Politics

As much as my politics and scholarship reflect the formative experiences of the 1960s and the resurgence of women's history, they also spring from my own background. From my current vantage point, I can reconstruct a personal genealogy that helps explain how I came to question hierarchy and value women. For one thing, growing up Jewish in post–World War II America supplied critical lessons about social hierarchies along with a deep grounding in identity politics. Despite their near silence about the Holocaust, my family and the tight-knit Jewish subculture in which I grew up communicated a historical lesson about the pitfalls of assimilationist survival strategies and the importance of establishing a strong communal base. We lived in central Pennsylvania, a region dominated by German Protestants. No adult had to state explicitly, "Look what happened to the Jews of Germany who thought they were safe," yet my elders communicated clearly a message about potential hostility around us. Only once as a child was I called a Christ-killer and only once did swastikas appear on the synagogue doors, but both left lasting impressions. More routinely, the public schools I attended outside Harrisburg inculcated a religious hierarchy when they required participation in celebrating only Christian holidays.

My Orthodox Jewish grandparents, Albert and Ruth Freedman, constituted a counterbalancing force in this social milieu. They insisted that I observe all of our own holy days — even some unheard of by most of my Jewish friends — and they monitored my Jewish education. A deeply religious immigrant who provided a moral compass for the family, my grandfather had little formal education, but he owned biographies of his two American heroes: the renowned lawyer Clarence Darrow, who fought for the underdog, and the talented baseball pitcher Sandy Koufax, who refused to play in the World Series during the Jewish High Holidays. Like my grandparents, our rabbi and other communal leaders socialized me to retain a Jewish identity in a gentile world. Participating in a range of Jewish institutions, from Hebrew school to youth groups to summer camp, furnished a safe harbor. Years later, when I heard a Jewish feminist remark that female separatism had supplanted the Jewish separatism of her youth, I realized how much that early community had affected my own political instincts.

By adolescence, I increasingly experienced the confinements, along with the comforts, of community. My immediate family had already begun to point me beyond our enclave, especially through my parents' cultural interests, which combined their bourgeois and bohemian longings. My mother,

Martha Freedman, loved words and wit; she published light verse, short stories, and nonfiction in magazines whenever she could. She and my father, Ted Freedman, shared a passion for American literature and theater, which they passed on to my older sister, Mickey, and myself. Our annual family pilgrimages to New York City exposed us to appealing new social worlds, including Broadway and Greenwich Village. During high school, the short-lived repertory theater my parents established in Harrisburg immersed me in an alternate cultural universe.

Like other Jewish girls in postwar America, my sister and I expected to finish college, which our parents had not been able to do during the depression. Unlike most of our peers, however, each of us would choose women's colleges, in part because they supplied more sustenance for our intellectual aspirations than had the intensely social worlds of our public high school. We each studied American history and, for a time, each looked to Emma Goldman as a heroine. Significantly, both of us chose to settle in metropolitan centers, far from our tight-knit Jewish community.

I should acknowledge that my subcultural base also offered a bridge from a fairly provincial to a broader worldview. The staff at the subsidized Jewish summer camp I attended from 1956 to 1961 introduced me to folk music, which would become a lifelong pastime, and to the civil rights movement. One of my counselors, who served as a mentor as I grew up, worked with Bayard Rustin when he organized the 1963 March on Washington. Her letters provided a lifeline to contemporary politics. The descriptions of the poverty she witnessed in Mississippi during the Freedom Summer of 1964 opened my mind to the daily indignities of racism. Still in high school, I imagined myself following in her footsteps. Because she had attended Barnard College, I applied there, and I expected that I too would participate in an interracial social movement.

When I got to Barnard in 1965, I encountered the growing separatism of the Black Power movement. Back home, racial integration had seemed radical, but at Barnard many black students were asserting their political identity by creating their own organizations. My first naive efforts to create programs for high school girls from Harlem revealed how much I had to learn about race and about organizing. As I wondered where a liberal white student fit in a radicalizing movement, studying African American history helped me sort through my dilemmas. At a critical moment in my education, my adviser at Barnard, historian Annette Baxter, encouraged me to expand my thoughts on racial separatism in a paper I had written about black and white abolitionists. That project led to my senior honors thesis on nineteenth- and early-twentieth-century black separatist movements, in which I differentiated between the separatisms of racial exclusion (such as colonization) and those rooted in self-determination (such as the Exodusters or the followers of Marcus Garvey).

In the process of writing my thesis, I learned that historical research brought me intellectual pleasure as well as insight into contemporary politics. For the first time, I contemplated graduate study, even though I had no notion of what academic life was like. For personal and financial reasons, however, I delayed graduate school. After college, I worked full-time in a national Jewish organization. In partnership with a network of black clergy, we organized local interracial projects to improve relationships between blacks and Jews in New York City neighborhoods at a time when the historic black-Jewish civil rights alliance was faltering. The job raised further doubts not only about the merits of liberal reform but also about the limitations placed on women in institutions dominated by men.

If working in a hierarchical religious organization was not enough to turn me into a feminist, the dilemmas of the sexual revolution were making me quite receptive to the message. In college during the 1960s, rejecting obligatory chastity often translated into accepting obligatory sexual availability. For example, I recall being asked by men, rather accusingly and more than once, "Why aren't you on the pill?" After a student activist I knew ignored my refusal to have sex with him, the liberal gynecologist who administered a "morning after" injection persuaded me that I would be safer taking oral contraceptives. It would be years before I acknowledged how violated, yet culpable, I felt at the time. Even in consensual relationships, however, I often longed for greater depth than the casualness allowed by the sexual freedom then in practice.

The revival of the women's movement would provide a language to describe my daily dissatisfactions, and I began to contextualize the personal within a political framework of gender hierarchy. While still an undergraduate, I had not been able to absorb fully the lessons communicated by my teachers, such as sociologist Mirra Komarovsky, who first alerted me to the disparities in male and female educational aspirations. When Annette Baxter suggested that I enroll in her women's history course, I had tactlessly explained that I preferred to study "real" history. By my senior year, however, I had sorely regretted that decision. The experiences of the work world after graduation deepened my hunger for insight into women's secondary status. In 1970, someone handed me a set of mimeographed papers then circulating in New York City called "Notes from the Second Year." As I read essays on consciousness raising, radical feminism, and "loving another woman," the proverbial light bulb began to illuminate my own consciousness.[3] I began to think politically about gender and sexuality.

The ideas of radical feminism in the early 1970s helped make sense of an unnamed hierarchy that I now observed everywhere. I realized how deeply I had internalized what has since been called "the sexual contract," in which (white) men had direct access to power, money, and authority while most women were supposed to procure indirect access to these prerogatives by being attractive, nurturing, and dependent on the men who possessed them. The flaws in this system could be detected in my own family history. My maternal grandmother, Jenny Pincus, had been widowed during the influenza epidemic of 1918 and had to raise two small children on her own; my mother had determined during the mid-1960s to return to full-time work, not only because of my father's faltering small business but also to achieve personal independence. When I became self-supporting at the age of twenty, I felt the constraints of social expectations begin to lift. Shifting my focus from male approval to self-determination had revolutionary consequences for my future and, no doubt, for the historical questions I would later address.

As women of my generation consciously withdrew from the old sexual contract, we expected to select romantic and sexual partners apart from economic considerations. For some, myself included, that choice made lesbianism not only less frightening but also an appealing alternative, particularly in the context of a feminist culture that affirmed the value of women. But it was only after becoming a feminist and, significantly, after I finally gained some economic security, that I consciously chose relationships with women over those with men and began to identify as a lesbian. My experience of sexuality as a choice and not merely a given contributed to my interest in social-constructionist interpretations, although I came to realize the very different paths to lesbian identity followed by other women.

Feminist consciousness, a kind of spiritual awakening, was by no means painless. Older connections suffered, including my ties to the Jewish community. In the early 1970s, I could not imagine acceptance of feminism, and later lesbianism, within the conservative form of Judaism and family-centered social world in which I had been raised. In addition, having to acknowledge pervasive media violence and the persistent limits on women's mobility made me highly sensitive, sometimes enraged, about threats to women's physical safety. Even as feminists tried to create alternative models, the dominant culture seemed constantly to reinforce women's lesser worth and greater vulnerability. Ultimately, I would ask historical questions about sexual violence, but only years after I had reestablished my sense of physical safety. Feminism supplied tools to overcome fear — women's self-defense classes, for example — and to unlearn the secondary status many of us had internalized as women. It also empowered me to trust my own intellectual, sexual, and political instincts.

My receptivity to feminist politics built upon a habit of questioning hierarchy that had deepened during my educational experiences at both Barnard and Columbia. While I was an undergraduate, the antiwar and student movements had challenged my liberal politics.[4] In 1968, the year I first marched for peace, I also made the decision to resist authority on campus. During that spring of international student protest, radicals at Columbia had occupied campus buildings to protest university policies, including support of military research and expansion into the neighboring Harlem community. Rather than resolve the sit-ins peacefully, the Columbia administration invited New York City police riot squads onto campus to clear the student protesters. Although I did not agree with the tactics of the militant students, I was hugely disillusioned by the administration's resort to force. And so, along with other students and faculty, I positioned myself outside one of the occupied buildings, Fayerweather Hall, to create a buffer zone where we passively resisted the police. The night of the Columbia "bust" was a political turning point for me. After midnight, mounted police chased groups of us down Broadway and away from campus, yet as I walked back to my dorm at dawn, I had a romantic inkling that a new university might arise from the ashes of the old and that I might become part of it.

Two years later, when I returned to Columbia as a graduate student in U.S. history, it was not clear that I would have a place in that academic world. At the first meeting of my introductory seminar, the professor announced that along with a Ph.D., Columbia also awarded a terminal M.A. degree, which might be especially appealing to the women in the class, who could leave after a year and "get a job downtown." I certainly thought of leaving, given his attitude toward women, but a few supportive faculty members made me feel more welcome. When I later thought of dropping out of graduate school because of mounting debts and an alienating department culture, Nathan Huggins (the first African American historian hired at Columbia) delivered a political pep talk based on his own graduate experiences at Harvard. Did I really expect these people to welcome me?, he asked. And if I left, wouldn't it simply perpetuate the old regime? It wasn't going to change, he insisted, until people like him, like me, stuck it out.

My graduate adviser, Kenneth Jackson, helped make it possible for me to stay by encouraging my interest in women's history and hiring me as a research assistant. My graduate cohort played a large part as well. We banded together to study, to play, to criticize faculty members for their sexism, to support research on women. The women graduate students formed a caucus, collected stories of discriminatory practices (such as faculty who favored male students in job recommendations), and then called a meeting with the faculty at which we cataloged their discouraging behavior. Above all, the relationship I formed at Columbia with fellow graduate student John D'Emilio helped me not only to survive personally but also to flourish intellectually. Our intimate friendship and energizing conversations about history, sex, and politics have continued for decades, surviving both long distances and later the process of coauthoring a book. John, who wrote one of the first dissertations on U.S. gay history, eased my own coming-out and helped kindle my curiosity about the history of sexuality.

In the mid-1970s, while I completed my dissertation, I began teaching at Princeton University, which was still a very patriarchal institution. Women students had been admitted only five years before I arrived, and the few female faculty tended to be at the bottom of the academic ranks. To survive what felt like a stifling environment, I relied on the small band of feminist graduate students and faculty who met in consciousness-raising and study groups. At Princeton, I learned a great deal about the craft of teaching from the faculty whose lectures I attended and then through preparing my first lecture course with my new colleague Elaine Tyler May, another Jewish feminist who became a lifelong friend. I also learned the joy of teaching my first women's studies courses, initiated by a handful of exceptional women undergraduates. A group of feminist faculty created a committee on women's studies, which eventually launched an undergraduate program. My Ph.D. in hand, I moved onto the tenure track. When Stanford University offered me a job in 1976, I was thrilled to leave the East and move to California. Even as I made the transition from struggling student to salaried professor at these elite schools, I continued to feel very much like an outsider — as a Jew, a woman, a feminist, and a lesbian — and I remained highly conscious of the social hierarchies that shaped academic privilege.

Expanding the Scope of Feminist History

My personal history fueled my historical curiosity about feminism. As the "second wave" of feminism washed over American culture in the 1970s, I could not imagine where all that energy had been stored for so long or why it had revived just then. Why had feminism seemingly waned in the 1920s, with so much unfinished business, a generation before I encountered it? What little I had read of U.S. women's history portrayed the slow but steady march of women's rights from Seneca Falls in 1848 to suffrage, always ending with national enfranchisement in 1920. Yet as an entering graduate student in 1970, keenly aware of the lack of women faculty at Columbia in contrast to Barnard, I sorely wanted feminism back. Perhaps, I thought, I could learn what had happened to that earlier movement, why it had effectively disappeared.

The question of "what happened to the women's movement" has been at the heart of at least half of my scholarship since that time. Beginning in a graduate seminar on the 1920s and 1930s, I asked how scholars had explained the postsuffrage era, surveying their interpretations of women's status and politics after 1920. What struck me most was that historians themselves had contributed to the silencing of feminism by declaring its irrelevance after suffrage. American society, most of these writers pronounced, had achieved gender equality with the stroke of a constitutional amendment (aided and abetted, perhaps, by a revolution in manners and morals). Ever since writing about the "New Woman," I have been suspicious about the way historians define periods and more aware of the implications of the benchmarks we create.[5]

Frustrated by the limits of a suffrage-centered history, I wanted to learn about the periods before and in between the "waves" of American feminism, so I turned to women's social movements other than suffrage. In my first book, *Their Sisters' Keepers*, I asked why and how religiously motivated, white middle-class women in the late nineteenth century had successfully created state prisons run largely by and for women.[6] By the 1920s, they had succeeded in establishing separate women's reformatory institutions for predominantly white inmates in most states and in creating the first federal women's prison. But, I concluded, the original reformers' vision of maternal rather than punitive institutions had not survived. In most states, the reform impulse—an amalgam of social justice and moralistic class uplift—had been supplanted by punitive and bureaucratic prisons not unlike the men's institutions from which women inmates had been initially transferred. Even well-intentioned social critics, I learned, had to conform in order to retain state funding. Like other scholars trying to restore historical agency to women by uncovering their activism (via temperance, antiprostitution, or Americanization efforts, for example), I learned that both the motives and the results of reform were complex and full of pitfalls.

As I wrote about women's prisons, I benefited greatly from the new women's history of the 1970s produced by scholars such as Gerda Lerner (whose summer school course I had taken at Columbia), Nancy Cott, Ellen DuBois, Elizabeth Hafkin Pleck, Mary Ryan, Kathryn Kish Sklar, and Carroll Smith-Rosenberg. From multiple directions, their work complicated inherited wisdom about what were termed the "separate sexual spheres" in which white middle-class men and women were supposed to operate in the nineteenth century. I was also influenced by interdisciplinary scholarship, particularly by feminist anthropologists such as Michelle Zimbalist Rosaldo, who would later become a treasured colleague at Stanford. Reading pre- and postsuffrage sources through these reconsiderations of "separate spheres" and "gender systems" helped produce the synthetic essay that opens this collection, "Separatism as Strategy." (The article originated in the lecture I gave during my job interview at Stanford University in 1976; I chose the subject in part because I wanted those doing the hiring to know exactly what they were getting.)

As I acknowledged in the article, my conceptualization of female separatism in the late nineteenth and early twentieth centuries rested in part on my observation of flourishing women's groups around me in the 1970s, and it was clearly influenced by the politics of lesbian separatism then being articulated by writers such as Charlotte Bunch. Surveying the historical literature in the United States, I argued that a major strength of the women's movement between 1870 and 1920 was its separatist strategy of female institution building, evidenced by women-run schools, clubs, clinics, and even prisons. After suffrage, however, premature pronouncements of equality had encouraged a dismantling of this separatist infrastructure, which depleted the strength of the white women's movement. The most often reprinted of my essays, this article has long provoked students to reconsider their integrationist tendencies and to value female social worlds. The historical literature has grown enormously since I wrote it, now incorporating diverse racial, ethnic, and working-class women's institutions before and after suffrage and exploring both the costs of sexual integration and the limits of sisterhood. I feel that illuminating the separatist strategy remains salient today, particularly in light of recurrent claims about postfeminism that ignore the continuing importance of women's organizations throughout American culture and internationally.

My early exposure to Jewish and then African American separatism, which I later applied to women, surely influenced my scholarly interpretations of both women's prison reform and feminist strategies. Later, my academic experiences reinforced the power of maintaining separate worlds while participating in larger institutions. My continuing education as a feminist scholar flourished in separate women's spaces, such as the Center for Research on Women at Stanford, where I helped edit the journal *Signs* and worked on two other cooperative feminist projects: the documentary collection *Victorian Women* (1981), my first foray into comparative women's history, and *The Lesbian Issue* (1985), a special edition of *Signs* that I coedited in order to call attention to the emergence of interdisciplinary lesbian scholarship. I found an intellectual and pedagogical home in the undergraduate Program in Feminist Studies, which we launched at Stanford in 1981. Our choice of "feminist" in the title consciously signaled our commitment to interrogating gender hierarchy along with documenting women's experiences. In addition, local feminist study groups, women's professional caucuses, and an annual conference on teaching U.S. women's history all nurtured my career. Whenever possible, I chose to publish my scholarship in feminist journals and to support the nascent women's studies movement. Training women graduate students, many of whom pioneered a multicultural women's history, provided additional rewards and a growing circle of feminist colleagues.

It turned out, too, that women's networks would be critical to sustaining me when, from 1981 to 1983, my "tenure case" escalated into a battle between a largely supportive history department and a hostile dean, an episode I recount in chapter 3, "Women's Networks and Women's Loyalties." Feminist scholars around the country weighed in on the merits of the sex discrimination grievance I filed, supplying much-needed affirmation. Along with my steadfast partner, Susan Krieger, close colleagues helped restore my spirits and shared my burdens during this difficult period. Several of them — Barbara Babcock, Diane Middlebrook, Nancy Stoller, and Barrie Thorne — deserve particular credit, as does my extraordinary lawyer, Marsha Berzon (who now sits on the Ninth Circuit U.S. Court of Appeals). Stanford graduate students mobilized to raise funds for legal fees by designing a T-shirt that paraphrased feminist abolitionist Abby Kelley Foster: "Sisters, bloody feet have worn smooth the path upon which you trod." Ever since my internal appeal succeeded in 1983, I have been called upon to advise all too many faculty members, female and male, who have struggled through similar ordeals. Along with feminist colleagues at Stanford, I have repeatedly tried to hold the university administration responsible for addressing gender and race inequities on our campus.

My tenure case ultimately brought me back to the study of prison reform and the question of how historians periodize women's movements. During the year in which I prepared my sex discrimination grievance, I found myself drawn to the papers of Miriam Van Waters, a prison reformer who in the 1940s waged a long and public battle to keep her job as the innovative superintendent of the Massachusetts State Reformatory for Women. Reading her letters and diaries at the Schlesinger Library while I awaited the outcome of my tenure appeal at Stanford, I found solace in the way she retained her perspective and ultimately triumphed. Several years later, I returned to Van Waters's papers, realized the rich evidence they contained, and made a commitment to write her biography. Doing so allowed me to revisit both prison reform and separatism. From the 1930s through the 1950s, Van Waters championed a redemptive and educational rather than punitive approach as superintendent of the Massachusetts State Reformatory for Women. Her career, which flourished after 1920, revolved around women's networks and fostered separate institutions, suggesting greater continuities with nineteenth-century reformers than I had previously acknowledged. During the 1980s, other scholars were also shifting attention to twentieth-century women's history and toward political life. Drawing on their work, my essay "Separatism Revisited" (chapter 2) synthesized this new literature as the context for a case study of Van Waters, whose career demonstrated the survival of women's institutions after suffrage.

My teaching also forced me to rethink the scope of women's history. In particular, I began offering FS 101, the introductory course in the Program in Feminist Studies, in 1988. Women's studies, like American feminism itself, had recently begun to expand beyond its Western cultural base. While a multiracial U.S. women's history had taken root in the 1980s, for an American historian, FS 101 required much greater attention to cross-cultural, international, and interdisciplinary scholarship. Along with making feminism compelling rather than forbidding for students, I tried to embed feminist politics within broader critiques of racial, class, sexual, and national hierarchies. Two essays in this book derive from that course, one on pedagogy (chapter 4) and one on the historical dynamics of feminism (chapter 5). I hope the former — about adapting the historical strategy of consciousness raising as a pedagogical tool — conveys the intensity of feminist classrooms, their rewards for teachers and students alike, and the relationship of gender to other sources of identity. The latter essay, "No Turning Back," is an overview of my book of the same title. Dedicated to my students, the book grew out of the lectures for this course, revised to incorporate students' probing questions and the growing literatures of interdisciplinary feminist scholarship. By writing it, I sought a broader audience, ranging from the parents of my students, to staff members, to colleagues who taught introductory women's studies courses.

No Turning Back (2002), though grounded in the United States, placed feminism within an international context. It represents a synthesis of interdisciplinary and historical literatures, including the contributions of political scientists who have theorized about comparative feminisms; postcolonial scholars who have questioned the Western monopoly on feminist politics; and historians who have explored past international feminist organizing.[7] The essay included in this volume presents my central arguments about feminist momentum over time and across cultures, namely that wherever democratic politics and wage labor systems have converged to transform societies, some form of feminism has attempted to extend the rejection of hierarchical rule by questioning the gender privileges retained by men. By 2000, those conditions were spreading throughout much of the world, along with communications networks among feminists, to produce a panoply of women's creativity and politics that is unlikely to disappear, despite intense backlash. Thus, from my initial interest in U.S. women's movements beyond suffrage, I had come to redefine the scope of feminism, both geographically and substantively.

Sexual Boundaries: Mapping the History of Sexuality

As a beginning graduate student intent on forging a new women's history, I had not yet made the analytic link between hierarchies based on gender (that is, socially constructed categories of male and female) and those based on sexuality (that is, erotic and reproductive practices and identities). Two incidents that occurred while I was in graduate school, both around 1972, reveal my early blinders. First, when a classmate announced in a seminar that he wanted to write about the history of sexuality, I felt embarrassed by his revelation. To me, women's history seemed important and grounded in abundant evidence, while the study of sexuality felt both indulgent and historically elusive. Second, while a group of us were editing a student newsletter article in which we called for a feminist history, a fellow graduate student suggested to John D'Emilio and me that perhaps we should also call for a gay history. Both of us ignored the comment. Just as I had reconsidered my early aversion to women's history, only a few years later, these reservations would lift.

Along with my personal disengagement from what Adrienne Rich has termed "compulsory heterosexuality," my reading of both socialist feminist and lesbian theorists such as Sheila Rowbotham and Gayle Rubin cleared the way toward rethinking the categories of biological sex, social gender, and sexuality. After moving to California in 1976, I joined a feminist study group that read sexual theory from Havelock Ellis to Michel Foucault. By the late 1970s, the feminist "sex wars" — largely a debate over defining female sexuality primarily as a source of power or as a source of vulnerability — loomed large. As I navigated through this political divide, I wanted to make sense of it historically as well.[8]

Around 1978, I joined the fledgling San Francisco Lesbian and Gay History Project, a small and intensely stimulating group of scholars, lay historians, and filmmakers committed to making gay history accessible to the public. Both sexual theory and the prospect of excavating past lesbian and gay experience opened new historical vistas for me.[9] As with the revival of feminism, I wanted to know why lesbianism had remained invisible to me until the contemporary political wave. Through the Lesbian and Gay History Project, I helped create a video for community and classroom use, *She Even Chewed Tobacco*, which illustrated women who had cross-dressed and lived as men in the nineteenth and early twentieth centuries.[10] At the same time, to make a place for lesbian history within the profession — and despite well-intentioned advice that I not do so, lest I appear to be "slumming" — I began to organize lesbian panels at history and women's studies conferences.

My work on women's prison reform strongly shaped my approach to the study of female sexuality in general and lesbian history in particular. Many of the women in jails and prisons were sexual offenders; their incarceration established a boundary that helped define a white middle-class purity ideal. Women served time for minor "crimes against chastity" that included not only streetwalking but also "manifest danger of falling into vice," a category intended to protect young women from sexual experience. Although the women's reformatories attempted to uplift these "fallen women," their founders accepted the line dividing pure and impure. Prison sources also revealed sexual liaisons between women, but heterosexual offenses dominated the early records. Over time, I became curious about how the boundary defining female sexual deviance shifted from a heterosexual purity divide to the criminalization of lesbianism.

Just a few years after my premature dismissal of sexual history, then, I was immersed in questions about sexual deviance and purity. By the early 1980s, after being invited to review recent scholarship on some aspect of women's history, I decided to map out the rapidly developing literature on subjects such as prostitution, contraception, abortion, and same-sex relationships.

As I drafted this article on the "history of sexuality," the territory kept extending beyond the confines of the assignment. One colleague who read the massive draft essay suggested that I could write a book on the subject, and I took her advice.[11] Given the scope of the project, I asked John D'Emilio to share this challenging task. At the time, we felt that collaborating on a book about the history of sexuality would, at the very least, allow us to continue our decade-long conversation about sexuality and engage in regular work during a period when we both anticipated unemployment (given my tenure case and his prolonged search for an academic position). In fact, we both soon found job security, but we had already decided to coauthor a synthesis of the emerging subfield of sexual history.

Intimate Matters: A History of Sexuality in America (1988) mapped the transition from a reproductive society in the colonial era to a sexualized society in the twentieth century. The book argued against a linear, progressive march from repression toward sexual liberation and emphasized instead sexual politics, particularly the ways that sexual regulation reinforced race, class, and gender hierarchies within the context of economic commercialization. We attempted to integrate same-sex relations throughout the narrative and to highlight both the sexualization of women and the politicization of sex by progressives and conservatives alike. Looking back over the literature in preparing the second edition, which appeared in 1997, we felt gratified both by the maturation of the field and by the staying power of our analytic framework. Lesbian and gay history, in particular, had begun to emerge from the margins of the profession. For this collection, I have selected my article, "The Historical Construction of Homosexuality in the United States" (chapter 6), to represent the analytic overview that characterizes *Intimate Matters*.

While our book mapped the broad contours of sexual history, I had also been exploring the treatment of sexual deviance in the twentieth century. I wanted to understand the effects on women when the boundaries of acceptable female behavior expanded to include heterosexual desire but simultaneously stigmatized homosexual possibilities. However, my research took an unexpected turn when I noticed how much attention the American public paid to male sexual crime after the 1930s. "Uncontrolled Desires" (chapter 7), my article about the waves of sex crime panics in the mid-twentieth century, corresponded to a broader historiographical turn toward the feminist analysis of men as well as women. It reflected as well the influence of Foucault in mapping new sexual discourses and interrogating shifting sexual boundaries. Like *Intimate Matters*, this article pays attention to the contradictory effects of sexual liberalization, such as the demonization of certain men as monsters amid the growing acceptance of "normal" male aggression and the heightened vulnerability of sexualized women and children. It also foreshadows my current work on the changing meaning of rape in American history.

I further examined the construction of deviant identities in "The Prison Lesbian" (chapter 8), which illustrates the racially specific impact of female sexualization. By the time I began my biography of Miriam Van Waters, both American feminism and women's history were expanding their scope beyond white middle-class lives, and explorations of racial and class distinctions permeated feminist scholarship. Reviewing my earlier prison research, along with sources in Van Waters's papers, I noted a shift in the racial meanings of lesbianism. In the early twentieth century, it was primarily African American women in prison who were labeled as aggressive homosexuals. After World War II, however, white working-class prisoners also came to represent the "lesbian threat." Moreover, by the 1950s, the earlier boundary between the pure (chaste women) and the impure (prostitutes, women of color, working-class women) competed with the line drawn between normal heterosexual and pathological homosexual women. Another essay reprinted here, "The Burning of Letters Continues" (chapter 9), explores the impact of the growing stigma surrounding lesbianism on elite women like Van Waters. Here, too, I wanted to show how identity can be complicated by layers of race, class, and sexual desire, using a close exploration of the sexual subjectivity of one woman to do so. Although I did not ground the essay in the queer theory that was infiltrating the academy in the 1990s, the themes of multiple, malleable, and elusive identities within that literature resonate with my interpretation.

The final essay in this book (chapter 10) addresses the dilemmas and the joys of applying historical research to contemporary policy issues. On several occasions I have done so, for example, when I offered expert testimony about the history of female institutions in a Canadian legal case in defense of a women's teachers union that wished to remain a single-sex organization. In response to Supreme Court nominee Clarence Thomas's charges of a "high tech lynching" at his 1991 confirmation hearings, I felt compelled to correct the record to include the equally horrendous history of violence against African American women, many of whom, like Anita Hill, survived sexual exploitation and were disparaged as sexually impure.[12] But my collaborations with other historians in several major court cases highlighted distinctions in the use of historical interpretations in legal arguments. In this chapter, I reflect on the tension between continuity and change in three episodes when historians have prepared amicus briefs: in *Webster v. Reproductive Health Services* (1989), which upheld state restrictions on access to abortion; in *Lawrence v. Texas* (2003), in which the Supreme Court overturned antisodomy laws; and in contemporary cases addressing the right to same-sex marriage. Bringing my exploration of history and politics full circle, this essay argues that historians cannot selectively emphasize positive and linear paths to current policies; we can look for precedents, but above all we must explain the process of change, including the contradictory lessons of the past.

LOOKING BACK over the essays collected here, I recognize the influences on my work of family, community, and mentors, as well as the energies unleashed by student movements and second-wave feminism. The theoretical insights of academic feminism and of theories ranging from social constructionism to postcolonial histories recur throughout these pages. But this narrative leaves out many of the personal encounters that have also shaped my thinking. Training graduate students, for example, continually enabled me to expand my own historical expertise. Directing the Program in Feminist Studies, as well as the faculty seminars it sponsored, fostered interdisciplinary literacy. In the early 1990s, the program also gave me a critical opportunity to rethink my own politics through workshops on intersecting identities and "unlearning oppression." And while time has tempered the utopian aspirations nurtured during my academic and feminist awakenings, the undergraduates who are drawn to my courses constantly renew my hopes that insight into the past can foster a more egalitarian future.

With this goal in mind, I offer these essays to explore the diverse ways in which women's history allows us to question social hierarchies and contribute to the process of social change. They illustrate the scholarship crafted by my generation, and for their influences, I am grateful to all of the feminists whose writing has so enriched both history and women's studies. I hope that this collection will introduce lay readers to the study of gender, sexuality, and feminism and that students reading it will be able to deepen their understandings of the connections among these subjects. At the same time, I would like these essays to inform the work of activists and policymakers who, I am confident, will put this scholarship to good use.

Part One | Feminist Strategies

1 | Separatism as Strategy | Female Institution Building and American Feminism, 1870 – 1930

At the time I wrote this essay, I had begun to question liberal feminism in light of the separatist "women's culture" of the 1970s. In the work of Emily Newell Blair, the feminist politician who in the late 1920s reconsidered the strategy of integrating women into mainstream political parties, I found historical precedents for applying the concept of women's culture to feminist politics. I continue to value female separatism but always with the caveats that we should distinguish carefully between women's and feminist institutions, remain aware of the costs of racial exclusiveness, and avoid romanticizing the past. My own revision of the argument about women's separatism, along with references to later studies, appears in chapter 2.

Scholarship and Strategies

The feminist scholarship of the past decade has often been concerned, either explicitly or implicitly, with two central political questions: the search for the origins of women's oppression and the formulation of effective strategies for combating patriarchy. Analysis of the former question helps us answer the latter. As anthropologist Gayle Rubin has wryly explained: "If innate male aggression and dominance are at the root of female oppression, then the feminist program would logically require either the extermination of the offending sex, or else a eugenics project to modify its character. If sexism is a by-product of capitalism's relentless appetite for profit, then sexism would wither away in the advent of a successful socialist revolution. If the world historical defeat of women occurred at the hands of an armed patriarchal revolt, then it is time for Amazon guerrillas to start training in the Adirondacks."[1]

Previously published as Estelle B. Freedman, "Separatism as Strategy: Female Institution Building and American Feminism, 1870 – 1930," *Feminist Studies* 5, no. 3 (Fall 1979): 512 – 29. Reprinted by permission of Feminist Studies, Inc.

Another anthropologist, Michelle Zimbalist Rosaldo, provided an influential exploration of the origins-strategies questions in her 1974 theoretical overview of women's status.[2] Rosaldo argued that "universal sexual asymmetry" (the lower value placed on women's tasks and roles in all cultures) has been determined largely by the sexually defined split between domestic and public spheres. To oversimplify her thesis, the greater the social distance between women in the home and men in the public sphere, the greater the devaluation of women. The implications for feminist strategies become clear at the end of Rosaldo's essay when she says that greater overlap between domestic and public spheres means higher status for women. Thus, to achieve an egalitarian future, with less separation of female and male, we should strive not only for the entry of women into the male-dominated public sphere but also for men's entry into the female-dominated domestic world.

Rosaldo also discusses an alternative strategy for overcoming sexual asymmetry, namely, the creation of a separate women's public sphere, but she dismisses this model in favor of integrating domestic and public spheres. Nonetheless, the alternative strategy of creating "women's societies and African queens" deserves further attention.[3] Where female political leaders have power over their own jurisdiction (women), they also gain leverage in tribal policy. Such a separate sexual political hierarchy would presumably offer women more status and power than the extreme male-public/female-domestic split, but it would not require the entry of each sex into the sphere dominated by the other sex. At certain historical periods, the creation of a public female sphere might be the only viable political strategy for women.

I would like to argue through historical analysis for the alternative strategy of creating a strong, public female sphere. A number of feminist historians have recently explored the value of the separate, though not necessarily public, female sphere for enriching women's historical experience. Carroll Smith-Rosenberg's research has shown how close personal relationships enhanced the private lives of women in the nineteenth century.[4] At the same time, private "sisterhoods," Nancy Cott has suggested, may have been a precondition for the emergence of feminist consciousness.[5] In the late nineteenth and early twentieth centuries, intimate friendships provided support systems for politically active women, as demonstrated by the work of both Blanche Cook and Nancy Sahli.[6] However, the women's culture of the past — personal networks, rituals, and relationships — did not automatically constitute a political strategy. As loving and supportive as women's networks may have been, they could keep women content with a status that was inferior to that of men.

I do not accept the argument that female networks and feminist politics were incompatible. Rather, in the following synthesis of recent scholarship in American women's history, I want to show how the women's movement in the late nineteenth and early twentieth centuries provides an example of the "women's societies and African queens" strategy that Rosaldo mentioned. The creation of a separate, public female sphere helped mobilize women and gained political leverage in the larger society. A separatist political strategy, which I refer to as "female institution building," emerged from the middle-class women's culture of the nineteenth century. Its history suggests that in our own time, as well, women's culture can be integral to feminist politics.[7]

What Happened to Feminism?

My desire to restore historical consciousness about female separatism has both a personal and an intellectual motivation. As a feminist working within male-dominated academic institutions, I have realized that I could not survive without access to the feminist culture and politics that flourish outside mixed institutions. How, I have wondered, could women in the past work for change within a male-dominated world without having this alternative culture? This thought led me to the more academic questions. Perhaps they could not survive when those supports were not available, and perhaps this insight can help explain one of the most intriguing questions in American women's history: What happened to feminism after the suffrage victory in 1920?

Most explanations of the decline of women's political strength focus on either inherent weaknesses in suffragist ideology or external pressures from a pervasively sexist society.[8] But when I survey the women's movement before suffrage passed, I am struck by the hypothesis that a major strength of American feminism prior to 1920 was the separate female community that helped sustain women's participation in both social reform and political activism. Although the women's movement of the late nineteenth century contributed to the transformation of women's social roles, it did not reject a separate, unique female identity. Most feminists did not adopt the radical demands for equal status with men that originated at the Seneca Falls Convention of 1848. Rather, they preferred to retain membership in a separate female sphere, one which they did not believe to be inferior to men's sphere and one in which women could be free to create their own forms of personal, social, and political relationships. The achievements of feminism at the turn of the century came less through gaining access to the male domains of politics and the professions than through the tangible act of building separate female institutions.

The self-consciously female community began to disintegrate in the 1920s just as "new women" were attempting to assimilate into male-dominated institutions. At work, in social life, and in politics, I will argue, middle-class women hoped to become equals by adopting men's values and integrating into their institutions. A younger generation of women learned to smoke, drink, and value heterosexual relationships over female friendships in their personal lives. At the same time, women's political activity epitomized the process of rejecting women's culture in favor of men's promises of equality. The gradual decline of female separatism in social and political life precluded the emergence of a strong women's political bloc that might have protected and expanded the gains made by the earlier women's movement. Thus, the erosion of women's culture may help account for the decline of public feminism in the decades after 1920. Without a constituency, a movement cannot survive. The old feminist leaders lost their following when a new generation opted for assimilation in the naive hope of becoming men's equals overnight.

To explore this hypothesis, I will illustrate episodes of cultural and political separatism within American feminism in three periods: its historical roots prior to 1870; the institution building of the late nineteenth century; and the aftermath of suffrage in the 1920s.

Historical Roots of Separatism

In nineteenth-century America, commercial and industrial growth intensified the sexual division of labor, encouraging the separation of men's and women's spheres. While white males entered the public world of wage labor, business, the professions, and politics, most white middle-class women remained at home, where they provided the domestic, maternal, and spiritual care for their families and the nation. These women underwent intensive socialization into their roles as "true women." Combined with the restrictions on women that denied them access to the public sphere, this training gave American women an identity quite separate from men's. Women shared unique life experiences as daughters, wives, childbearers, childrearers, and moral guardians. They passed on their values and traditions to their female kin. They created what Smith-Rosenberg has called "the female world of love and ritual," a world of homosocial networks that helped them transcend the alienation of domestic life.[9]

The ideology of "true womanhood" was so deeply ingrained and so useful for preserving social stability in a time of flux that those few women who explicitly rejected its inequalities could find little support for their views. The feminists of the early women's rights movement were certainly justified in their grievances and demands for equal opportunity with men. The Seneca Falls Declaration of Sentiments of 1848, which called for access to education, property ownership, and political rights, has inspired many feminists since then, while the ridicule and denial of these demands have inspired our rage. But the equal rights arguments of the 1850s were apparently too radical for their own times.[10] Men would not accept women's entry into the public sphere, but more important, most women were not interested in rejecting their deeply rooted female identities. Both men and women feared the demise of the female sphere and the valuable functions it performed. The feminists, however, still hoped to reduce the limitations on women within their own sphere, as well as to gain the right of choice — of autonomy — for those women who opted for public rather than private roles.

Radical feminists such as Elizabeth Cady Stanton and Susan B. Anthony recognized the importance of maintaining the virtues of the female world while eliminating discrimination against women in public. As their political analysis developed at mid-century, they drew upon the concepts of female moral superiority and sisterhood and affirmed the separate nature of woman. At the same time, their disillusionment with even the most enlightened men of the times reinforced the belief that women had to create their own movement to achieve independence. The bitterness that resulted when most male abolitionists refused to support women's rights in the 1860s, and when the Fifteenth Amendment failed to include woman suffrage, along with the introduction of the term "male citizen" into the Constitution in the Fourteenth Amendment, alienated many women reformers. When male abolitionists proclaimed in defense, "This is the Negro's hour," the more radical women's rights advocates followed Stanton and Anthony in withdrawing from the reform coalition and creating a separatist organization. Their National Woman Suffrage Association had women members and officers; supported a broad range of reforms, including changes in marriage and divorce laws; and published the short-lived journal, *The Revolution*. The radical path proved difficult, however, and the National Woman Suffrage Association merged in 1890 with the more moderate American Woman

Suffrage Association. Looking back on their disappointment after the Civil War, Stanton and Anthony wrote prophetically in 1881:

> Our liberal men counselled us to silence during the war, and we were silent on our own wrongs; they counselled us to silence in Kansas and New York (in the suffrage referenda), lest we should defeat "Negro Suffrage," and threatened if we were not, we might fight the battle alone. We chose the latter, and were defeated. But standing alone we learned our power: we repudiated man's counsels forevermore; and solemnly vowed that there should never be another season of silence until woman had the same rights everywhere on this green earth, as man. . . .
>
> We would warn the young women of the coming generation against man's advice as to their best interests. . . . Woman must lead the way to her own enfranchisement. . . . She must not put her trust in man in this transition period, since while regarded as his subject, his inferior, his slave, their interests must be antagonistic.[11]

Female Institution Building

The "transition period" that Stanton and Anthony invoked lasted from the 1870s to the 1920s. It was an era of separate female organization and institution building, the result on the one hand of the negative push of discrimination in the public, male sphere and on the other hand of the positive attraction of the female world of close, personal relationships and domestic institutional structures. These dual origins characterized, for instance, one of the largest manifestations of "social feminism" in the late nineteenth century—the women's club movement.

The club movement illustrated the politicization of women's institutions as well as the limitations of their politics. The exclusion of women reporters from the New York Press Club in 1868 inspired the founding of the first women's club, Sorosis. The movement then blossomed in dozens and later hundreds of localities, until a General Federation of Women's Clubs formed in 1890. By 1910, it claimed over one million members. Although club social and literary activities at first appealed to traditional women who simply wanted to gather with friends and neighbors, by the turn of the century, women's clubs had launched civic reform programs. Their activities served to politicize traditional women by forcing them to define themselves as citizens, not simply as wives and mothers. The clubs reflected the societal racism of the time, however, and the black women who founded the National

Association of Colored Women in 1896 turned their attention to the social and legal problems that confronted both black women and black men.[12]

The Women's Christian Temperance Union (WCTU) had roots in the social feminist tradition of separate institution building. As Ellen DuBois has argued, the WCTU appealed to late-nineteenth-century women because it was grounded in the private sphere — the home — and attempted to correct the private abuses against women, namely, intemperance and the sexual double standard.[13] Significantly, though, the WCTU, under Frances Willard's leadership, became a strong prosuffrage organization, committed to righting all wrongs against women, through any means, including gaining the right to vote.

The women's colleges that opened in these same decades further attest to the importance of separate female institutions during this "transition period." Originally conceived as training grounds of piety, purity, and domesticity, the antebellum women's seminaries, such as Mary Lyon's Mt. Holyoke and Emma Willard's Troy Female Academy, laid the groundwork for the new collegiate institutions of the postwar era. When elite male institutions refused to educate women, the sister colleges of the East, like their counterparts elsewhere, took on the task themselves. In the process, they encouraged intimate friendships and professional networks among educated women.[14] At the same time, liberal arts and science training provided tools for women's further development, and by their examples, female teachers inspired students to use their skills creatively. As Barbara Welter noted when she first described the "cult of true womanhood," submissiveness was always its weakest link.[15] Like other women's institutions, the colleges could help subvert that element of the cult by encouraging independence in their students.

The most famous example of the impact of women's colleges may be Jane Addams's description of her experience at Rockford Seminary, where she and other students were imbued with the mission of bringing their female values to bear on the entire society. Although Addams later questioned the usefulness of her intellectual training in meeting the challenges of the real world, other women did build upon academic foundations when, as reformers, teachers, doctors, and social workers, they increasingly left the home to enter public or quasi-public work. Between 1890 and 1920, the number of professional degrees granted to women increased 226 percent, three times the rate of increase for men. Some of these professionals had attended separate female institutions such as the women's medical colleges in Philadelphia,

New York, and Boston. The new female professionals often served women and children clients, in part because of the discrimination against their encroachment on men's domains but also because they sincerely wanted to work with the traditional objects of their concern. As their skills and roles expanded, these women would demand the right to choose for themselves where and with whom they could work. This first generation of educated professional women became supporters of the suffrage movement in the early twentieth century, calling for full citizenship for women.

The process of redefining womanhood by the extension rather than the rejection of the female sphere may be best illustrated by the settlement house movement. Although both men and women resided in and supported these quasi-public institutions, the high proportion of female participants and leaders (approximately three-fifths of the total), as well as the domestic structure and emphasis on service to women and children, qualify the settlements as female institutions. Mary P. Ryan has captured the link these ventures provided between "true womanhood" and "new womanhood" in a particularly fitting metaphor: "Within the settlement houses, maternal sentiments were further sifted and leavened until they became an entirely new variety of social reform."[16] Thus did Jane Addams learn the techniques of the political world through her efforts to keep the neighborhood clean. So too did Florence Kelley of Hull House welcome appointment as chief factory inspector of Illinois to protect women and children workers; Julia Lathrop, another Hull House resident, entered the public sphere as director of the U.S. Children's Bureau; and one-time settlement resident Katharine Bement Davis moved from the superintendency of the Bedford Hills Reformatory for Women in 1914 to become the first female commissioner of corrections in New York City. Each of these women, and other settlement workers who moved on to professional or public office, eventually joined and often led branches of the National American Woman Suffrage Association (NAWSA).[17] They drew upon the networks of personal friends and professional allies that grew within separate female institutions when they waged their campaigns for social reform and suffrage.

Separate female organizations were not limited to middle-class women. Recent histories have shown that groups hoping to bridge class lines between women existed within working-class and radical movements. In both the Women's Trade Union League and the National Consumers League, middle-class reformers strived for cooperation rather than condescension in their relationships with working women. Although in neither organization did reformers entirely succeed, the Women's Trade Union League did provide valuable services in organizing women workers, many of whom were significant in its leadership. The efforts of the Consumers League, led by Florence Kelley, to improve working conditions through the use of middle-class women's buying power were probably less effective, but efforts to enact protective legislation for women workers did succeed. Members of both organizations turned to suffrage as one solution to the problems workers faced. Meanwhile, both in leftist organizations and in unions, women formed separate organizations. Feminists within the Socialist Party met in women's groups in the early twentieth century, while within the clothing trades, women workers formed separate local unions that survived until the mid-1920s.[18]

As a final example of female institution building, I want to compare two actual buildings—the Woman's Pavilion at the 1876 Centennial Exposition in Philadelphia, analyzed recently by Judith Paine, and the Woman's Building at the 1893 World Columbian Exposition in Chicago. I think that the origins and functions of each illustrate some of the changes that occurred in the women's movement in the time interval between those two celebrations.

Originally, the managers of the 1876 Centennial Exhibition in Philadelphia had promised "a sphere for woman's action and space for her work" within the main display areas. In return, women raised over $100,000 for the fair, at which point the management informed the members of the Women's Centennial Executive Committee that there would not be any space for them in the main building. The women's response surprised the men: they raised money for a separate building. Although they hoped to find a woman architect to design it, no such professional existed at the time. From May through October 1876, the Woman's Pavilion displayed women's achievements in journalism, medicine, science, art, literature, invention, teaching, business, and social work. It included a library of books by women; an office that published a newspaper for women; and an innovative kindergarten annex, the first such day school in the country. Some radical feminists, however, boycotted the building. Elizabeth Cady Stanton claimed that the pavilion "was no true exhibit of woman's art" because it did not represent the product of industrial labor or protest the inequalities of "political slavery."[19]

By 1893, there was less hesitation about the need for a woman's building and somewhat less conflict about its functions. Congress authorized the creation of a Board of Lady Managers for the Columbian Commission, and the women quickly decided on a separate Woman's Building, to be designed by a woman architect chosen by nationwide competition. Contests were also held to locate the best women sculptors, painters, and other artists to complete the designs of the building. The Board of Lady Managers also planned and provided a Children's Building that offered nursery care for over 10,000 young visitors to the fair. At this exposition, not only were women's artistic and professional achievements heralded, but industrial organizations were "especially invited to make themselves known," and women's industrial work, as well as their wages and the conditions they encountered, was displayed. Feminists found this exhibit more agreeable. Antoinette Brown Blackwell, Julia Ward Howe, and Susan B. Anthony all attended, and Anthony read a paper written by Elizabeth Cady Stanton at one of the women's symposia. Members of the Board of Lady Managers fought long and hard to combine their separate enterprise with participation in the rest of the fair. They demanded equal representation of women judges for the exhibitions and equal consideration of women's enterprises in all contests. They had to compromise some of these goals, and, equally important, they failed to heed African American women's petitions for inclusion on the Board of Lady Managers. Thus, the Women's Building at the 1893 World's Fair represented a form of separatism that both demanded equal status for white women and reflected the racial exclusivity of American society.[20]

The Political Legacy

The separate institution building of the late nineteenth century rested on a belief in women's unique identity that had roots in the private female sphere of the early nineteenth century. Increasingly, however, as its participants entered a public female world, they adopted the more radical stance of feminists such as Stanton and Anthony who had long called for an end to political discrimination against women.

The generation that achieved suffrage, then, stood on the border of two worlds, each of which contributed to its ideology and politics. Suffragists argued that women needed the vote to perform their traditional tasks — to protect themselves as mothers and to exert their moral force on society. Yet they also argued for full citizenship and waged a successful, female-controlled political campaign to achieve it.

The suffrage movement succeeded by appealing to a broad constituency — mothers, workers, professionals, reformers — with the vision of the common concerns of womanhood. The movement failed, however, by not extending fully the political strengths of woman bonding. For one thing, the leadership allowed some members to exploit popular racist and nativist sentiments in their prosuffrage arguments, thus excluding most black and immigrant women from a potential feminist coalition. They also failed to recognize that the bonds that held the constituency together were not "natural" but social and political. The belief that women would automatically use the vote to the advantage of their sex overlooked both the class and racial lines that separated women. It underestimated the need for continued political organization so that women's interests might be united and realized.

Unfortunately, the rhetoric of equality that became popular among men and women (with the exception of the National Woman's Party) just after the passage of the suffrage amendment in 1920 subverted the women's movement by denying the need for continued feminist organization. Of course, external factors significantly affected the movement's future, including the new Freudian views of women; the growth of a consumer economy that increasingly exploited women's sexuality; and the repression of radicalism and reform in general after World War I.[21] At the same time, many women, seemingly oblivious that these pressures necessitated further separate organizing, insisted on striving for integration into a male world—sexually, professionally, and politically.

Examples of this integrationist approach can be found in the universities, the workplace, and politics. In contrast to an earlier generation, the women who participated in the New York World's Fair of 1939 had no separate building. Woman, the fair bulletin explained, "will not sit upon a pedestal, not be segregated, isolated; she will fit into the life of the Exposition as she does into life itself—never apart, always a part." The part in this world's fair, however, consisted primarily of fashion, food, and vanity fair.[22] In the universities, the success of the first generation of female academics did not survive past the 1920s, not only because of men's resistance but also, as Rosalind Rosenberg has explained, because "success isolated women from their culture of origin and placed them in an alien and often hostile community." Many academics who cut off their ties to other women "lost their old feminine supports but had no other supports to replace them."[23]

The lesson of women's politics in the 1920s is illustrated by the life of one woman, Emily Newell Blair, who learned firsthand the pitfalls of rejecting a separatist basis for feminism.[24] Blair's life exemplified the transformation of women's roles at the turn of the century. Educated at a woman's college, Goucher, this Missouri-born, middle-class woman returned to her hometown to help support her family until she married and created her own home. Between 1900 and 1910, she bore two children, supported her husband's career, and joined in local women's club activities. In her spare time, Blair began writing short stories for ladies' magazines. Because she found the work, and particularly the income, satisfying, she became a freelance writer. At this point, the suffrage movement revived in Missouri, and Blair took over state publicity, editing the magazine *Missouri Woman* and doing public relations. Then, in World War I, she expanded her professional activities further by serving on the Women's Council of the U.S. Council of National Defense. These years of training in writing, feminist organizing, and public speaking served Blair well when suffrage passed and she entered politics.

In 1920, women faced three major political choices: they could become a separate feminist political force through the National Woman's Party, which few did; they could follow the moderates of the NAWSA into the newly formed, nonpartisan League of Women Voters, concentrating on citizen education and good government; or they could join the mainstream political parties. Emily Newell Blair chose the third option and rose through the Democratic Party organization to become national vice chairman in the 1920s.

Blair built her political life and her following on the belief that the vote had made women the political equals of men. Thus, she thought the surest path to furthering women's goals was through participation in the party structure. Having helped found the League of Women Voters, Blair then rejected nonpartisanship and urged women not to vote as women but as citizens. In her 1922 lecture "What Women May Do with the Ballot," Blair argued that "reactions to political issues are not decided by sex but by intellect and emotion." Although she believed that lack of political experience and social training made women different from men temporarily, she expected those differences to be eliminated after a few years of political activity. To hasten women's integration into the mainstream of party politics, Blair set up 30 "schools of democracy" to train the new voters during the early twenties, as well as over 1,000 women's clubs. Her philosophy, she claimed, was one of "boring from within." Blair rejected the "sex conscious feminists" of the Woman's Party and those who wanted "woman cohesiveness." Although she favored the election of women, she wanted them to be chosen not as women but as politicians. "Give women time," she often repeated, and they would become the equals of men in politics.

By the late 1920s, however, women had not gained acceptance as men's political equals, and Blair's views changed significantly. Once she had claimed that the parties did not discriminate against women, as shown by her own powerful position. After she retired from party office in 1928, however, Blair acknowledged that the treatment of women by the parties had deteriorated since the years immediately after suffrage passed. As soon as male politicians realized that there was no strong female voting bloc or political organization, they refused to appoint or elect powerful women, and a "strong masculine prejudice against women in politics" surfaced. Now they chose women for party office who seemed easiest to manage or who were the wives of male officeholders.

By 1931, Blair's former optimism had turned to disillusionment. She felt herself "ineffective in politics as a feminist," a term that she began to use positively. Blair realized that women could not command political power and the respect of their male colleagues unless, like the suffrage leaders, they had a visible, vocal following. "Unfortunately for feminism," she confessed, "it was agreed to drop the sex line in politics. And it was dropped by the women." In the pages of the *Woman's Journal*, Blair called for a revival of feminism in the form of a new politics that would seek to put more women in office. Reversing her former stance, she claimed that *women* voters should back *women* candidates and use a *women's* organization to do so. They could remain in the parties but should form "a new organization of feminists devoted to the task of getting women into politics."

The development of Emily Newell Blair's feminist consciousness may have been unique for her time, but it is a familiar process among educated and professional women today. Having gained access to formerly male institutions but still committed to furthering women's struggles, today's "new women" are faced with political choices not dissimilar to those of the generation that achieved suffrage. The bitterness of Stanton and Anthony in their advice to the younger generation in 1881 and the strategy that Emily Newell Blair presented in 1931 may serve as lessons for the present.

The Lessons of Separatism

The strength of female institutions in the late nineteenth century and the weaknesses of women's politics after the passage of the suffrage amendment suggest to me that the decline of feminism in the 1920s can be attributed in part to the devaluation of women's culture in general and of separate female institutions in particular. When women tried to assimilate into male-dominated institutions without securing feminist social, economic, or political bases, they lost the momentum and the networks that had made the suffrage movement possible. Women gave up many of the strengths of the female sphere without gaining equally from the male world they entered.

This historical record has important implications for the women's movement today. It becomes clearer, I think, why the separate, small women's group, organized for consciousness raising or political study and action, has been effective in building a grassroots movement over the past ten years. The groups helped reestablish common bonds long veiled by the retreat from women's institutions into privatized families or sexually integrated but male-dominated institutions. The groups encouraged the reemergence of female networks and a new women's culture, which in turn have given rise to female institution building — women's centers, health collectives, political unions, even new women's buildings, like the ones in Los Angeles and San Francisco.

The history of separatism also helps explain why the politics of lesbian feminism have been so important in the revival of the women's movement. Lesbian feminism, by affirming the primacy of women's relationships with each other and by providing an alternative feminist culture, forced many nonlesbians to reevaluate their relationships with men, male institutions, and male values. In the process, feminists have put to rest the myth of female dependence on men and rediscovered the significance of woman bonding. I find it personally gratifying that the lesbian feminist concept of the woman-identified woman has historical roots in the female friendships, networks, and institutions of the nineteenth century.[25] The historical sisterhood, it seems to me, can teach us a great deal about putting women first, whether as friends, lovers, or political allies.

I find two kinds of political lessons in the history of the separatist trend. In the past, one of the limitations of separate female institutions was that they were often the only places for women to pursue professional or political activities, while men's institutions retained the power over most of the society. Today it is crucial to press for feminist presence both outside and within the bastions of male dominance, such as politics, the universities, the professions, and the unions. But it is equally important for the women within mixed institutions to create female interest groups and support systems. Otherwise, token women may be either co-opted into traditionally deferential roles or assimilated through identification with the powers that be. In the process, these women will lose touch with their feminist values and constituencies, as well as suffer the personal costs of tokenism. Thus, in universities we need to strengthen our women's centers and women's studies programs and to form women's groups among faculty as well as students. In all of our workplaces, we need women's caucuses to secure and enlarge our gains. And unlike much of the movement in the past, we need to undertake the enormous task of building coalitions of women's groups from all classes, races, and cultures.

I argue for a continuation of separatism not because the values, culture, and politics of the two sexes are biologically, irreversibly distinct but rather because the historical and contemporary experiences that have created a unique female culture remain both salient for and compatible with the goal of sexual equality. Our common identities and heritage as women can provide enormous personal and political strength as long as we claim the power to define what women can be and what female institutions can achieve. I argue for renewed female institution building at this point in the contemporary women's movement because I fear that many feminists — faced with the isolation of personal success or dismayed by political backlash — may turn away from the separate women's politics that have achieved most of our gains in the past decade. And I argue as well for both greater respect for women's culture among political feminists and greater political engagement on the part of cultural feminists because we now face both external resistance and internal contradictions that threaten to divide our movement.

The contradictions faced by contemporary feminists are those experienced by an oppressed group — in this case, women — which needs both to affirm the value of its own culture and to reject the past oppression from which that culture in part originated.[26] To survive as a movement, we must avoid two kinds of pitfalls. In this essay, I have concentrated on the dangers of rejecting our culture through individualist integration of the kind that undermined feminism after the first wave of political and educational progress. The other pitfall is that of embracing our culture too uncritically, to the point of identifying with the sources of our own oppression. Rayna Rapp has warned that "as we excavate and legitimize women's history, social organization, and cultural forms, we must not allow our own need for models of strong female collectivities to blind us to the dialectic of tradition" in which women are both supported and constrained.[27] Although we must be self-critical of women's culture and strive to use female institutions to combat inequality, not to entrench it, at the same time, we must not be self-hating of that which is female as we enter a world dominated by men. Even as women retrain in the skills that men once monopolized — in trades, professions, and politics — we should not forsake but rather we should cherish the values and institutions that were once women's only resources. Even if the Equal Rights Amendment someday legally mandates equality, in the meantime and for some time thereafter, the female world and separatist politics will still serve the interests of women.

2 | Separatism Revisited | Women's Institutions, Social Reform, and the Career of Miriam Van Waters

Women's prisons differ significantly from voluntary separatist institutions, but they reveal larger patterns in the history of female reform. I had written about the origins of these institutions in my first book, Their Sisters' Keepers, *and a decade later I returned to the subject to write a biography of Miriam Van Waters. By then, an expanding historical literature on twentieth-century women's politics was calling into question the usefulness of national enfranchisement in 1920 as a turning point, especially for women outside the white middle classes. As I explored Van Waters's career, I was struck by similarities between her values and those of earlier women prison reformers. This essay builds upon Miriam Van Waters's exceptional story to generalize about the survival of women's personal and political networks in the era between the 1920s and the 1960s.*

IN NOVEMBER 1945, a group of college students who were conducting research on women and social reform paid a visit to the Framingham, Massachusetts, women's prison. They went to meet with the superintendent, Miriam Van Waters, a prominent juvenile justice and prison reformer. In 1927, Van Waters had served as president of the National Conference on Social Work, and she currently presided over the American League to Abolish Capital Punishment. Talking with the students about their projects gave Van Waters a chance to reflect back upon her career. That night, writing in her journal, she posed an intriguing historical question: Why, she wondered, were there no longer any great women leaders in social work, women of the stature of Florence Kelley, Jane Addams, and Julia Lathrop?[1] Van Waters's sense that the

Previously published as Estelle B. Freedman, "Separatism Revisited: Women's Institutions, Social Reform, and the Career of Miriam Van Waters," in *U.S. History as Women's History: New Feminist Essays*, edited by Linda K. Kerber, Alice Kessler-Harris, and Kathryn Kish Sklar (Chapel Hill: University of North Carolina Press, 1995), 170–88. Reprinted by permission of the University of North Carolina Press.

golden age of women and reform had passed by the 1940s has been echoed by historians, who generally date the ascendance of American women's public moral authority in the mid-nineteenth century and its decline sometime after the enactment of suffrage in 1920. Yet both Van Waters's own career and recent scholarship on the twentieth century suggest the persistence of women's contributions to social reform in the postsuffrage era. Even during the rise of professionalized social work and the provision of welfare by state and national governments, women's local, voluntary associations continued to play an important role in sustaining progressive reform. To explore this premise, I would like to look more closely at continuities in women's contributions to social reform after 1920. I draw particularly on the career of Miriam Van Waters to do so, placing her life within a larger historical landscape.

THE ROLE OF WOMEN in American social reform has a long and complex history. In the antebellum period, religiously motivated middle-class women began to provide the impetus for local and national reform movements. White women formed associations to achieve temperance and prison reform, while black and white female antislavery societies appealed to women to work for abolition. At the turn of the century, African American women's clubs crusaded against lynching and provided critical local social services such as health, education, and day care in southern black communities. In the North, elite and working-class white women cooperated in movements for protective legislation for workers, while white middle-class women's clubs sponsored a variety of "child-saving" measures, including local juvenile courts and state child labor laws. Women's voluntarism and reform campaigns not only filled a significant gap in American political life but also gave disfranchised women a degree of public authority. In the settlement houses, through the National Consumers League, and in the U.S. Children's Bureau, reformers like Addams, Kelley, and Lathrop brought women's maternal vision of social justice into the mainstream of American life and helped lay the groundwork for a welfare state.[2]

After the waning of progressivism and the attainment of suffrage in 1920, however, organized womanhood seemed to play a less influential role in social reform. Women's clubs, which had once led the movement for juvenile justice, now gained a reputation as mere recreational groups. Rescue homes founded by nineteenth-century Protestant women missionaries closed or were taken over by male authorities during the 1920s and 1930s. Even as women entered the new profession of social work, they lost a measure of their older moral authority. Among professional social workers, male domination began to "insinuate itself" in the 1920s, and it deepened during the depression.[3] What one historian has termed the "female dominion in American reform" may have culminated in the New Deal steps toward a welfare state, but in the process, male officials attained increasing state authority over concerns once left largely in the hands of women volunteers. According to another historian, women "surrendered to government functions that had belonged to the woman's sphere" and thus lost their separate political culture.[4]

The explanations for this shift from female to male authority in reform vary, from the personal — for example, a decline in women's interest in serving — to the structural — such as economic competition for social work jobs during the depression. I have previously argued that women's postsuffrage efforts to integrate into male organizational structures undermined their autonomous political base since separate women's networks and institutions are critical to the survival of the women's movement.[5] New historical research, however, has shown the ways that separatism, or female institution building, did, in fact, survive as a reform strategy after 1920. Indeed, where separatism in some form persisted, women continued to influence social reform and politics to an extent that earlier histories have underestimated. The persistence of women organized for reform complicates and challenges a monolithic interpretation of the decline of women's moral and political authority after the suffrage victory.

As historians have shifted attention from the private, female sphere of the nineteenth century to the public, political activities of women in the twentieth century, they have clarified the contours of that amorphous term, the "women's movement." We now recognize the coexistence of many social movements led by women — some to protect women and children in the family or workplace, some to benefit larger social groups (such as workers or African Americans), and others committed solely to the goal of gaining equal political rights for women.[6] Given this broadly defined women's movement with overlapping memberships, the suffrage victory in 1920 seems like a narrow and inappropriate benchmark for periodizing women's history.

Continuity as much as change characterized the pre- and postsuffrage decades for African American women, for example. In the South, suffrage did not usher in a new era, for political, economic, and social discrimination persisted, necessitating local social service and self-help programs that continued to rely on female leadership. After World War I, in response to the northern migration, middle-class black women formed new clubs that provided service to urban communities, and in several cities, working-class women organized Housewives Leagues to support black-owned businesses. In addition, educated black women worked within interracial groups, such as the Consumers League, the local juvenile courts, and the League of Women Voters; in the Young Women's Christian Association (YWCA), black women waged a fervent though largely unsuccessful campaign for racial equality.[7]

Among privileged white women, a variety of postsuffrage organizations continued to influence reform. Some groups — such as women's clubs and the Consumers League — drew upon an older ideology of female difference, using maternalism as a basis for their contributions to politics and social reform. Others, such as the National Woman's Party, embraced the newer ideology of "feminism," which claimed that women merited political authority because they were equal to, not different from, men. Despite their ideological differences, however, both groups of women frequently relied on the separatist institutions of the earlier women's movement to achieve their goals.[8]

The legacy of separatism can be seen, for example, where women reformers continued to draw upon the kinds of close personal networks that had long nurtured activists such as Jane Addams and Florence Kelley. The "emotional anchor" of friendship helped buttress women's social service efforts within African American communities. Personal networks advanced women's political goals in the 1920s and especially during the New Deal, when middle-class reformers such as Molly Dewson and Frances Perkins worked to extend the benefits of the welfare state to working women. In addition, formal women's institutions, such as the Children's Bureau in the Department of Labor and the Women's Joint Congressional Committee, maintained the "female dominion" of reform through the New Deal era. At the other end of the ideological spectrum from these "social feminists," the National Woman's Party also drew on close personal networks and separate female organizing to support its lobbying efforts for the passage of the Equal Rights Amendment, providing a critical link to the reemergence of liberal feminist politics in the 1960s.[9]

Separate networks and institutions also sustained women's quests for economic opportunities in the postsuffrage era. The National Federation of Business and Professional Women's Clubs, founded after World War I, sought equality at work through a separate women's organization. Among working-class women, recent scholarship suggests, separate women's locals best served the interests of unionized women, such as waitresses. Among California cannery workers, the continuing sexual segregation of labor helped create a female workplace culture of predominantly Mexican and Jewish women, which in turn facilitated union organizing during the 1930s and 1940s.[10]

Women's social-service and social-reform organizations provide another example of continuity in separatist institution building after suffrage. Although the YWCA had nineteenth-century origins as a separate women's organization, it flourished after 1920, resisting efforts by the Young Men's Christian Association to subsume it and adopting more explicitly political goals. In the 1920s, the college division of the YWCA took the lead in opposing racial segregation in the South, and by the 1940s and 1950s, black and white leaders struggled over how to integrate the segregated YWCAs without inadvertently taking autonomy away from important black community institutions.[11]

A final legacy of separatism is the survival of women's intimate relationships in the twentieth century. Historians once argued that the emergence of a medical and psychiatric definition of lesbianism as a sexual perversion served to suppress the loving friendships that once flourished among white middle-class women.[12] Although prescriptive literature may have stigmatized homosexuality in the early twentieth century, the naming of lesbianism simultaneously granted to women the capacity to have sexual relations with members of their own sex. More important than labels, when opportunities for economic self-support freed women from dependence on marriage, female couples proliferated. In settlement houses, during the Harlem Renaissance, among political activists of the New Deal, in the women's armed forces during World War II, and in the lesbian bars of the 1950s, lesbian subcultures gradually emerged, laying the groundwork for the homophile and lesbian-feminist political movements. Although female couples did not necessarily claim a lesbian identity, particularly before 1950, intimate relationships between women nonetheless continued to provide one means of support for activists, including social reformers.[13]

These examples of women's networks and female institution building in the postsuffrage era, along with the women's peace movement and the southern white women's antilynching movement, force a revision of the modern history of women and reform.[14] Rather than portraying only decline or erosion of women's organizations and their role in social reform after 1920, we may need to tell a story that includes pockets of quiet persistence. Understanding where and why separate women's organizations did survive may help explain the contours of reform in the twentieth century as well as the reemergence of feminism in the 1960s.

THE CAREER OF Miriam Van Waters (1887–1974) illustrates the continuing importance of women's networks and women's institutions in modern American social reform. A nationally known juvenile justice reformer in the 1920s, Van Waters made headlines in 1949 when she successfully defended herself from dismissal as superintendent of the Massachusetts Reformatory for Women in Framingham. A series of dramatic public hearings inspired both a popular biography and the classic women's prison film, *Caged* (1950), in which Agnes Moorehead created a remarkable facsimile of the high-minded superintendent. Miriam Van Waters continued to direct Framingham until her retirement in 1957.[15] Throughout her career, she chose to work with and for women, and female institutions provided critical support for her reforms. An examination of separatism in her life suggests that historians may need to rethink the periodization of modern women's history by looking more closely at women's voluntary and political institutions between 1920 and 1960.

Like other middle-class women activists of the nineteenth and twentieth centuries, Miriam Van Waters developed her commitment to serve women and children within the broader context of liberal Protestantism. Growing up in the rectory of her father's Episcopal church in Portland, Oregon, Van Waters was exposed to both the late-nineteenth-century social gospel and support for the rights of women. In 1904, she graduated from an Episcopal girls' school and entered the University of Oregon. Suffrage activism was gathering strength in Oregon, and as editor of the campus literary magazine, Van Waters urged women to participate in student government lest they be unprepared to vote.[16] A strong dean of women may have provided a model for Oregon students, for in addition to Van Waters and several of her women friends, a disproportionate number of the university's female graduates pursued advanced degrees.[17] After completing her M.A. in psychology at Oregon in 1910, Van Waters entered Clark University to study with the country's leading psychologist, G. Stanley Hall.

Three years later, disillusioned with Hall's scientific methods and dismayed by the second-class status accorded academic women, Miriam Van Waters completed her doctorate in anthropology. She joined a small but growing elite of highly educated American women. Like other early women social scientists, Van Waters wanted to put her academic expertise to "constructive" use.[18] Inspired by Jane Addams, the suffrage movement, and juvenile court reformers, she began a lifetime career of working with delinquent women. After an internship at Boston Children's Aid, she returned to the West in 1914 to direct the Frazer Detention Home in Portland, Oregon.

There she implemented sweeping reforms in education, recreation, and self-government. After 1917, Van Waters worked at the Los Angeles Juvenile Court, which, like its predecessor in Chicago, was the product of a reform campaign led by local women's clubs. She directed Juvenile Hall and, as one historian has written, "quickly transformed this institution into one of the leading progressive detention centers in the country."[19] From 1920 to 1930, she served as court "referee," a quasi-judicial position. In her capacity of recommending the disposition of cases of all girls and the younger boys brought to court, she favored probation rather than incarceration.

At Juvenile Hall, Van Waters worked with both girls and boys, but the project dearest to her was El Retiro, an experimental school for adolescent girls brought to the juvenile court. In 1919, she helped transform this former sanatorium into an unenclosed, rural, residential high school for girls, operated on a system of student self-government. El Retiro stressed education and economic self-sufficiency for its residents. Van Waters served as a surrogate mother to many of its students and as their advocate in juvenile court. She proselytized the El Retiro model nationally through the liberal press and in her influential studies of delinquency, *Youth in Conflict* (1925) and *Parents on Probation* (1927). Van Waters also investigated girls' reformatories around the country, exposing punitive conditions and calling for improvements.[20]

As did reformers of an earlier generation, Miriam Van Waters found support for her work within a network of like-minded women. For over a decade, she operated within a circle of women lawyers, judges, and social workers who staffed the juvenile court and participated in an elaborate community of professional women in Los Angeles. Van Waters herself belonged to the Professional Women's Club, the Women's Athletic Club, and the Los Angeles Business Women's Club. She shared a communal house with former juvenile court referee Orfa Jean Shontz and two classmates from Clark University, University of California at Los Angeles psychology professor Sara Fisher and Los Angeles school psychologist Elizabeth Woods. When Van Waters adopted a daughter, members of the household helped raise her. All supporters of the presuffrage "woman movement,"[21] the housemates continued to seek greater public authority for women in the criminal justice system and equal treatment of female delinquents. In the 1920s, their suburban home, "The Colony," served as a latter-day salon for women reformers from around the world, such as Chicago philanthropist Ethel Sturges Dummer, who visited The Colony whenever she went to Los Angeles. Similarly, when Van Waters traveled around the country, she stopped at Hull House to stay with her colleague Jessie Binford and meet with Jane Addams, Edith Abbott, and other reformers. In Los Angeles or Chicago, these women exchanged information on the juvenile court movement and social legislation to improve the conditions of women and children.

The community of women reformers in Los Angeles during the 1920s extended beyond paid, professional workers like Shontz, Fisher, Woods, and Van Waters. An extensive network of women's clubs, whose members came from both elite and middle-class families, took up the cause of the female juvenile delinquent, largely at the urging of Van Waters in her frequent addresses to local women's organizations. For example, the Friday Morning Club — with 1,000 members, the largest women's club on the West Coast — offered political support for her efforts to improve conditions at Juvenile Hall. Van Waters chaired the juvenile court division of the California Federation of Women's Clubs and took special pride in her relationship with the Colored Women's Federation, which sought to establish a training school for "colored girls."[22] Church-affiliated women's auxiliaries sustained both the social gospel and the moral authority of Protestant women when they brought pressure to bear during recurrent conservative attacks on the El Retiro experiment. Van Waters also made an ally of the local Council of Jewish Women, which funded a court social worker. In her most effective use of women's professional networks in the 1920s, she helped convince the Los Angeles Business Women's Club to fund a residential home where young women released from El Retiro could live on their own while they became self-supporting, thus preventing their return to hostile or abusive families. Through such efforts, separate women's organizations in Los Angeles supported both the professional and political advancement of women like Miriam Van Waters and maintained a female voice within social-reform efforts.

However supportive the Los Angeles women's community, local politics ultimately impinged on Van Waters's reform efforts, destroying the El Retiro experiment in 1927. Frustrated by the failures she witnessed in the juvenile court movement and drawn into national service on both President Herbert Hoover's crime commission and a Harvard Law School crime survey, Van Waters shifted her career in two directions: from California to Massachusetts and from juvenile to adult corrections. In 1932, at the age of forty-four, she accepted the position of superintendent at the Massachusetts Reformatory for Women in Framingham. For the next twenty-five years, she made Framingham a testing ground for her reform philosophies and innovative social work methods. Van Waters vowed "to bring our neighbors into our planning, to have the community flow into us, and our institution into the community."[23] She drew local students, college faculty, clergy, and women's groups into the prison as volunteers; introduced psychological counseling and therapeutic recreational groups for inmates; and established intensely close familial relations with the women whom she called "students" and in whom she invested unusual trust and responsibility for their daily lives. Her efforts to create an alternative correctional institution at Framingham echoed the visions of the nineteenth-century women prison reformers who had founded the reformatory, but her methods contrasted sharply with the disciplinary style of prison administration that prevailed during the 1930s and 1940s. Critics accused Van Waters of coddling prisoners and defying state authority. Even some supporters marveled at the extent of her regal command over the Framingham reformatory. Repeatedly Van Waters conflicted with the parole board and the Massachusetts Department of Corrections, and as in Los Angeles, she often mobilized women's networks to support her reforms.

Although the Framingham prison was an involuntary women's institution, under Van Waters it often resembled a voluntary community. Hundreds of women, imbued with a mission to rehabilitate incarcerated women, chose to work there as interns and staff members. In many ways, Van Waters modeled Framingham as much on Hull House as on El Retiro. Indeed, over the years, residents of various settlement houses visited or interned at Framingham, as did women college students in search of meaningful work. One such woman, a recent graduate of Cornell, recalled her first impression of Framingham in the mid-1930s: "I think from the moment I walked in there was something about the atmosphere. I just thought . . . 'This is wonderful.' . . . It was more like a progressive school. There was no prison atmosphere whatsoever. . . . The whole atmosphere was one of growth and excitement and new experience, you know, and people coming in and out."[24] This woman stayed as an intern, then joined the staff; after receiving a social work degree, she spent the rest of her career as a devoted employee of Van Waters at Framingham. Similarly, interns from Vassar, Smith, Wellesley, Simmons, and other colleges went to the reformatory to teach classes on current events, ceramics, art, and psychology. Van Waters herself enjoyed the opportunity to lead weekly literary study groups. Like progressive educators, she tried to make the entire institution a learning experience. The nursery, which housed children born in prison, became a training ground for teachers and health workers. The nearby woods provided an incentive for well-behaved and trusted inmates who aspired to join the nature study club that took weekend hikes. In the 1940s and 1950s, Van Waters incorporated elements of group therapy and the self-help model of Alcoholics Anonymous into her programs for inmates. "Only delinquents can solve the problems of delinquents," she wrote, and so she offered jobs to former "students," some of whom chose to return to the institution as staff members.[25]

As much as it was like a school, Framingham was also a social welfare institution in the broadest sense. Many of the women committed by the courts were simply homeless, pregnant, or alcoholic. Van Waters and other staff members preferred to view them as women in need of supportive services instead of as women in need of punishment. "Framingham presents all the problems of the modern world," Van Waters once reflected, noting that its residents shared with other women the dilemma of finding adequate child care to enable them to go to work.[26] Since poverty and inadequate health care plagued the residents, Van Waters pressed for both medical and mental health personnel to address their problems. Job training became a central goal, and she developed a "furlough system" that allowed many "students" to work for pay on the outside.

Material support was only part of Van Waters's program. A deeply spiritual woman, she spoke of her mission as "Christian Penology." As she recorded in her journal: "Here I intend to build — 'a kingdom of heaven on earth' — that is to say — a world of order, protection, fluid understanding, where both spontaneity and discipline — express the service of justice."[27] Central to achieving her goal of creating "The Framingham Symphony" was the personal charisma of conductor Miriam Van Waters. As one observer noted, the "faith and friendship of the superintendent" were key to the "informal rehabilitation" that characterized Framingham. In the words of one inmate, "The Superintendent has so much faith in me that I can't ever let her down."[28] Van Waters maintained a sincere respect for "the child of God" in each woman in the institution. In many cases, her charges responded to this personal approach with extreme loyalty, deep adoration, and idealization of their saintly superintendent.

Personal charisma alone could not have maintained such an unusual institution. Van Waters repeatedly relied on a variety of middle-class women's networks and organizations to support her earthly kingdom. Smith, Wellesley, and other women's college graduates, who often worked for room and board plus a small stipend, made possible the educational programs at Framingham. Outside the institution, club women offered support. In 1947, the Altrusa Club of Boston, consisting of fifty-four prominent businesswomen, raised money to hire women workers from the reformatory since, as one club member wrote, "men in institutions have the privileges of earning and saving money through their labors while such privileges are not given to women."[29] Similarly, the Massachusetts League of Women Voters protested both the injustice of imposing heavier penalties for women offenders (for crimes such as adultery and cohabitation) and the fact that "only poor women are prosecuted for these crimes," many of whom were "foreign speaking."[30] Van Waters also mobilized church women to support her reforms, as she had learned to do in Los Angeles. In a state with long-standing tensions between Catholics and Protestants, she won the respect of every denomination. A striking example of how club women's networks operated appears in a letter to Van Waters from Willa W. Brown, who had once heard the superintendent give a college commencement address. Learning that Van Waters might lose her job in 1949, Brown wrote to offer help. "You do not know me," she began. "I am a member of the Boston Wheelock Club, the Florence Crittendon League, the Women's Charity Club, the Bright and Helmstone Women's Club, & the Women's Association of the Brighton Congregational Church. So you see I would be able to obtain a great many signatures in your behalf."[31]

Aside from relying on community support, Van Waters turned to religious, personal, and political networks to bolster her efforts. At the invitation of settlement worker Vida Scudder, she joined the Society of the Companions of the Holy Cross, a select group of reform-minded Episcopalian women who nurtured a spiritual commitment to social justice and class reconciliation.[32] Professionally she remained in touch with her former Los Angeles colleagues and with her first benefactor, Ethel Sturges Dummer, who funded small research projects at Framingham. After 1930, however, Van Waters's main emotional and political sustenance came from her "dearest love," Geraldine Morgan Thompson (1872–1967).

A former suffragist and an activist in the New Jersey women's club movement, Geraldine Thompson devoted her life and her considerable wealth to the cause of charitable institutions. She helped found the Monmouth County Organization for Social Services in 1912 and served on its board until 1952. Thompson took a special interest in the treatment and cure of tuberculosis and in juvenile justice and women's prisons. As a member of the Board of Control of the State Department of Institutions and Agencies (the first woman appointed to a state board in New Jersey), she helped oversee the women's reformatory at Clinton Farms. Although a lifelong Republican and a national committeewoman during the 1920s, Thompson had close ties to the New Deal White House for she had grown up near Hyde Park and remained a warm friend of Eleanor and Franklin Roosevelt.[33]

Geraldine Thompson met Miriam Van Waters in the mid-1920s, and the two women gradually became intimate friends as well as reform allies. Thompson supported Van Waters's reform efforts at Framingham. She often visited the institution and addressed staff meetings and student assemblies, speaking about politics and public service. Thanks to Thompson, Eleanor Roosevelt also spoke at the institution. Thompson's philanthropy provided stipends for interns, funded a part-time psychiatrist, and supplemented the educational and nursery budgets.

In addition to involving herself in the life of the institution through contributions and visits, Thompson provided a physical and emotional refuge for Van Waters. When the superintendent felt overwhelmed by institutional responsibilities and the stress of providing for the close relatives who lived with or near her, she could recuperate at Brookdale, the Thompson estate near Red Bank, New Jersey. The two friends would take early morning horseback rides and long walks, talk of their work and their spiritual beliefs, and take comfort in each other's love. Thus, after a day at Brookdale, Van Waters wrote in her journal: "I am deeply at peace, cherished and blessed beyond words by Geraldine's love and care."[34] After Thompson's husband died in 1936, the two women regularly vacationed together, and they continued to attend conferences throughout the United States and in Europe. Through letters and telephone calls, Thompson provided a well of "strength" for Van Waters. As they aged in the 1950s, Van Waters and Thompson, along with close women friends from the reformatory staff, spent weekends at Audubon Camps in New England and delighted in the company of nature and each other.

Thompson also provided a link to larger women's political networks. Van Waters met Eleanor Roosevelt when the couple dined at the White House in 1940. When Massachusetts politics threatened to undermine the mission at Framingham, Thompson would remind Mrs. Roosevelt of Van Waters's good works and ask her to intervene. In 1945, for example, when Thompson feared that the governor might remove Van Waters from office, she wrote to Roosevelt. "Miriam," Thompson explained, "is not only a liberal, but a radical, and a fighting radical, at that. . . . She is, and has always been, an ardent supporter of yours and Franklin." A brief note to the governor, Thompson suggested, could let him know how much Mrs. Roosevelt appreciated "the type of philosophy and administration which has made Framingham the outstanding Women's Reformatory in this country."[35] Van Waters remained in office, at least partially due to Eleanor Roosevelt's intervention.

Although Miriam Van Waters staved off political attack through the 1940s, her methods had long infuriated conservatives in the Department of Corrections. From 1947 to 1949, critics of the reformatory made her the subject of state investigations, newspaper exposés, and a series of three public hearings at which she defended her administration. The attack began in 1947, when state officials charged that Van Waters had exceeded her authority by indenturing women in jobs outside the reformatory and allowing some of them privileges such as occasional dinners and movies in town. They also attacked the superintendent for hiring former inmates and for allowing released "students" to visit friends at the reformatory. The most controversial charge was that she condoned homosexual relationships between inmates, a practice that, opponents claimed, had led to the suicide of one inmate. In January 1949, the commissioner of corrections dismissed her from office.

Van Waters defended herself against these charges effectively, standing up in public hearings for her belief in educational rather than punitive treatment and gaining national attention for her work at Framingham. Meanwhile, influential friends throughout the country rallied to stand by her. Testimonials and contributions arrived from women active in reform and politics, including Geraldine Thompson, Ethel Sturges Dummer, Eleanor Roosevelt, and Frances Perkins. Both men and women in the field of social welfare mobilized on her behalf, as did dozens of Boston area Episcopal, Catholic, and Jewish clergy and local college faculty and students. Organizational endorsements included those of the Massachusetts State Federation of Women's Clubs, the National Council of Jewish Women, the Massachusetts Society for Social Hygiene, the YWCA, the Massachusetts Council of Churches, and the Americans for Democratic Action. Outpourings of faith and admiration arrived daily—in handwritten notes from former inmates, on engraved stationery from the wives of prominent men, and in typed letters from professional women. When Van Waters won reinstatement as superintendent in March 1949, letters from supporters around the country poured into her office. Her close friend Felix Frankfurter claimed that the cause of democracy was served through her reinstatement. Having withstood the attack by conservative politicians, Van Waters became a symbol of "progressive penology." Along with her prominent liberal supporters, dozens of former prisoners, local housewives, and complete strangers wrote to congratulate the superintendent on the "vindication of your principles."[36]

At Framingham, Van Waters continued to mobilize local middle-class women's organizations to support her reforms. In the 1950s, for example, members of the Friends of Framingham not only volunteered at the prison but also lobbied the state legislature to preserve the day work system. But hostile state officials, resentful of Van Waters's victory, monitored the prison closely and tried to impede her most innovative reforms. Like other Cold War politicians, her critics repeatedly raised the specter of sexual deviance, claiming that homosexuality was rampant at Framingham in order to sensationalize their charges. In 1957, just two months before Van Waters retired, Boston newspaper headlines charged: "Sex Fiends, Boozers Run Wild in Women's Prison." A state legislative investigation soon condemned "aggressive homosexuals" at the facility and led to the resignation of the deputy superintendent, a protégé of Van Waters.[37] These attacks reflected a new climate for women reformers that was in many ways symptomatic of a larger postwar critique of women's work outside the home, women's sexual independence, and female political authority. The Van Waters case and its aftermath left a public image that conflated wage-earning women, lesbians, and the threat that strong female leaders encouraged both.

EACH STAGE OF Miriam Van Waters's dramatic career — first as an influential figure in the juvenile justice movement, then as a champion of women's prison reform, and finally as a reformer under attack — illuminates the history of women and social reform in modern America. Van Waters's decision to apply her education to the provision of social services, and in particular her work with female clients, made sense in terms of the tradition of women's reform. By the time Van Waters came of age professionally, however, the relationship between women reformers and the state had begun to change in critical ways. Women like Florence Kelley and Julia Lathrop had moved beyond the voluntarism and outsider politics of the past, while the expansion of state social services during the Progressive Era, and later during the New Deal, drew women into paid, professional, and often highly politicized roles. As voluntary reformers, settlement workers such as Jane Addams and Vida Scudder had enjoyed a measure of immunity to male political authority. With the professionalization of social work and its centralization within state agencies, a younger generation of reformers, including Miriam Van Waters, entered administrative hierarchies, usually headed by men, under the watchful eyes of state legislators. As a result, women expanded their public authority through integration into the male political culture but lost some of the administrative autonomy that earlier, voluntary reformers had enjoyed. Thus, new obstacles confronted Van Waters at critical points in her career, in the 1920s and the 1940s, when state officials attempted to undermine her reforms or oust her from office because of her sympathies toward prisoners and her innovative methods.

The career of Miriam Van Waters illuminates not only new obstacles but also certain continuities in women's reform strategies. Van Waters repeatedly relied on women's personal and political networks to advance her programs. Before suffrage, she both created and was supported by strong ties to women — in her family, in school, and in the juvenile court movement. After 1920, she continued to draw on both close personal ties to women and extensive outreach to women in churches and in social service organizations. That Van Waters could bring such an array of women's community-based organizations into a prison reminds us of the rich yet still largely untapped history of middle-class women's voluntary associations in the twentieth century.[38] Among the women in these organizations — few of whom joined the expanding female paid labor force or the small feminist movement — separate institution building persisted, as did support for women's social-reform efforts.

Van Waters's individual character, the nature of women's prison reform, and the local contexts in which she operated might account for the continuing influence of separatism throughout her career. But the fact that she could mobilize so many women's voluntary, religious, and political organizations from the 1920s through the 1950s suggests that Van Waters's story may not be entirely unique. Rather, her life may reveal larger patterns that require at least two kinds of further historical inquiry: first, to learn what common experiences inspired and sustained the work of this cohort of reformers; and second, to compare the approaches of pre- and postsuffrage women reformers.

Van Waters belonged to a generation of women reformers who followed in the shadow of Addams, Kelley, and Lathrop. These activists continued to work for women's interests, often based in women's institutions though constantly maneuvering through the obstacles of male political authority. In the labor movement, this generation included women who came out of the workers' education movement of the 1920s, such as organizer Rose Pesotta and researcher Theresa Wolfson, as well as Women's Bureau director Esther Peterson. In civil rights, it encompassed the careers of Mary McLeod Bethune and Charlotte Hawkins Brown, each of whom remained rooted in African American women's clubs as they worked through the 1940s to achieve racial equality. In criminal justice, Edna Mahon, a protégé of Van Waters, drew on women's organizations to protect her reforms at the New Jersey Reformatory for Women. The career of Dorothy Kenyon, a feminist lawyer and public official, illustrates the devastating impact McCarthyism could have on this generation.[39]

Common dilemmas and survival strategies characterized members of this generation of reformers. Despite the decline of the old social gospel, religious values continued to inspire and sustain reform efforts for Van Waters, as it did for others, such as another minister's daughter, labor activist Mary Van Kleeck, who also belonged to the Society of the Companions of the Holy Cross. Intimate female partnerships among white middle-class women survived the modern "lesbian taboo" to nourish reformers — as did the Van Waters–Thompson relationship and the partnerships of Lillian Smith and Paula Snelling, Mary Dreier and Frances Kellor, and psychologists Jessie Taft and Virginia Robinson.[40] Whatever degree of consciousness these women had about their sexual identity, like Van Waters, they could become vulnerable to veiled accusations of lesbianism, especially during the antigay atmosphere of the McCarthy era.[41] Whether in couples or alone, some women of Van Waters's generation resolved the family-career dilemma by raising adopted children, often with the support of women friends, as did, for instance, Assistant Attorney General Mabel Walker Willebrandt.[42] Whatever personal strategies supported them, I suspect that the members of this generation provided an unrecognized legacy for the founding mothers of the new feminism. How often do the YWCA, Hadassah, black women's church clubs, the Women's Bureau, and the League of Women Voters appear in the genealogies of later activists who were inspired, as was historian Ann Scott during the 1940s, by "women of such force and power"?[43]

In addition to revealing the survival of women's networks and institutions in the twentieth century, turning our historical attention to the generation of postsuffrage women social reformers that included Miriam Van Waters may revise our understanding of continuity and discontinuity in reform strategies from the Progressive Era to the Cold War. To compare pre- and postsuffrage reform movements requires at least three kinds of historical analyses: analyses of institutions, ideology, and political authority. The clearest evidence of continuity in women's reform is the survival of separate women's networks, clubs, and formal institutions. Despite the emphasis on political integration in the 1920s and the professionalization of women's reform, particularly through social work, older forms of voluntary associations continued. While many professional women worked within male institutions after 1920, nonemployed and nonprofessional women kept up local, voluntary, and often church-based female institutions. In addition, the formation of national institutions such as the Women's Bureau, the Children's Bureau, the League of Women Voters, the National Woman's Party, and the Business and Professional Women's Clubs suggests that not all politically active or professional women were willing to turn over the tasks of social service and policymaking to men.

The ideology underlying these women's institutions, however, did not necessarily resemble that of their predecessors. In the nineteenth century, women's reform rested in large part on ideals of female difference from and moral superiority to men, as well as on a social authority based on the common experience of motherhood. Within a modern gender system that no longer rested solidly on an ideology of separate spheres, women's moral authority had to derive from more than gender. As Nancy Cott has shown, the idea of a unitary female identity gradually disintegrated after 1910 as feminists both claimed equality with men and recognized diversities among women.[44] The rhetoric of both professional and voluntary women's groups reflected this shift. Although Van Waters and others continued to focus on service to women and children, they were less likely to invoke their own womanhood as a justification for their efforts. Even as Van Waters drew women's groups to her aid, she called on their humanitarian (or, in her terms, "Christian") sympathies; an earlier generation would have called on Christian "womanhood." Privately, however, gender consciousness did not disappear; in her journal, for example, Van Waters compared her minority status as "an isolated female Penologist" to the status of a racial minority, and she once — but only once — requested that a public official testify on her behalf by invoking his support for "the rights of women."[45] Her public rhetoric often played down gender and spoke in neutral terms of the parenthood of the state and the importance of scientific insight into delinquency. I suspect that other reformers similarly mixed their strategies in order to survive in the climate in which they operated. At a time when female bonding was suspect rather than esteemed, reformers relied on women's separate support systems even as they denied the significance of gender in their reforms. Perhaps women's institutions seemed to disappear in the postsuffrage era because separatism had disappeared from women's rhetoric, if not always from their sustenance.

Women's institutions survived, their rhetoric modified, but what kind of political authority did they wield, especially in comparison with women's authority during the era of Addams, Kelley, and Lathrop? Historians have suggested that red-baiting undermined women's political authority during the early 1920s and that by the end of the decade, the national women's lobby failed to maintain its gains, as evidenced by the loss of state support for maternal health care with the defeat of the Shephard-Towner Act in 1927. Even the New Deal, which can be seen as a culmination of women's social welfare goals, fell far short of meeting the needs of working and poor women.

Whether through the success or the shortcomings of welfare politics, women's political authority on the national level suffered serious blows.

Nonetheless, two important questions about the persistence of women's reform influence are suggested by the career of Van Waters. First, to what extent did women maintain legislative influence and administrative authority at the state and local levels after 1930? Only further case studies will reveal how many women like Van Waters remained in office, how they did so, and what obstacles they faced. Recent revisionist histories suggest that separate institutions did support women who were able to maintain formal political authority. Susan Hartmann has pointed out that many female legislators who sponsored bills to advance women's opportunities in the 1940s (such as Representative Chase Going Woodhouse of Connecticut and Senator Margaret Chase Smith of Maine) gained their political expertise in the League of Women Voters, the Women's International League for Peace and Freedom, the women's colleges, or the Business and Professional Women's Clubs.[46] For them, postsuffrage women's institutions fueled female political authority. The second question concerns women's power outside traditional political institutions. When did women wield authority in neighborhoods, communities, unions, churches, and nascent social movements, and did their power derive in part from separate women's institutions? Again, historical inquiries have just begun, but, as Sara Evans notes, during the 1950s, diverse groups of women mobilized their private networks for political ends, ranging from New Mexico Chicanas who took leadership in the miners' strike depicted in *Salt of the Earth*, to San Francisco lesbians whose social network formed the basis for the Daughters of Bilitis, to southern black members of the local Women's Political Council, which became critical to the Montgomery bus boycott.[47]

As in the past, separate women's institutions did not have a unified politics, nor did they always work to promote the interests of women and children. Women's organizations, informal or formal, could support class or race supremacy and gender inequality, and they could be used by conservative politicians.[48] My focus here, however, is the role that separate women's institutions have continued to play in the service of social reform. In this essay, drawing on the career of Miriam Van Waters, I have tried to suggest that where women continued to organize as women — even without an explicit ideology of gender difference — they had the power to facilitate social reform in their local communities and even in state and national politics. Although women's movements for reform were smaller, more beleaguered, and more vulnerable after 1920, they developed new strategies for navigating within male political cultures, strategies that in turn helped lay the ground-work for yet another surge of women's political activity after 1960.

In 1945, when Miriam Van Waters lamented the passing of great women leaders in social reform, she was at least partially correct in her historical assessment. Gone were Addams, Kelley, and Lathrop, the nationally visible leaders of movements to protect women and children through state-sponsored reforms. Yet Van Waters may have overlooked an equally important historical phenomenon that flourished in her own backyard: grassroots, local, and voluntary women's institutions. These separate organizations continued to nurture an American women's reform tradition well into the twentieth century.

3 | Women's Networks and Women's Loyalties | Reflections on a Tenure Case

In the midst of my tenure case, I was asked to speak to the Committee on Women Historians at the 1983 meeting of the American Historical Association. The previous year, I had filed an internal grievance charging that a Stanford dean's reversal of my department's vote to grant me tenure discriminated against me as a woman and reflected biases against my research on women. During the next year and a half, until the university decided in my favor, I was sustained by the emotional and financial support of hundreds of friends and colleagues. I agreed to speak at the 1983 meeting in order to share my experiences with many of them. I present this talk as a historical document that offers personal testimony about the pitfalls women face in attempting to integrate male-dominated institutions. The recurrent distrust of both women's loyalties and feminism that I discuss here also reveals the influence of homophobia on academic life.

LAST SPRING, when I was asked to speak at this meeting, I had serious reservations about whether I should do so. For one thing, I believed at the time that, come December 1983, I would most likely be engaged in a sex discrimination suit, and I was not sure how much I would be able to say in public about what was coming to be known as the "Estelle Freedman Case." Aside from this strategic reservation, I felt very uncomfortable about being asked to speak to my professional colleagues about what seemed like a personal crisis—we all have them, I thought, but why should I get up in public and talk about mine? My feminist instincts—and my feminist colleagues—soon helped me overcome the latter hesitation, for I realized that the university's denial of my tenure was not simply a personal problem; it was a deeply political one that has affected many members of the community of women historians and feminist scholars. It was also an event that needed to be placed in historical perspective, for it might serve as a measure

Previously published as Estelle B. Freedman, "Women's Networks and Women's Loyalties: Reflections on a Tenure Case," *Frontiers* 8, no. 3 (1986): 50–54. Reprinted by permission of Frontiers Editorial Collective.

of both women's position within the historical profession and the status of women's studies in the 1980s.

Just a decade ago, there were few women historians and fewer still who specialized in women's history, and yet the signs of change were clear — the formation of the women's caucuses, the revival of the Berkshire Conference on the History of Women, the entry of women into graduate programs, and the outpouring of articles and books by or about women. Despite the tightening job market, many history departments did hire their first women historians and/or historians of women, giving an impression of expanding opportunities. As we know, however, women disproportionately entered the profession at the lowest and least secure ranks rather than through tenure track appointments. Moreover, in the early 1980s, the generation of junior faculty hired in the 1970s began to come up for tenure in more troubled economic times and in a political climate that was increasingly hostile to feminism and to the principle of affirmative action. As a result, the phenomenon of "last hired, first fired" struck feminist scholars in a number of disciplines, including history. In response, bitter tenure fights and legal suits have too often taken energy away from the very scholars we have needed to continue building our profession and our field.

My own case sent ripples through the network of feminist scholars who know from personal experience, or from the experience of colleagues at their own universities, that we must now fight a defensive battle in order to maintain the limited professional gains we have made over the past ten years. We do so not only for ourselves but also because we risk losing the next generation of women graduate students who might well fear that there is no equal opportunity in the university for them.

For these reasons, I think, the Estelle Freedman Case drew national attention from a wide audience of women scholars and their male supporters. And largely because of that interest, because of that support — for which I am deeply grateful — I was able to fight the decision to deny me tenure. Given these larger concerns and given the role of the community of women historians in my case, I did finally decide that it would be fitting for me to address the Committee on Women Historians today, in what will be my first and, I hope, my last public statement about my tenure case.

Happily, I do not stand here today as a litigant in a sex discrimination suit. As many of you know, in July 1983, after a year and half of delays and reconsiderations, the denial of an internal grievance, and submission of a formal appeal, the provost of my university recommended that I be granted tenure and promoted to the rank of associate professor; in September, the president and the trustees approved my promotion, and the Estelle Freedman Case came to a long overdue and very welcome conclusion. When I learned of the positive decision, amid my feelings of relief and anger I often found myself thinking about this audience, using it as an imaginary sounding board for taking stock of that painful year and a half.

Today I will share only a small portion of the thoughts that have come to me — there are limits of time, propriety, and relevance to this audience.[1] This morning, I want to talk about three questions that might be of particular interest to other women historians. First, what was the role of the community of women historians and other feminist scholars in this case? Second, in what ways was my predicament related to problems that we all face in our jobs? And third, what did my tenure fight mean for the rest of you — the graduate students, colleagues, and allies who wrote to me during the past year and a half to offer support and to share your feelings?

I have often thought that if I had to choose a title for this talk, I would want to borrow one from an article by Mary Ryan called "The Power of Women's Networks."[2] I am convinced that in many ways it was the existence of strong women's and feminist networks that made it possible for me to fight and then to win this tenure dispute. The university will, of course, officially deny that outside pressure had anything to do with its reversal of the original negative decision. But that is not really the point, for I know that the mobilization of the women's history community and its allies was a critical factor in enabling me to file an appeal, to get the legal help I needed, and, above all, to survive the overwhelming pressures that the denial of tenure places on one to withdraw entirely from the university and from one's work.

Women's networks proved to be powerful in this instance in a number of ways. The most basic and crucial was the personal support I received from feminists at Stanford and around the country who let me know that it was important to fight back. At the same time, it was clear from the outpouring of letters to the Stanford administration — which admitted that it had never received so much commentary on any individual decision — that women's history was not some isolated, quirky, or "narrow" field. Rather, the university was going to have to contend with a widespread recognition within the historical profession that women's history is "real" history. That these letters came not only from the practitioners of women's history but also from their colleagues, both male and female, carried important weight, I think, for it let the administration know that a sizable chunk of our profession was watching Stanford to see how it evaluated not just me but, especially, my field.

At least three other powerful women's networks helped sustain me and influence public opinion in my case. Both women lawyers and women journalists empathized with my position and offered their professional help at critical moments. They wrote or called to give me advice, drew upon their own professional networks to let others know what was happening at Stanford, and encouraged me to pursue my case for the sake of their careers as well as my own. In addition, a small and seasoned group of "tenure case survivors" — women like Louise Lamphere and Nancy Shaw — each in her own way offered assistance: tips from previous and current grievances at other universities, leads to financial and legal support, and personal inspiration. Finally, both old and new women's organizations mobilized to support the tenure cases — the American Association of University Women (AAUW) has set up a fund for academic women's tenure suits, and the National Women's Studies Association (NWSA) now has the Fund for the Defense of Women's Studies, begun with money from Annette Kolodny's settlement in her academic sex discrimination case.[3] Knowing about these resources made it possible to envision the long legal fight that I anticipated.

Several years ago, I published an article entitled "Separatism as Strategy," in which I suggested that when women integrate into mixed but male-dominated institutions, we have to be particularly careful not to lose our separate, female-dominated organizations, which have been, historically, the basis of our power.[4] My experience over the past few years has confirmed this belief. Without the separate organizations of women — the Coordinating Committee on Women in the Historical Profession (CCWHP), the Committee on Women Historians of the American Historical Association (CWH), the NWSA, the AAUW, and women's studies and feminist studies programs around the country — I, for one, would have given up long before I received tenure. That is why it is so important to me that we are gathered here today and that we continue to meet as women and as feminists — even as we continue to draw male allies into our movement and try to convince our nonfeminist colleagues of the need to combat discrimination against women scholars and against scholarship on women.

But there is also an interesting irony about the strength of our networks, one that brings me to my second question: in what ways did my case relate to problems we all face in our jobs? To put it another way, how did my being a woman, a feminist, and a historian of women affect the denial of tenure? (It might be pertinent to explain here that the Department of History voted to recommend my promotion with tenure; the denial came from a set of administrators and faculty who were not historians and who, until I began my grievance, were traditionally all male. One outcome of my case is that Stanford finally appointed a woman dean and, for a time, one woman sat on the committee that reviews departmental hiring and promotions.)

If I had to choose a title that captures my answer to the question of what difference it made that I was a woman, and a feminist scholar, I would take it directly from a memo to the deans written by an unsympathetic department member who questioned the value of my work by stating that I seemed to have "other loyalties." "Other loyalties." The phrase implied, I believe, that being a feminist, a cofounder of the Feminist Studies Program at Stanford, and a faculty member known for supporting women's and feminist issues on campus must in some way detract from my loyalties to the values of the university as a whole and to those of the historical profession.

This characterization of feminist academics is both dangerous and in some ways accurate. It is dangerous to the extent that it presupposes that there is one appropriate set of loyalties that academics must share — loyalties to the traditional patterns of academic life, patterns that we well know have excluded women and minorities from full access to that life. To attempt to transform those patterns is to risk being labeled, essentially, a subversive. But the characterization is at the same time an accurate one, for, indeed, I do want to subvert traditional academic life in order to encourage both the advancement and the study of women within it. By associating with the subgroup of academics and historians who consider ourselves feminist scholars, we risk being seen as traitors. And yet it is our very identification with each other, our networks and our organizations, that often gives us the strength to remain in the profession. I believe that the only resolution of this seeming dilemma is to obtain recognition of the *legitimacy* of our loyalties to other women, and to women's studies, so that we are appreciated rather than penalized for our work in these fields. That is what ultimately happened at Stanford — the legitimation of feminist loyalties. But before I speak of happy endings, let me dwell for a moment on the ways that discrimination against women who have "other loyalties" operated in my case and likely operates in many of our lives.

In my case, two related interests — women's history and women's studies — made my record suspect and led the deans to downgrade the department's evaluation of my teaching and my scholarship. For one thing, my participation in the Stanford Program in Feminist Studies was not considered part of my academic work. Rather, these activities — which I knew to be intellectually challenging and important to my scholarly development — were labeled as a commitment to a "cause" that could, at best, be relegated to the category of "university service" but that could not count toward tenure. In a long, defensive letter sent during spring 1983 to people who had written in my support, Dean Norman Wessells explained that feminist studies has not yet proven itself as a legitimate academic concern and may simply be a temporary fad; therefore, the university should not invest its resources in the careers of feminist scholars. Obviously, if the university does not do so, women's studies is destined to wither away for lack of support, and the prophecy will be neatly fulfilled. Under this logic, whatever good I may have done for feminist scholarship, my teaching and research on women, however highly rated, could only hurt, not help, my status at Stanford. To me, this mentality reeked of a regrettable cultural phenomenon, namely, the nearly universal devaluation of that which is female. What women do together, for or about women, simply does not count as much as what is done with, for, or about men. It is not, so to speak, of comparable worth.

This devaluation of the female hits even closer to home when it is applied to the study and teaching of women's history. In my case, although I had previously received the university's two awards for excellence in teaching, although my department had evaluated my teaching as excellent, the next administrative level downgraded that judgment to only "very good" — that is, not good enough to get tenure. The only grounds I could find in all the documents I received about the decision — and these grounds were stated explicitly — were that my teaching was too narrowly focused on women. In fact, less than half of the courses I had developed at Stanford focused on women, but even this amount of attention to my specialty was perceived as too much. Similarly, my scholarship was faulted for being, like my teaching, narrowly concerned with women. Women, it was implied, are simply not that important.

In a long and rather legalistic appeal that I prepared last winter, I developed these points thoroughly, along with a discussion of the ways that discrimination operates to exclude women and minorities from the university. In response to my appeal, the provost ruled, quite interestingly, that although he found that no discrimination had taken place, he was recommending my promotion because it was proper for him to take into account my contribution to the university as a feminist scholar and teacher. However different his logic was from mine, we were, in a sense, in agreement on the crucial points I have been raising here: that is, that women's history, feminist scholarship, and women's studies must count fully in the evaluation of scholarship and teaching. The message of the decision to the university and to the academic world at large, I would like to think, is that our loyalties to women are legitimate ones and should be supported by the institutions in which we work.

Thus far, I have been speaking purely from my own experience and presenting my own interpretations of my case. Others who were involved would see things differently — and indeed further considerations influenced both the denial of tenure and the ultimate success of my appeal. For the moment, I want to turn to the thoughts of scholars who were not directly involved in the case but who wrote to me over the past year and a half, often commenting on the meaning of my case for themselves and for the profession. I want to close with this summary of *your* reactions to what happened to me, in part because I think it provides a measure of how we now see ourselves and, admittedly, because I felt I had a wonderful "data set" — a file of well over a hundred letters — that I wanted to reread in order to get some perspective on what had happened.

In reading through all of the correspondence I received about my case, I detected four kinds of responses. The first and most frequent was an emotional response that can be easily summarized as empathetic anger, along with compassion for my feelings of anger and my sense of injustice. The recurrence of words like "fury," "outrage," "rage," and "frustration" was affirming; these words also indicated an enormous backlog of anger that many of us carry around as we maneuver our way through unfamiliar and often demoralizing academic rituals. As one historian wrote, "It is anger against what has happened to you. . . . It is also a reaction against a blow that feels aimed at all of us as a group. I feel that it is part of a nationwide reaction, and all the more frightening because of it."

Along with this wonderful outburst of collective rage came offers of support — a willingness, frequently stated, to "do anything," to "fire off letters," to send money, and to support whatever legal actions I took. Many colleagues urged me to file a grievance and go to court if necessary. "Whether you grieve or not," one wrote, "you have my strong support." A third and related response was that of advice, some of which I liked better than others. The best advice I want to be sure to recall for those who find themselves in similar situations, but really for all of us, on all of our working days: *Do not internalize this judgment!* Women who had been denied tenure and those who had filed grievances or lawsuits were especially clear about the danger of accepting, even as we fight, that we somehow deserve all of this trouble. We don't. The next best advice was to carry on with my work rather than become totally absorbed in the process of fighting the decision. I think this advice, too, has to be recalled in all of our daily political struggles lest we undermine the larger cause for which we fight: the right to do this work.

One set of advice I found very problematic. It was that, at all costs, I should determine to advance my career, move anywhere, write what would most please the powers that be, and generally "clean up my act" lest I never get a tenured position elsewhere. Powerful individuals offered variations on this theme out of sincere concern for my welfare. As much as I appreciated their concern, I feel strongly that we must not ask each other to forget either our personal lives or our political commitments in the name of achieving professional "success."

The final and perhaps most telling response came in the form of interpretation of what was happening. The most frequent commentary was that a backlash had begun to hit women historians and feminist scholars. One former student asked, is getting rid of the feminists "part of the new look on campus"? A scholar in another discipline put it somewhat differently: "The rejection seems to go beyond you individually to all women who have academic appointments at elite universities AND real commitments to feminism." Letters from both women and men in various disciplines informed me of other cases of tenure denials, some of which have been resolved and others of which may go on to the courts. Frequently, the grievant had been active in women's studies as well as in her discipline.

A subtheme running through a number of letters suggested that my denial of tenure was, for some, a clarifying event. "Your experience has outlined with merciless clarity the perils and politics of academia," wrote a graduate student in women's history. Another explained, "They don't see the world the way we do (we were foolish to forget that) and the way we see the world threatens . . . them." Or, as one local feminist explained, "I suppose I should stop being surprised that institutions correctly perceive feminism as such a threat." A feminist political scientist suggested to me that this recognition could be strategically useful. "One can only hope," she wrote, "that the experience will make clear to some of your supporters what kind of thing has to be done to crack open 'men's studies.'"

The recognition that we are indeed different from many of our colleagues also led to affirmations of that difference and its value. For example, a recent Ph.D. in women's history made my day when she wrote that my situation was "a useful reminder to me not to shape my work too much to conform to conventional standards of what is an important issue. . . . This may sound paradoxical, but it has convinced me to follow my own inclinations and do what I think is right. If the . . . establishment doesn't approve, they won't approve no matter how I dress it up!" Several senior scholars in women's history offered fascinating commentary on the question of how we judge our own work. As one wrote, "Who's to say what makes scholarship 'good'? I think that for feminists, engaging in nonscholarly activities, simply LIVING . . . gives us different sorts of insights." Another, in one of my favorite letters, explained, "Fortunately, as feminists we have learned the limits of male acknowledgment (and the limits of its true value), and have learned to treasure our own. Unfortunately, the bums still have the fucking power (NO pun intended)."

All of these themes — empathy, a sense of common struggle, a commitment to fighting discrimination, and a belief in the value of feminism and feminist scholarship — recurred in the congratulatory letters I received when the denial was reversed. Predictably, some viewed the victory as evidence that "the system works," to which I must add that it does so only under intense pressure and at great — possibly unbearable — costs to individuals. The decision, a former colleague wrote, "restores my faith in justice . . . and in the strength of scholarship about women and by women making headway, slowly but surely." Many people correctly perceived the victory as one "for feminist scholars nationally" and for "the movement at a time when our spirits need uplift." As a historian wrote from another elite university (one that has hired and promoted all too few women), "It is so elating and, unfortunately, so rare to feel oneself part of a WINNING cause!"

In closing, I want to quote at length from one final letter that I received from a woman journalist who has followed women's politics and women's history over the past decade. I think she expressed better than I can what *could* be the outcome of this story, but only if we continue to recognize discrimination when we encounter it, refuse to let it immobilize us, and utilize the power of our networks to combat it. She wrote:

> I remain appalled that you had to go through what you went through, but your victory helped lock in feminist studies as a discipline to reckon with. It is difficult for people — especially male people — who have taught one way for years to acknowledge that they may not have known it all and furthermore that they may have to change what they know in the future. The work, in short, is not done and they can't coast. The whole point of scholarship, as I understand it, is to open doors, not close them, and that is what you [feminist scholars] have done and they haven't.
>
> This is 1983 and none of us should have to be working so hard just to stay in place, but little by little there are these victories. Perhaps eventually the people

who cannot stand change will find we have our hooks in granite and won't let loose!

Meanwhile . . . HOORAY.

I share her relief and her vision for the future, and I thank all of you, here and elsewhere, who helped make *this* victory possible, for all of us. May it help strengthen our networks and our loyalties for the ongoing tenure cases, in which we seek to make women and feminism legitimate within the university.

4 | Small Group Pedagogy | Consciousness Raising in Conservative Times

This essay applies some of the historical lessons about feminism to teaching. Long before the consciousness-raising groups of second-wave feminism, women relied on personal networks and separate organizations to support the work of transforming society. In teaching "Introduction to Feminist Studies," I sought to have the students, both male and female, rely on each other's insights in small self-reflective groups. Over the years since I began to assign small groups, national politics have become even more conservative, but students enter this class with less fear of feminism than in the past. They also increasingly have adopted the multiple identities associated with postmodern, queer, and third-wave feminist politics. Lesbianism, however, remains a tense subject for many of them.

IN THE FALL OF 1988, I began teaching the introductory course in the Feminist Studies Program at Stanford University. "Introduction to Feminist Studies: Issues and Methods" (FS 101) had grown from a small discussion class to a medium-sized lecture course with separate section meetings for sixty-six students. The subject matter ranged from the origins of sexual inequality and the history of feminism to contemporary paid and unpaid labor, race and feminism, reproductive rights and sexuality, and violence against women. Because many of these topics raise both emotional and political sensitivities, I felt that FS 101 required a forum in which students could discuss their personal reactions to classroom learning. Even more than the U.S. women's history classes I had taught previously, "Introduction to Feminist Studies" permitted, and indeed necessitated, the integration of the personal and the academic.[1]

In preparing the course, I wondered how I might use consciousness raising (c.r.) in the classroom to achieve this end and whether my 1970s experience of c.r. would work with the more conservative students of the late 1980s.

Previously published as Estelle B. Freedman, "Small Group Pedagogy: Consciousness Raising in Conservative Times," *NWSA Journal* 2, no. 4 (Autumn 1990): 603–23. Reprinted by permission of Indiana University Press.

By "consciousness raising" I mean the sharing of personal experience with others in order to understand the larger social context for the experience and to transform one's intellectual or political understandings of it. Once before, in a women's history class, I had experimented with the explicit use of c.r. in the classroom. On the day we discussed documents from the feminist movements of the 1960s and 1970s, I spontaneously turned the class into a consciousness-raising session. We formed a circle and spoke in turn about how one article or idea in the readings had affected each of us personally. The experiment took over an entire week of the course, as students shared feelings of both anger and inspiration, revealed personal experiences with sexism on campus, and reacted to the differences that emerged in their views. The evaluations of the exercise were enthusiastic, so the next year, I built a consciousness-raising session into the syllabus. Again, the students reported that they not only understood the historical experience of feminism more clearly but also made important connections between the past and the world around them.

In addition to this and other positive models, I had more defensive reasons for incorporating c.r. into the introductory course.[2] The preceding year, a hostile male student had tried unsuccessfully to disrupt FS 101, and at the University of Washington, one male student had placed the entire women's studies program under attack by claiming that classes discriminated against men. I wanted to forestall such disruptions as much as possible by creating a place outside the classroom where emotional responses might be shared with peers and not simply directed at faculty. Aside from hostile students, I worried about the feelings of alienation that students of minority race, class, ethnicity, sexual identity, or physical ability would experience in a predominantly white, middle-class, heterosexual, and able-bodied classroom.[3] Consciousness-raising groups might allow these students to acknowledge their feelings and make personal and intellectual connections between gender and other forms of social hierarchy.

To faculty who are veterans of 1970s women's studies classes or who work in public universities or small liberal arts colleges committed to teaching, my rationale for incorporating c.r. into the classroom may seem unnecessary. But I work within an extremely elitist university in which pedagogy is rarely discussed and academic advancement depends almost exclusively on scholarship. At this university, opponents of the term "feminist studies" shudder at such a self-conscious reference to the political nature of knowledge and associate feminist scholarship with a political radicalism they consider anti-intellectual. Indeed, even a colleague at a feminist studies meeting reacted to my plans for setting up c.r. groups by warning that it was inappropriate and unprofessional for me to attempt to do "therapy" in my classes.[4] Students who signed up for FS 101 in the fall of 1988 arrived in a state of extreme fear of feminism. Most associated the term with an unpleasant militancy and refused to accept the label "feminist" even if they believed in the liberal goals of the movement.

In this setting, I feel that the use of c.r. has to be handled carefully, not only for its pedagogical value but also for the political well-being of the course and the program. Even on more liberal campuses, these conservative times might make faculty wary of the explicit use of c.r. groups. I believe that now more than ever, however, we need to confront students' fears of feminism and social change. As women's studies courses become part of general education and distribution requirements on many campuses, we can expect more conservative or nonfeminist students in our classes. From my experience teaching FS 101, I believe that c.r. can be an extremely effective way to address the fear of feminism held by many of these students. This essay, then, is an effort to share my own and the students' experience with c.r. in the late 1980s in order to encourage the careful incorporation of personal experience into academic classes wherever this might be appropriate.

WITH ADVICE FROM feminist colleagues, I devised a structure for making c.r. central to FS 101. Required biweekly group meetings supplemented an already demanding course — three lectures, heavy reading, a weekly discussion section, and three papers during the quarter.[5] Thus, to make clear from the outset that the groups were not extracurricular but integral to the process of learning, I spelled out on the syllabus the rules for attendance and the format of sessions and I stressed the importance of a final paper evaluating the groups. On the recommendation of several colleagues, this paper would not be graded lest students feel judged for either their emotions or their politics. Knowing Stanford students' sensitivities about language and politics, I called the process "small groups." Although I referred to consciousness raising in my lectures, students continued to speak of their "small groups" rather than "c.r. groups."

The major dilemma I faced, however, was not about naming but about whether to create random groups that would mix students from various backgrounds or to create minority support groups — for women or students of color, lesbians and/or gay men, or disabled, male, ethnic, or working-class students. As much as I wanted to diminish minority alienation, I felt that it was more important for each group to confront the issues of difference with as much firsthand information as possible. In addition, many students had multiple or overlapping identities; constructing separate groups would force them to choose only one basis of support. For these reasons, the groups were formed by a random sorting of names into thirteen sets of four or five students each. (I hoped that the small size, compared to discussion sections of up to twenty-one students, would make scheduling easier, allow students to meet in a dorm room, and help to build friendships.) Each group had to meet five times during the ten-week quarter, for a session lasting about two hours, at a time to be arranged by group members.

I assigned readings for the first session only: Pam Allen's "Free Space" and Irene Peslikis's "Resistances to Consciousness."[6] I also recommended a rotating timekeeper, leaderless groups, and an uninterrupted five to ten minutes for each member to speak at the outset of sessions. Suggested topics paralleled the syllabus and attempted to link course readings and lectures with everyday life. The question "How does your personal experience of race, class, and ethnicity affect your response to what you are learning?" followed the lecture on race and feminism and coincided with a required "unlearning-racism" workshop.[7] When we studied women and work, the suggested question asked students to relate readings and lectures to jobs, families, and campus life. I left one week open for student topics and closed with a question to parallel our reading of Marge Piercy's utopian novel, *Woman on the Edge of Time*: "What one thing would you most want to change about our current world?" Students were asked to keep private journals after groups but not to submit them. The final paper evaluating the groups was to draw heavily upon the journal.[8]

During the quarter, several incidents on campus, in the community, and in the classroom intensified the importance of c.r. and expanded it beyond the groups and into the lecture sessions. On campus, two white students posted racist slurs in the Afro-American residential theme house, igniting a year-long debate over the action and the administration's response and heightening awareness of racism. Then, against the backdrop of the Bush-Dukakis campaign, a few anti-abortion activists mobilized conservative women to join Operation Rescue's blockade of local abortion clinics, while campus feminists formed a prochoice alliance. In the classroom, students responded to the readings on lesbian feminism with such a profound silence that I felt compelled to challenge their homophobia. Borrowing a technique from a colleague at an even more conservative university, I asked students to write hypothetical "coming-out letters" to their parents, drawing on their readings about lesbianism and homophobia.[9] At the same time, the students' presumption of their instructor's heterosexuality made me extremely uncomfortable about "passing" as straight and raised my own consciousness to the point that for the first time I came out in a classroom as a lesbian.

Thus, for me, as well as for the students, FS 101 took unexpected turns. On two occasions, for example, students raised my consciousness about issues that personally affected them. First, shortly before my lecture on sexual violence, I received a call from an incest survivor in the course who was distressed by the lack of readings on incest. I asked her permission to discuss the call, anonymously, in class and used the episode to talk about my own preconceptions about violence.[10] Second, in anticipation of the lecture on women and food, a student volunteered to speak in class about her own struggles with anorexia and bulimia. Her moving, expert presentation provided both personal testimony and information about support groups on campus. Inspired by her offer, I invited other students in the class to speak about their personal involvement with issues we studied. Members of the Rape Education Project did so, and since no students came out in the lecture class, I invited representatives from the Gay and Lesbian Alliance to speak on available student support services.

Meanwhile, students managed the small groups independently. Every other week, I asked for feedback on the groups during the lecture. Although students made few concrete comments at the time, they suggested that the groups were going well and were important to them. Only at the end of the course, after I read the set of sixty-six papers describing and evaluating the groups, did I realize how critical they had been to the educational process. Several students felt that the groups were as important as the class itself; for some, they were "the best part," and for at least one, "the most personally enriching part of the class."[11] Not every group, however, succeeded in establishing a sense of purpose and facilitating growth. Several groups had difficulty finding meeting times or sharing personal experiences; their members felt disappointed when they compared their experiences with those of the majority of students. Generally, though, papers from eleven of the thirteen groups testified to the power of the small groups for enhancing student understanding of issues raised in class and for contributing to both self-understanding and greater understanding of others.

AS THEY DID FOR second-wave feminists of the 1960s and 1970s, c.r. groups in FS 101 functioned to move students from silence to speech, from isolation to community, and sometimes from political ambivalence to political commitment. Once empowered to explore ideas and feelings, a number of students were able to confront personal dilemmas, especially those concerning sexuality and race. As a result, their definitions of feminism expanded. By the end of the course, the majority of students reported that they had shifted from discomfort with the word "feminism" to enthusiastic embrace of the term and its complexity. A few made commitments to political activism. One small group continued meeting throughout the year to support the feminist activism of its members.

Although the degree of change varied greatly, the majority of students reported that initially they had been "skeptical," "wary," "a little leery," "worried," "nervous," or "doubtful" about going to these "weird" and "extra" groups. "We all began by saying that we could not possibly talk as long as we were supposed to," one woman recalled. "We then proceeded to talk longer than that, amazed that we each had so much to say."

Student papers provide many clues about why the groups offered safety so quickly. For one thing, a supportive environment was especially necessary for members of this class, given the hostility to feminism in the culture at large and the university itself. Even enrolling in a feminist studies course could be stressful. Because many students "met with nervous responses from family and friends over taking the course," they "found it was helpful to discuss these problems with others" in the small group. Most members of one group thought that "our fathers felt threatened by our studying feminism," and the students shared their responses from family members.

Male students, who made up just under one-fifth of the class, may have been particularly vulnerable to stigma. A freshman explained at his first group meeting "how difficult it was being a guy feminist," for "not only did he get badgered by guys, but also he got heat from women who saw his feminist comments sometimes as pickup lines." Another man discovered from the different reactions of male and female friends "the extent to which" his enrollment "was viewed as a political decision." The experience of one male student illustrated the extent of male resistance on campus. While distributing pamphlets from the Rape Education Project in his dorm, he was typically asked by men, "Oh, are you going to teach us how to rape?" In another group, every member wrote about an incident that demonstrated firsthand the kind of chiding directed at male students who took feminist classes. While they met at an outdoor eating area, a student described by one woman as "a domineering white male" approached his buddy in the group. Learning what the small group was doing, the outsider "started to tease" his friend, "hollering disbelief." After one woman accused the intruder of sexism, the group had a forty-five-minute debate on the meaning of the attack, the usefulness of the counterattack, and the way the incident clarified points about oppression made during the unlearning-racism workshop.[12]

As might be expected, for men the experience of groups tended to be more intellectual than personal. One man wrote that he "felt somewhat alienated" in the group because he did not share the experience of gender with others. Another felt at the first meeting that the issues "did not always seem to affect me directly," but at a later session, discussions of the readings on the politics of housework engaged him quite personally.[13] By the third meeting, he "spoke at length" of the struggle to create an "equalitarian" relationship in living with a woman. At least one man, already aware of being a member of a "targeted" racial group, now saw how gender affected women daily. "I've come to realize what kind of stuff women have to go through," he wrote, "and more importantly, how gender affects me."

In addition to feeling conflicted about enrolling in the class, reading about issues such as rape, racism, sexual identity, body types, and standards of beauty proved disturbing to many students. Other instructors had warned me that heightening student consciousness of discrimination and sexual vulnerability often creates emotional stress in women's studies classrooms. The students echoed this theme in their papers. "We all agreed that [by the] third meeting the class had changed our lives in a profound way; we now felt surrounded by sexism." Or, as another student explained, "the material in this class was overwhelming, which made it particularly important to have a place to express reactions to it as we went along."

Anger was a primary reaction to the readings but one that evoked deep conflict, especially for women. At the beginning of the course, many students stereotyped feminists as "angry" and feared being so labeled. The small groups functioned to legitimize anger and make it less overwhelming. "Our first group meeting can be summed up in one word: ANGER," a student recalled. "Unfortunately," she continued, "most of us felt defensive when speaking about feminism, as if we needed to prove something to men, but could not channel the anger into well articulated arguments. . . . We hoped that this class and our upcoming small group meetings would help articulate our thoughts, explain why we were angry, and how we could feel 'offensive' by presenting a clear definition of feminism and its goals." Even a student who was more reluctant to identify as a feminist shared similar feelings: "Being able to air my feelings and hear the impressions of the other women in the group helped me to resolve some of the anger that I formed while reading the materials on violence against women." Another student recalled thinking that "at last, here were some people who I could talk to about those things that make me angry that no one seems to understand. I felt somewhat empowered." Speaking about the experiences of the past week "was good for me," a minority woman wrote, because "I found that I had a lot of unvented anger that I could let loose at these meetings." One group applied the reading of Virginia Woolf's *Three Guineas* to the problem of anger. Because Woolf "encouraged people to understand the background people are coming from," a student wrote, she talked of her father's traditional upbringing. "The group discussion," she concluded, "helped bring out that I should be angry at the socialization structure that my father grew up in, not merely at my father himself."[14]

Finding the support for taking the course and for processing both the knowledge of sexism and the anger it evoked made meetings valuable and a source of growth. One student explained, "As a result of the support I received during the meetings, I quickly began to look forward to them. If I were religious I might say that the meetings were a bit like going to church, in that I felt stronger, more self-loving, and more confident after leaving." The sole man in another group wrote that he had "the courage to persevere in my studies because I had a support group. I had the drive to share so that I could see reflections of myself in others, even if the reflections had the faces of a different gender." Drawing on Bernice Johnson Reagon's ideas in "Coalition Politics," one student described the small groups as "the 'room' that we all went back to in order to discuss strategies on how to change the world."[15] The ability to feel safe, relaxed, and candid was due "no doubt," one student suggested, "to the absence of a TA or other authority figure."

Activism brought its own lessons about feminism. Well into the quarter, one group of five white women devoted a meeting to writing a collective letter to the student newspaper to criticize "examples of sexist humor and negative depictions of women" in a recent campus production. The effort brought out group differences that surprised them. As they struggled "to transform our anger into a well-articulated argument," the group learned firsthand the difficulties of feminist process and politics. They debated language and strategies, and they discovered their limits when some members were reluctant to sign the letter. "Many of us," one member explained, "although willing to speak up in a small group, still feared taking a 'feminist' stance and being labelled a 'feminist.'" The group never produced a letter "that satisfied us all," and at least one member left discouraged. Another woman felt, however, that the "exercise was still an important one" because the group had collectively articulated its feelings, which, she believed, was more important than publishing a letter. "From the standpoint of political consciousness-raising," a member began her evaluation paper, "we may not have been very effective, but the group was invaluable as a place to laugh and sound off without having to justify our feminist point of view." Although the letter was never sent, she wrote, "it was a wonderful, and sometimes tense, exercise in coalition-building."

REFLECTING THE feminist politics of the 1980s — when women of color moved feminism from its white middle-class focus to a more inclusive political worldview — FS 101 attempted to emphasize the intersections of race and gender inequality. Along with the readings on race and feminism, the unlearning-racism workshop and campus incidents made race and racism highly charged topics in the class. The small groups offered a potential space for understanding racial difference and patterns of domination. The demographic composition of the groups, however, strongly influenced the tone and depth of their discussions of race. Because three-quarters of the students were white, minorities were either absent or rare in small groups. Predictably, all-white groups had the least insightful discussions; highly unbalanced groups placed the burden of education on the few minority students; and highly mixed groups had the most valuable sessions on race.

The all-white groups tended to focus on the shared experiences of women and on nonracial differences between members. A man in one of these groups regretted its racial composition. Although he enjoyed the comfort and intimacy of his group, he realized that it "felt more like a womb than a coalition," in the terms of Reagon's article. Had the group been more diverse, he felt, members would have been forced to deal with differences in other ways. Often, these groups sought ways to resolve their discomfort over white privilege, with some interesting results. For instance, one white student used the concept of "simultaneous oppression" in her own way. Rather than referring to the multiple and simultaneous oppression of women of color (by gender, class, and race), she took the term to mean that white women were both oppressed and oppressors. With this interpretation, she identified through her gender with subordinate groups, while she accepted responsibility for her position of racial dominance.

For both mixed and all-white groups, the themes of white guilt and feelings of helplessness recurred in the papers.[16] White students in a mixed group felt immobilized by the realization, as one wrote, that "at one time in our lives we are all the oppressor." "Our group teeters on the brink of an intellectual abyss," she wrote of the unsatisfactory conclusion. "We say nice things to each other and depart." Or as the one black member of the group put it, the white women "all admitted to feeling guilty for being white." Another white member acknowledged that recognizing difference within feminism "was really very eye-opening and made some of us feel as though we had been pretty spoiled and blind." Similarly, a white woman in another group commented after listening to a Chicana describe the dual effects of racism and sexism: "It was hard for the white people in our group to accept that we would never be able to truly identify with the minority women's experience."

The racial imbalance in mixed groups placed a special burden of explanation on black, Asian American, and Chicana members. "It seemed that [X] and I, who were the two people of color in our group," wrote one man, "did most of the talking on the subject of racism." The woman to whom he referred illustrated the educator role when the group discussed Betty Friedan's attitude toward housework. Other students, she explained, "felt sorry for housewives," but since her own mother had been on welfare and then struggled in a service job, she longed for "my mom to be a housewife and to live in a house like the 'Brady Bunch.'" The man in the group shared with her "the alienation minority children feel when they are taught by the media to value a white middle-class lifestyle over their own."

Other women of color reported the frustrations they felt when placed in the role of racial educators. When the four white women in one group "all looked to" the one black member to discuss race, "she turned the question around" by asking her classmates if "we would all have the same response given our similar whiteness." In another group, a woman of color learned that her white classmates were surprised when she spoke of the internalized racism that leads to straightened hair and plastic surgery among minorities. "Although it hurts to have these things go unnoticed," she reflected, "I was encouraged by their acknowledging that when you have a prevalence of white, blond, blue-eyed skinny models, dolls, and characters in story books, these facts should not be shocking."

The most successful discussions of race — that is, the ones that elicited deep responses, as well as conflicts — occurred in the most diverse groups. A group with two minority women, two white women, and one white man achieved a degree of safety in discussing difference and racism. As the Chicana member wrote, the group "seemed to me to be a microcosm of the feminist movement — where people work for many of the same goals for differing reasons." Having made her "'foreign' experiences and ideas accessible to people through small group," she now felt ready to "move to this next stage of a potentially more hostile environment" in the world at large.

These episodes reflected the dilemmas of mixed groups. On the one hand, these groups did the most to educate white students and sometimes helped alleviate their guilt. In the process, they risked relying on students of color as racial educators who explained differences among women rather than addressing the deep personal and structural barriers to race equality. On the other hand, the few minority students in these groups learned a great deal about white attitudes toward race and how these attitudes affect them personally. Given the race and class stratification of our society, students of color will no doubt confront these views throughout their lives; small groups can serve as testing grounds for clarifying their responses. Overall, the racially mixed groups worked at identifying the dilemmas of difference better than the all-white groups, but they would have been even more effective if they had a greater proportion of students of color. That way, the minority students would feel less isolated and less targeted as racial educators. At a more racially mixed campus or in a course with greater minority enrollment, groups could go even further in raising consciousness about racism. In this setting, mixed groups can go only so far toward exploring the relationship between gender and racial inequality.

WHATEVER PROGRESS the lesbian and gay movement has made since the 1970s, for most Stanford students, lesbianism remains a frightening topic. In signing up for FS 101, a woman student said she risked being labeled "the feminist dyke." Another woman told her group she "felt funny because people who knew she was taking the class would think of her as a lesbian." The association of feminism with lesbianism ran deep among students who brought to the class strong prejudices about homosexuality. Several expressed their religious opposition to gay sex or, in response to viewing the film *Choosing Children*, to lesbians or gay men raising children. Even liberal students wanted to distance themselves from homosexuality by defending feminists against the label of lesbianism.

Not surprisingly, the coming-out letter challenged the class enormously, and students said it proved to be "harder than we had thought." Everyone expressed discomfort about doing the assignment. Students who had thought they were tolerant of lesbians and gay men found themselves hiding the assignment from roommates; some wrote "'Fem-Stud Assignment' across the top in big letters" in case friends passed by as they wrote. In the words of one student, we "were continually worried that somebody was going to look over our shoulder and misinterpret what we had written."

The small group following the letter-writing assignment was, for many, "by far the most tense of the quarter." One of the most highly political groups seemed to spend little time discussing the letters. One member was reportedly "speechless" and "couldn't imagine how others managed to do it." Another woman became "very depressed" writing hers, and for telling reasons: "I knew my parents would go off on another fit, and that once again I had to face the fact that their love and financial support is conditional." Fear of parental disapproval loomed large in the discussions and helps explain the tone of so many of the letters, well summarized by a freshman who wrote critically that several members of his group had made "a total emotional plea to their parents telling them of their misfortune and asking for acceptance." The members of another group "all agreed that it took a while to finally get around to actually saying 'I am lesbian'" — a term that many letters avoided altogether.

However difficult, the exercise, and especially the group discussion of it, brought home the depth and the costs of homophobia. "If we feared so much that someone might find our letter, did that indicate that we were homophobic?," one student asked. The discussion of the letters led another group to realize that "by denying our feelings of homophobia, we were only perpetuating them." It also helped to undermine homophobic responses. During the discussion of hiding the assignment, for example, one woman said she "gradually realized that my fear of being stereotyped wrongly had greatly diminished since the beginning of the course."

For other students, the assignment brought homosexual feelings to the surface. The group discussion forced one man to "think about my own homophobic fears — did I harbor those feelings because being homosexual is not being a man?" In another group, the question "Have you ever thought about being homosexual?" produced "some defensive reactions." At least one woman admitted to the thought but found that she could not "envision a sexual relationship" with another woman. In response to the question, another woman contemplated her unsatisfactory relationships with men and wondered if she might be lesbian. At that point, she recalled: "Two of the other members looked like they thought I was going to come out right then and there and didn't know what to do, and the other member looked grateful that I had responded to her question honestly, and did seem to sincerely understand my confusion at the time." The speaker found it a "rewarding moment" because she was not ostracized for her honesty or her suspicions about her sexuality.

If the coming-out assignment created the most tension, it also seemed to have had the most consciousness-raising effect. In one group, a woman who had recently "stopped identifying . . . as heterosexual" rated this session as the "best meeting" because it "produced the most consciousness raising." Other members (a straight man and two straight women) agreed that it was the "most rewarding," in part because the letter gave a "concrete experience" about which to relate feelings and "a bonding experience" for students who struggled with the assignment. In several groups, attitudes toward coming out seemed to have changed for many students. One group member "concluded that many more people would come out if there weren't such a stigma in society. We admired those who are strong enough to."

Only two students came out in their groups. In one case, a gay man was relieved to find that he was "among pretty gay-sensitive people." The group later turned to him to tell them what was and what was not "offensive" in their behaviors and whether their fear of having their coming-out letters seen constituted homophobia. Accepting the educator role, he both criticized and reassured his peers. "We all sort of agreed," he wrote, "that this was another form of homophobia but acknowledged too, that individuals are forced to make choices under duress in a deeply homophobic society." In another group, a woman cataloged the responses when she "told the group that I am a lesbian." "Unfortunately, the person who I expected to have a negative reaction had to go to a funeral. . . . One seemed unimpressed. . . . One asked me what lesbians looked like, was obviously uncomfortable, but made a very noble attempt to pretend that she wasn't, and the other felt very comfortable and proceeded to ask me lots of questions." The discussion shifted when this same student also revealed that she was an incest survivor and explained that she was not alone among Stanford students. Group members, she reported, "were more shocked by this than the lesbianism, and had a hard time dealing with it. . . . As for myself, I didn't think I could deal with talking about either subject without being honest about it. I also felt I owed [it] to other lesbians and to other incest survivors to speak out." In the small group setting, she was able to do so.

Just as all-white groups had more superficial discussions of race, the overwhelmingly heterosexual groups often began with the question of homosexuality but soon moved to the general topic of sexuality and relationships.

In two of the women-only groups, the coming-out discussion turned to comparable fears of rejection or exposure among straight people. "Just as gay people are expected to be ashamed of their sexuality, fat women are supposed to view their weight as a transitory state," explained one student. Another group moved from discussing lesbians' fear of rejection by their families to memories of their own childhood rejections by other girls and the lasting fear of being different. The parallels gave them insight into homophobia in the absence of firsthand accounts from lesbian or gay male students.

I was surprised by how few lesbian and gay male students either took this class or came out in it; fear of disclosure by association with feminism may have kept them away or in the closet. Nonetheless, the predominantly straight groups learned more about homophobia than they had expected, in large part due to the letter-writing assignment. Despite their resistance, once students tried on a homosexual identity, they had at least a glimpse of the firsthand experience that was missing in most groups. Forced to identify with the sexual minority, students seemed to confront their homophobia more personally, and with less guilt, than they confronted their racism. Thus, although the presence of minority students within groups did not necessarily raise consciousness dramatically, an assignment that encouraged personal identification with minority vulnerability had strong potential to do so.

DURING THE FIRST lecture of the quarter, before I distributed the syllabus, I had asked each student to write a paragraph or two about how they defined and reacted to the term "feminist." The overwhelming majority of the class described the goals of liberal feminism positively but found the label "feminist" too frightening to adopt for themselves. At the beginning of the small groups, students addressed these feelings. "All of us stereotype a feminist negatively," one black woman explained, "that is, as a militant person." One student summarized the reaction to feminists voiced by members of her small group: they "hated men," "did not want to appear attractive," and "were radical and rebellious."

In analyzing their prejudices in class discussion, many students credited the media with shaping their image of angry, militant feminists. I would add that Stanford's student culture not only emphasizes the importance of being attractive to the opposite sex but also encourages conformity to a model of self-satisfaction (the "no one has problems at Stanford" syndrome, as a counseling center flier labels it). In this atmosphere, political rebelliousness—especially when it addresses personal issues rather than, say, U.S. foreign policy—can be dismissed as a sign of personal failure.

I sensed from the student papers that the small groups were perhaps the most critical element in the process of unlearning earlier stereotypes. "I used to think that all feminists were either lesbians or militant man-hating women," wrote an Asian American woman. "After taking this class, I am proud to say that I am a feminist and I also do not hesitate to inform others of my feminist views and beliefs." Similarly, another woman confessed that "I'm quite sure that I wrote one of the least flattering definitions of and reactions to feminism at the beginning of the quarter" and "would certainly never have said that I was a feminist." During the course, she had adopted a definition of feminism that made her able to identify with the term: "A feminist recognizes differences between men and women, but does not always value either male or female attributes and qualities more than the other." She concluded her paper by embracing a new identity: "Now all I have to do to know how I respond to the word feminist is to look in the mirror and see someone whom I respect and like very much." One male student shifted from "a negative gut reaction" to a positive one: "I now consider myself a feminist, which I hadn't even considered before the class." Another man reported, "For the first time, I openly consider myself a feminist—with pride."

The disappearance of defensive reactions to feminism recurred as a final theme in the small group papers. "Now I really consider myself a feminist, it has become a part of who I am. I am not defensive about it. The word has lost its negative connotations," wrote one woman. In another group, a feminist studies major explained that "now more than ever, when I hear or see the word 'feminist' I feel proud. Most of my defensive reactions are entirely gone and I feel positive and connected with the title and its meaning to me." Yet another student felt that she "no longer need[ed] to back away from this name or label. I no longer need to put it in quotes." More rare was the student who expressed a commitment to advocating feminism in public, such as the woman who declared feminist studies as her major and said she felt "very relieved that I have exorcised most of my fears about defending [feminism] publicly."

The final paragraphs of the papers often spoke of pride and even joy in the students' transformation into feminists:

When I see the word "feminist," I feel like celebrating and crying at the same time. I feel a sadness because I know that many people will react to it negatively. . . . I also respond with a feeling of happiness because I know that through education, the incredible ideas of feminism have and will break through the negative stereotype. . . .

Now, when I see or hear the word feminist I invariably respond positively. I feel a bond with the person it is directed toward, and proudly feel a renewed women-centered identity.

When I hear the word feminist, I think: this is a person I want to get to know.

To be sure, when I see or hear the word feminist, I respond with a proud, warm, connective feeling. I myself am a feminist and it's nice to know that I have sisters and brothers who are the same.

Another student echoed this student's historical insight: "I now understand why feminist consciousness-raising groups in the 1970s were so effective in generating women's energies."

While most students claimed a greater willingness to identify as feminists, to themselves or to others, and a more complex definition of feminist constituencies and goals, others addressed the limits of their politics. Unlike the generation that initially adopted c.r. in an era when radicalism was fashionable, today's students shy away from any taint of political rebelliousness. "Even after having taken this class," a woman wrote, "I have yet to conquer my enduring uneasiness with the word 'feminist.' . . . I do still feel a deep and vague discomfort with the word . . . and continue to have difficulty saying 'I am a feminist'" because of the connotation of "radicalism, rebelling, and a touch of 'man-hating' that I am not yet able to accept or overcome."

In a different way, other students expressed how, by the end of the course, they had become acutely aware of their political limitations. As one woman of color reported of her group, "Each of us were entrenched in our inner conflict about our own capitalistic desires and urges." The most frequent conflict women addressed concerned standards of beauty. "We agreed that since taking this class we have often felt like complete hypocrites as we put on our makeup," one white woman revealed of her group. "I grapple with my difficulty of redefining beauty," wrote another woman; "perhaps I need to accept my silly definitions of beauty as dictated by the society I live in." The challenge of differentiating between the messages of the culture and their own beliefs confounded the members of this woman's group, as it did other feminists of the 1980s. The free classroom copies of MS magazine drove home the point — today's political feminism came packaged with contradictory messages extolling traditional femininity and consumer capitalism.

Whatever the limitations of student political consciousness, this experiment in the use of small group, personally based learning proved even more rewarding than I had anticipated. I agreed with the student who wrote that while she "expected these consciousness-raising sessions to change each of us, the rate and degree to which it occurred surprised and inspired me." Small groups had clearly played an important role in allowing internal, emotional shifts to occur gradually in students who had been resistant to feminism. Although the purpose of the groups was to enhance classroom learning and not necessarily to achieve political conversion, the two seemed to happen simultaneously. The intellectual challenge of readings, discussions, and papers certainly contributed to the process, but c.r. provided something that traditional academic work could not: a safe space for discussing personal differences and connecting these differences to gender inequality. Given the complexity of feminist identity that emerged in the 1980s, as well as the negative stereotypes of feminists that persist among students, c.r. offers a unique method for learning the very things feminism espouses.

Finally, in addition to emphasizing the importance of c.r. as a form of pedagogy and urging its adoption in other classes, I want to credit the students in this course with making c.r. work. Those who were willing simply to enroll in FS 101 at a campus that was generally hostile to feminism had to be exceptional students. Revealing their own fears of feminism, their anger and guilt about racism, and their discomfort with homosexuality took courage and entailed risks. The requirement of attending c.r. groups may have motivated change, but the students themselves made possible the personal and political growth that their papers document. For a feminist teacher, their learning has been an inspiration and a source of faith that feminism will survive, even in these conservative times.

5 | No Turning Back | The Historical Resilience of Feminism

A central theme in my feminist studies course is that feminism is a process, not an in-
herited dogma; only continual reinvention has allowed it to flourish. I also stress this
point in No Turning Back, *the book based on my course, which documents the histori-*
cal momentum of women's activism throughout the world. In class and in speaking
publicly about the book, I have found that one of the hardest points to communicate is
the theme of paradox. In addition to exploring a key tension in feminism between uni-
versalistic and particularistic politics, I try to show how the staples of modern Western
history — democracy and capitalism — simultaneously disadvantaged women and
enabled feminist political critiques to form.

SOON AFTER THE revival of the women's movement in the late 1960s,
American journalists began proclaiming the death of feminism. In 1976,
Harper's magazine declared a "Requiem for the Women's Movement"; in
1980, the *New York Times* assured readers that the "Radical Days of Feminism Are Gone"; in 1990, *Newsweek* trumpeted "The Failure of Feminism."
Unconvinced by two decades of obituaries, in 1998 *Time* magazine asked
readers to respond online to the question "Is Feminism Dead?" So ubiqui-
tous is this story that a feminist journalist recently labeled it "False Feminist Death Syndrome."[1] Perhaps these writers notice feminism only during
periods of mass public protest and overlook its quieter but more pervasive
forms. Or perhaps they are engaging in a form of wishful thinking, for given
the power of the media, declaring the death of feminism could become a
self-fulfilling prophecy.

Surveying the interdisciplinary scholarship on women's movements suggests to me that, contrary to the views of contemporary pundits, feminism
has never been more widespread or more politically influential than at this
point in history. In some countries, feminist concerns have moved from the
margins of alternative culture to infiltrate mainstream politics, whether mea-
sured by women's increased office holding or the importance of controversies
over subjects such as veiling, abortion, and lesbian and gay rights. In contrast
to issuing premature obituaries for feminism, the news media now regularly

cover the very subjects raised a generation ago only by radical feminists, such as domestic violence, breast cancer research, eating disorders, and rape in both wartime and peacetime. Moreover, just beyond the headlines, we find stories about the ongoing work of nongovernmental organizations (NGOs) around the world, such as Women in Law and Development in Africa, the Indian movement against dowry deaths, international lesbian rights groups in Taiwan and South Africa, and myriad others that advance women's legal and economic equality. Quietly, grassroots movements are transforming cultures, such as the successful village-based health campaigns in Senegal to end the practice of female genital cutting.

Turning to the United States, the social consequences of political change are so pervasive that we sometimes forget how recently women's opportunities have expanded. In the past generation, women's athletics finally achieved public recognition and enthusiastic participation, in large part because of the legal push for gender equity in school funding. Women's professional education has expanded enormously: from under 10 percent a generation ago, women's representation in law and medical school classes has risen to nearly 50 percent. To give a personal example of the impact of this change, in 1976, when I moved to a liberal community in California, I could not locate a woman doctor to serve as my primary care physician, nor could I find a female gynecologist under my health plan. Today, however, both my primary care provider and several of my health specialists are female. When I ask audiences about their own doctors, from half to three-quarters report having at least one female provider. Health care by women practitioners is now widespread because in the 1970s feminists succeeded in removing admissions quotas at medical schools, and qualified women flocked to the profession.

Another measure of change can be found in the public response to violence against women, evidenced recently by the worldwide impact of Eve Ensler's play, *The Vagina Monologues*. A few years ago, Ensler brought her "V-Day" benefit performance to the San Francisco Bay area. In one evening, with the help of a cast of feminist luminaries, she raised half a million dollars to donate to local antiviolence projects and to aid women in Afghanistan. As impressive as the fund-raising itself is the fact that San Francisco, like many other communities, now has an extensive feminist infrastructure that is ready to put that money to good use: shelters for battered women; rape crisis phone lines; groups like Women against Rape; self-defense classes; girls' empowerment programs; and men's groups conducted in county jails to prevent recurrent violence. These resources simply did not exist a generation ago. Although feminists have not ended violence against women, they have named it, provided services, changed legal practices, and created "zero tolerance" campaigns against rape, wife beating, and sexual harassment, all of which were once considered the inevitable price of being born female. At the same time, the continuing need for these antiviolence campaigns, given the ongoing abuse of women, belies the claims that we live in a "postfeminist" era. This term implies that women have already achieved equality, that women's movements are obsolete. Feminists like Ensler and those who staff antiviolence programs refuse to resign from the unfinished challenge of undermining patriarchy.

In short, both the historical record and contemporary politics suggest strongly that the momentum of feminism remains powerful. In the United States, public opinion polls conducted in 2000 revealed that although only 29 percent of Americans called themselves feminists, 85 percent agreed with the goals of the women's rights movement. Setting aside the labels, we find that aspirations for equal pay and political representation for women, as well as sexual and reproductive choice, have never been greater. Moreover, in a 2001 poll, 64 percent of adult American women responded positively to the word "feminism." Looking beyond the United States, in the European Union, over 80 percent of adults polled in 2005 agreed that women deserved higher education and jobs as much as men do.[2] Throughout the world, more women hold elected office than at any time in history, while in some northern European countries, men's willingness to take responsibility for household work and child care has risen significantly.

I want to be very clear, however, that I am *not* suggesting that we have arrived at a state of gender equality. Indeed, feminists have a great deal to do in the industrialized regions to address women's economic status, political representation, athletics, and health care — especially for women of color — as well as sexual violence and shared parenting; we have only begun to recognize the importance of securing full human rights for women in many parts of the world. Nor am I ignoring the formidable backlash that confronts us every time women gain power, for change is threatening, especially to those who fear they will lose power as a result. What I am pointing out is that the fruits of past feminist movements should be noted rather than denied and that the momentum of history convinces me that there is no turning back from the movement toward full citizenship and full human rights for women. In this essay, I argue that the malleability and diversity of feminism have produced sufficient strength to help feminism infiltrate mainstream political cultures and withstand recurrent opposition. To make my case for feminist resilience, I turn first to the political and economic histories that initially shaped feminism, then to a survey of how multiple feminist strategies have been redefined over time and place, and finally to both the prospects for and the obstacles to a feminist future.

Historical Origins of Feminism

The title of this essay and of my book, "No Turning Back," refers to the historical momentum that has propelled feminism, a word I use to describe broad efforts to achieve full political and economic citizenship for women.[3] Feminist movements reject a political theory of patriarchy, which assumes that men should naturally have authority over women. Although the term "feminism" has specific origins in nineteenth-century France, it has acquired multiple meanings over time. Moreover, not all efforts to empower women originated in modern Europe, nor do they all necessarily adopt the feminist label. Thus, at the outset, I want to acknowledge that long before explicitly feminist movements formed, women in all world regions resisted or modified patriarchy, finding unique ways to appropriate authority for themselves. They continue to do so today, alongside formal social movements.

Women's historical resistance to patriarchy has taken many forms. Some scholars use the label "indigenous feminisms" to refer to customary female authority or forms of women's resistance that preceded or paralleled explicitly political movements. In peasant communities, for example, women banded together to exert group pressure on abusive husbands or withheld economic services to gain leverage within the family. Beginning long before colonial rule, West African women who acquired wealth as traders could regulate personal and economic disputes in the marketplace. In Europe and Asia, women who wished to avoid marriage joined Christian or Buddhist convents, where some exercised important spiritual, intellectual, or creative authority. Throughout the world, even when denied formal education, women have used their minds and the arts, as did poets in early modern Japan and mystics in medieval Europe. Rather than challenging patriarchy through social movements, however, most of these women resisted it as individuals.

Formal critiques of patriarchy did not appear until two historical transformations — one political and one economic — made them both possible and necessary. Wherever democratic politics and wage labor systems have converged to transform societies, some form of feminism has emerged. Politically, feminism calls for extending the democratic rejection of hierarchical rule by questioning the gender privileges retained by men. Economically, the transition from a family to a market economy fueled feminism by creating a double bind for women, as mothers and as wage workers.

Feminist politics have repeatedly responded to the contradictions in women's lives wrought by democracy and capitalist economic growth. In parts of Europe and North America, where these transitions first converged after 1800, feminists began to agitate for education, property rights, and full citizenship. By 1900, an international women's movement was beginning to advance these goals in urban areas of Latin America, the Middle East, and Asia as well. In the twentieth century, anticolonial and democratization movements, as well as a global economy, continued to extend these historical processes. Today, transnational communications have brought ideas about women's rights to regions that have neither democratized nor industrialized. While no single narrative can do justice to the complexities of unique regional histories, a framework that emphasizes the recurrent effects of democratization and wage labor, along with international communications, illustrates the multiple, malleable politics that constitute feminist histories.

POLITICAL IDEAS

The roots of feminism in democratic political theory, the first element in this framework, have long been recognized by historians. Since at least the eighteenth century, the shift from hierarchical rule by elites to representative government—based on the theory of the natural rights of man—has inspired demands for self-representation and full citizenship that extend these rights beyond the Western, propertied, white males who first articulated the ideal. Like movements to abolish slavery in the Americas or to emancipate serfs and Jews in Europe, arguments for women's rights rested upon these democratic principles. As more European and American men gained the right to vote and run for office in the nineteenth and twentieth centuries, the exclusion of women from voting, office holding, and jury duty stood out as signs of incomplete democracy, vulnerable to feminist critiques. In other world regions, such as parts of Latin America, Asia, and postcolonial Africa, whenever educational opportunities exposed women to emerging democratic ideals, they too expected full citizenship. Thus, in the 1880s, when Kishida Toshiko resigned from her position at the Japanese empress's court and began to speak in public about women's rights, she joined a growing international movement to recognize the value of women's lives, whether in the family or in public life. Kishida's 1883 speech, "Daughters Confined in Boxes," demanded educational and economic choices for women, whose horizons, she believed, should be "as large and free as the world itself."[4]

But even burgeoning democratic societies resisted the extension of self-determination to women (Kishida, for example, was considered so radical that she was arrested and imprisoned). Keep in mind that both the European Enlightenment and the revolutionary ideas that gave birth to women's longings for emancipation rested upon contradictory views. The movement for universal rights promised emancipation from the Old Regime of inherited status; simultaneously, however, the principle of natural law drew biological distinctions between the sexes and among races. In other words, in Enlightenment thought, the flip side of "natural rights" was "natural sex" and "natural race." Thus, when women or Africans or Asians claimed universal rights, white male critics could respond that their biological differences disqualified them from inclusion as citizens. This contradiction in modern political thought, as historian Joan Scott has pointed out, required a dual strategy on the part of feminists.[5] On the one hand, they emphasized universalism and demanded inclusion in the language of rights; on the other hand, they pointed to particularistic, biologically rooted female claims to political authority, which historians now refer to as "maternalism."

The exclusion of women from the body politic, a staple of Western democracy since the classical era, required the use of these paradoxical strategies for achieving inclusion. How else could women claim full citizenship, when their reproductive roles in families created the kind of dependency that seemed antithetical to exercising democratic rights? Thus, a balancing act between universalism and particularism recurred throughout Western feminist history.

Historians have identified at least three dominant feminist strategies. In the first approach, beginning in the eighteenth century and increasingly in the nineteenth century, middle-class liberal feminists — whether in England, the United States, Chile, or Japan — emphasized women's need for greater access to education, property rights, and jobs. In this vein, manifestos such as the Declaration of Sentiments adopted at the 1848 Seneca Falls Convention in the United States called for the extension of the rights of white male citizens to women. Two other simultaneous frameworks addressed the dual concerns of women as workers and as mothers. Socialist feminism originated among European labor activists concerned primarily about the plight of wage-earning women, both in their families and in their jobs. In Germany, Clara Zetkin organized working women within leftist parties, while Alexandra Kollontai, commissar of social welfare in the early

Soviet Union, tried to address family as well as workplace dilemmas, decreeing free maternity care, for example. A third strain, maternalism, built upon women's public authority as mothers to argue for social welfare policies, ranging from better schools to public child care to pacifism. Thus, Amanda Labarca of Chile reported to a U.S. women's group in 1922 that she expected "a new feminist creed" to arise in the southern continent, one "more domestic, more closely linked to the future of the home, the family, and the children," than that marked by the "exaggerated individualism" of what she called "Saxon feminism."[6] While liberal and Marxist feminists emphasized the integration of women into middle-class or working-class male politics, maternalists turned to women's unique experiences in the family to justify female citizenship.

These identifiable strains, however, were never mutually exclusive, for demands for universal rights often rested on the particularistic needs of women. For example, when Mary Wollstonecraft called for women's education in eighteenth-century England, she insisted it would help them become "sensible mothers"; Flora Tristan pressed for education for French working women in the nineteenth century in part "because women have the responsibility for educating male and female children"; in 1890, the Brazilian feminist Francisca Diniz wrote that the sanctity of maternal love and wifely fidelity proved women's superiority rather than inferiority and required equal treatment by men. Early-twentieth-century American suffragists echoed these particularistic arguments when they insisted that women voters would insure a more peaceful and nurturing society. For Charlotte Perkins Gilman, because life-giving women (preferably, in her view, those of Teutonic stock) would improve the man-made world, they deserved suffrage.[7] Overlapping strands of feminist ideas about equal rights thus continually defied the long-standing Western political distinction between the private realm of the family and the public world of politics.

ECONOMIC REALITIES

The expanding definition of citizenship proved a necessary but not sufficient cause for feminist movements to form. An economic motor reinforced these ideas — the transition from agricultural, family-based economies to commercial, and later industrial, market economies based on wage labor. Over time, women joined the ranks of paid workers, but it was not wage earning per se that fomented feminism, for capitalism by no means liberates women; rather, it requires them to perform the dual tasks of domestic and wage labor. Female wage earning had the potential to weaken the patriarchal family because women's economic contributions might provide greater leverage in the home. However, the lingering ideology of female dependency—the fiction of the "private woman" supported in the home—survived the demographic and economic transition to female wage labor. Because women earned lower wages than men in sexually segregated job markets (and had limited rights to property and little access to credit), they could not in fact support themselves. Lower wages in turn insured women's dependence on fathers and husbands, thus reinforcing patriarchy. As in the realm of citizenship, the discrepancies between male and female opportunities ignited feminist critiques.

The economic processes that created dilemmas for women workers occurred at different times throughout the world. With the exception of early textile workers, the initial transition to industrial production in Europe and North America excluded most women, reinforcing maternal identities within the middle class and employing working-class women largely to perform domestic labor outside their own homes. In response, male workers and the early labor movement promulgated an ideal of the "family wage" in which a male breadwinner earned enough to support his dependent wife and children. Over the twentieth century, light manufacturing, clerical and service jobs, and later information economies drew women of all classes and ages into formal labor markets.

In industrializing societies, the pool of available female workers grew as women's reproductive labor declined. In the United States, for example, average marital fertility rates dropped from around eight children in 1800 to under two children in 2000. Whenever an expanding sector of the economy sought cheap wage labor, women, who now had fewer reproductive labors, filled the jobs. As a result of worker availability and employer demand, female wage labor changed from exceptional to commonplace in most industrializing cultures. First, it was younger and single women who worked for wages; later, older and married women, and then mothers of small children, began to spend longer periods of their lives earning wages. By 1999, 70 percent of married women with children were working for wages in the United States. By then, 46 percent of U.S. workers and 42 percent of western European workers were women.

Given the global reach of market economies, this process was not limited to the West. By the 1990s, women constituted 43 percent of the wage labor force in East Asia, the Caribbean, and sub-Saharan Africa. Significantly, their jobs clustered in "female" sectors of the economy: light manufacturing, clerical and sales, and services once offered in private homes, such as preparing and serving food, cleaning, caring for children, and sex work. During every transition from agricultural to industrial economies, sexual commerce has drawn women from rural areas to cities, where restrictions on women's jobs keeps the pool of sex workers full.

The legacies of the private home have meant that even when women earn wages, they continue to have primary responsibility for caring for family members. This unpaid work in the home has perpetuated economic inequality in the wage labor force at every stage of economic development. Women's association as primarily unpaid caregivers has masked their full economic contributions, just as it has masked men's capacity for familial labors. In addition, it creates the double day for most women workers, who continue to absorb the social costs of family care. Data on the division of housework throughout the world, even for dual-earning couples, documents this disparity. Wage-earning women do most of the caring work within families. Even when socialist states have offered some relief, such as child care, women's domestic responsibility remained powerful. The domestic legacy has also led to employer biases that women are not dedicated to their jobs, simply by virtue of being potential or actual mothers. Women's secondary political status and this dual economic burden have meant that women increasingly chafe against the limitations on their full participation as citizens and as workers.

Competing feminist strategies have addressed the disparity between the ideal of political and economic democracy and the second-class status of women. Just as the paradox of female citizenship required a dual strategy that balanced universal and maternal claims to authority, labor inequalities have inspired multiple responses. In the nineteenth and early twentieth centuries, when most women worked within their own families, even liberal feminists recognized that as long as women remained economically dependent on men, motherhood represented a very powerful justification for protecting and empowering women. Like maternalists, the liberal feminists who sought public authority through woman suffrage felt comfortable invoking maternalist rhetoric to justify their demand for the vote; they accepted women's difference as a strength. Before the mid-twentieth century, most suffragists and socialists also supported the protection of women as mothers through laws that regulated women's hours of labor and the tasks they could perform for pay.

Until the 1920s, most American women accepted these particularist arguments, with the significant exception of the young militants who first claimed the label "feminist" around 1910. These women later formed the National Woman's Party, and in the 1920s, they introduced the Equal Rights Amendment to abolish all gender distinctions in the law. Only after the surge in women's wage labor force participation would equal rights laws grow in popularity. With so many women facing obstacles to jobs and professions, liberal feminists began to rely on a universalist strategy of promoting equal rights legislation. After its founding in 1966, for example, the National Organization for Women concentrated on supporting laws that would expand women's economic independence by opening new jobs and careers. Despite the failure of the Equal Rights Amendment, they succeeded in breaking down many legal barriers to women's economic opportunity. In the process, however, many American feminists shifted motherhood from the center to the periphery of their politics. Yet the double day persisted for working women who could not afford full-time domestic help, and even those who could hire caretakers often chafed at the conflicting claims of job and family.

By the end of the twentieth century, liberal feminists in the United States recognized both the benefits and the limitations of integrating into male work patterns. They began to articulate a new model of interdependence, in which women and men share both caregiving and breadwinning tasks. Drawing on policies long advocated by socialist feminists in Europe, U.S. activists increasingly called for paid family leave, workplace child care, and other forms of support from employers and the state to help parents combine wage labor and family life.[8] Unlike earlier maternalist politics, this recent approach avoids the pitfall of gender essentialism (which assumes that only women can parent) by assigning caregiving work to both men and women. Today, American feminists advocate family-friendly workplaces, adequate child care, and welfare policies that value children's education. Whether they will succeed in establishing the kind of social policies long in effect in parts of Europe and whether these services will survive where they originally flourished depends not only on feminist priorities but also on broader political realities and the alliances feminists are able to build with other social movements.

Which Women?

In addition to revising its labor policies in the face of structural change, feminism has shifted other central agendas after confronting internal challenges. Because the category "woman" is by no means universal but rather masks internal social hierarchies, conflicts among women of diverse racial and cultural backgrounds have repeatedly forced redefinitions of feminist politics. Those who insist on expanding the composition of the movement beyond the white, Western, middle classes have forced feminists in the United States and internationally to ask not only about gender disparity but also about "which women" feminism serves.

Two key internal conflicts derived largely from the legacies of colonial relations. The first concerns racial justice: Would feminism make race subordinate to gender concerns or recognize opposition to racism as central to its politics? The second pertains to national liberation from European dominance: Would Western feminism reject the "white woman's burden" of "civilized morality" — Gilman's Teutonic bias, for example — and acknowledge the political integrity of non-Western women and former colonial subjects? These questions have continually redefined feminism. Indeed, the historical strength of feminism often correlates with its attention to broader social justice concerns, while its weak periods are often those in which feminism is isolated from other critiques of social hierarchies.

In the United States, for example, strong ties between movements for gender and racial justice characterized the antislavery and early women's rights movements. Yet the initial alliance of abolitionists and feminists before the Civil War largely crumbled after 1870. During the postwar era of white-supremacist politics and Jim Crow segregation, the suffrage movement reflected the racial biases of the larger culture. The National American Woman Suffrage Association excluded black women as speakers to keep white southern members in the fold, and both suffrage and women's temperance movements had segregated chapters. African American activists, however, never stopped pressuring white feminists to reject the racial hierarchy that relegated black women to the back of the American suffrage parades and the margins of the political agenda. Tentative interracial coalitions reemerged in the twentieth-century civil rights movement, as activists in churches, the Young Women's Christian Association, and the antilynching movement finally heeded African American women's call for allies. Later, the involvement of young white women in the civil rights campaigns of the 1960s helped revive feminist politics by providing models of strong black female leaders and lessons in community organizing.

After the 1960s, when the United States had a more diverse population, not only African American but also Mexican American, Native American, and Asian American women — as well those who identified as lesbian and disabled — insisted that feminism dismantle all social hierarchies that impeded women's full citizenship. In the words of activist Barbara Smith, speaking in 1979, "Feminism is the political theory and practice that struggles to free all women. . . . Anything less than this vision of total freedom is not feminism, but merely female self-aggrandizement."[9] During the 1970s and 1980s, a repeated process of naming differences, organizing separately, and working toward political coalitions challenged U.S. feminism. Separate groups of women of color identified the issues most pressing for their communities, such as health care and welfare. Books like *This Bridge Called My Back: Writings by Radical Women of Color* (1981) helped educate white women about these priorities and about the effects of racism within feminism. Rather than splintering, many feminists have tried to learn, in the words of the African American lesbian poet Audre Lorde, "how to take our differences and make them strengths."[10] But feminism can do so only if it remains vigilant about opposing racism both inside and outside its ranks.

Racial inclusion meant that the U.S. feminist agenda had to change. Reproductive rights, for example, came to include not only contraception and abortion but also an end to the sterilization abuse that denied reproductive choice particularly to Native American, African American, and Mexican American women. The women's health movement had to address the particular concerns of women of color and make health care available in their communities. With so many women of color living in poverty, welfare reform had to become a feminist issue. While large swaths of American feminism still reflect a white and middle-class membership, at its best, the movement now works in alliance rather than in competition with movements for universal civil and human rights.

Internationally, colonialism set the stage for most global encounters among women, leaving a powerful legacy of unequal relations across regions. Although women in Africa, Asia, and the Middle East had historically forged individual routes to authority, European feminists often failed to appreciate the power held by these women. They tended to assume that imposing their own ideas about clothing, education, and family life would rescue colonized women, a project that could serve their own political goals. Just as some American women called for woman suffrage as one means of counteracting African American and immigrant male voters, British suffragettes incorporated the language of white racial superiority when they argued that as "mothers of the race" white women needed the vote to support the work of imperialism and to uplift native women.

Nonetheless, Western critiques of political hierarchy did appeal to many colonial subjects who questioned both foreign rule and patriarchy. In India and Egypt, for example, concerns about women's rights paralleled anticolonial movements. Pandita Ramabai, a widowed scholar in Bombay who worked for Indian independence, drew on Mary Wollstonecraft's ideas about education when she founded a training institute for teachers and called for women's medical schools. When women became involved in Egyptian politics in the early twentieth century, they often sought both national independence and women's education and citizenship rights. Thus, Huda Sha'arawi not only mobilized women to resist the British but also rejected the practice of veiling and successfully campaigned for women's access to Egyptian universities; in 1923, she founded the Egyptian Feminist Union.

Not all nationalist movements empowered women. In Turkey and Iran, male leaders tried to co-opt feminism. In the name of modernization, they imposed certain Western practices — such as rejecting the veil and establishing formal education for women — but at the same time, their regimes either crushed or took control of feminist political organizations. Elsewhere, successful national liberation movements proclaimed feminism a form of Western imperialism and took steps to overturn women's rights. In Algeria, a history of forced, public unveiling of women by the French colonial powers made the reveiling of women a symbol of national resistance. Even though the women who had struggled alongside men to win independence gained suffrage, in the 1960s, the leaders of the new Algerian state called for a nationalistic return to one version of local "tradition," namely, patriarchy, enforced through a family code that restricted divorce and contraception.

As women mobilized to gain their rights in former colonial regions, they communicated with European and North American feminists. Not surprisingly, given the history of European dominance and anticolonial critiques of the West, the international feminist organizations of the early twentieth century remained international largely in name only. In addition, what has been termed "feminist orientalism" on the part of European women, who treated all colonized women as if they were passive victims, hampered their outreach efforts. Women of color continually protested these condescending attitudes. At an international conference in 1935, for example, Shareefeh Hamid Ali of India spoke for women of "the East" when she explained to women of "the west" that "any arrogant assumption of superiority or of patronage on the part of Europe or America" would alienate "the womanhood of Asia and Africa."[11] Again, internal critiques pushed feminists to recognize the legacy of colonialism.

Growing internationalism after World War II expanded opportunities for women's communication across cultures. In its charter in 1945, the United

Nations endorsed "the equal rights of men and women." Since then, the organization has been instrumental in facilitating transnational feminist organizing, particularly during the Decade for Women (1975–85), which produced three international conferences, with concurrent NGO forums. From these conferences came the Convention to Eliminate All Forms of Discrimination against Women, as well as international dialogues about global grassroots projects to address women's needs. Interactions at the U.N. conferences forced Western feminists to begin to decenter their priorities and to recognize multiple strategies for empowering women. As the newsletter for the NGO forum in Copenhagen reported in 1980, "To talk feminism to a woman who has no water, no food and no home is to talk nonsense."[12] Poverty, illiteracy, and homelessness — critical women's issues throughout the world — had to become central to international feminist movements.

Transnational feminisms now try to acknowledge cultural differences among women and form alliances across those differences. This approach has made some activists more comfortable embracing feminism as a political identity. From the Feminist Peasant Network in Mexico to the Feminist Networks in eastern Europe, the term itself has been incorporated to describe NGOs. When the Women's League of the African National Congress (ANC) returned from exile in 1990, it proclaimed that "feminism has been misinterpreted in most third world countries. . . . There is nothing wrong with feminism. It is as progressive or reactionary as nationalism." With the establishment of a democratic government, the group dropped its call for "liberation before feminism" and began to negotiate for equal representation of women in the ANC.[13]

By the time of the U.N.'s Fourth World Conference on Women, held in Beijing in 1995, both NGOs and states had created extensive feminist infrastructures concerned with women's economic inequality and physical vulnerability and committed to gaining greater political representation and creative opportunities for women. A broad range of projects now address these issues by organizing domestic workers in Latin America; monitoring the treatment of migrant domestics internationally; exposing domestic violence in India through street theater as well as legislation; expanding microenterprise in South Asia; and empowering women economically. Grassroots movements seek to eradicate female genital cutting in Africa and expand female literacy in Asia. Women seek marriage and divorce reform in Egypt and Turkey. Women's arts, theater, publishing, and performance spaces promote creativity throughout the world. In countries ranging from Canada to

Zimbabwe, male feminists have organized, particularly in the fight against sexual violence or to reclaim parental, caring work.

WOMEN'S RIGHTS AS HUMAN RIGHTS

In addition to addressing the particular needs of women, international feminisms have insisted that human rights be understood from women's perspective. In a sense, this strategic move helps to resolve the Western tension between universal and particularist claims by redefining the universal as the female. In some cases, the impact on world and local politics has been transformative. For example, in response to a campaign by the Women's Caucus for Gender Justice, the 1998 Rome Statute that created the International Criminal Court outlawed gender-based violence in wartime. Despite strong opposition, the caucus succeeded in including as war crimes rape, sexual slavery, enforced prostitution, forced pregnancy, and enforced sterilization, and it acknowledged the vulnerability of men, as well as women, to sexual violence. Equally transformative, the statute required that the court include both female and male judges who had expertise on violence against women and children.

Another measure of the transformative impact of international feminisms can be found in the arena of electoral reform. The current French system of *parité* withholds state funding for political parties that do not nominate equal numbers of male and female candidates. A related mechanism of reserving a proportion of electoral seats for women can be found throughout the world. The recent Afghan and Iraqi constitutions, for example, not only require woman suffrage but also propose quotas for female political participation as one means of implementing democratic reforms in cultures in which women previously have been denied access to the political sphere.

The case of India illustrates the transformative implications of electoral reform. Because a proportion of seats on municipal councils are reserved for female and lower-caste candidates, today close to a million poor, rural women now hold village offices. Once elected, one study has found, these women try to allocate village resources to address the most pressing needs of poor women by creating better water and sewage infrastructure.[14] This structural reform is critical to feminist goals for it allows girls to spend less time hauling water and more time attending school. Education helps close the literacy gap (two-thirds of those who are illiterate throughout the world are female, and the figure is higher in rural South Asia). In turn, female education correlates highly with family planning. Rooted in feminist goals, both female literacy and family planning enable not just women but also their entire families to escape poverty. In a world in which 70 percent of those living in poverty are female, these political reforms can help narrow the global gap between the wealthy and the poor. In short, the particularist strategy of empowering women can have universal consequences; instead of serving as a justification for exclusion from rights, women's difference has become a basis for redefining rights, with implications for all.

The Future of Change

The varied forms of feminist activism that I have surveyed in this essay support one of the major themes of my book *No Turning Back*: that feminism is neither static nor monolithic. Indeed, I have found that much of the historical resilience of feminism derives from its malleability. As the following examples illustrate, feminism is a politics in process, ever-changing and ever-adapting to new ideas and local circumstances. However, it is also important to acknowledge the current obstacles to its survival. Despite recurrent backlash, I argue, feminism can endure, as it has in the past, through continual transformation.

REVISIONIST POLITICS

Overlapping and shifting strategies have recurred throughout this historical survey. Feminists who once concentrated on liberal demands for women's access to male jobs now call for men to share the valuable labor of caregiving. Another case of political adaptation can be found in the realm of reproductive rights. In the United States, the language employed to defend access to abortion has shifted over time from "abortion on demand" to "pro-choice" politics, not only in response to opponents' use of the term "pro-life" but also in recognition of the fact that abortion is not so much something women desire as an option they may require, albeit a difficult one. In other revisions, middle-class, white feminists came to recognize that for women of color and poor women, sterilization abuse is as important in reproductive choice as are contraception and abortion, while for lesbians, the right to parent (by insemination or adoption) must be part of the reproductive rights agenda.

Internationally, a quest for "reproductive health" rather than "reproductive rights" has proven to resonate more strongly in regions such as eastern Europe. As African activist Adetoun Ilumoka explained, the concept of reproductive rights "doesn't mean an awful lot to the average Nigerian woman. They are concerned with their health, certainly with their ability to make a living."[15] International feminist organizations have learned that only by addressing the underlying economic disparities between wealthy and poor nations, as well as between men and women, will women truly exercise reproductive choice.

A final example of changing ideological frameworks can be found among younger, "third-wave" feminists in the United States, many of whom have rejected any conformist politics concerning fashion, culture, sexuality, or gender identities. An earlier generation's penchant for politically correct language and styles may have fostered internal cohesion, but it left many feeling excluded from the feminist fold. To the third wave, who came of age in the 1990s, feminists come in myriad and protean forms—whether stylishly chic, punk, or tailored; female, male, or transgendered; heterosexual, lesbian, gay, or bisexual. At a time when academic theorists were challenging the legitimacy of any kind of unified identity, including that of "woman," third-wave activists claimed overlapping, multiple, and malleable identities that could enhance coalition politics rather than preclude activism.

In my view, feminism has grown stronger through redefining itself and rethinking its politics. Rather than the "death of feminism" story with which I opened, I wish to emphasize the various reinventions of women's movements. Not everyone who participates in these multiple challenges to gender hierarchy will necessarily identify as a feminist. Labels aside, I would argue that women who have access to and control of wages, make their own marital and sexual choices, exercise political rights, and can engage in artistic and intellectual, as well as parental, tasks (as well as men who defend women's rights and reclaim parental work for themselves) are both the beneficiaries of past feminisms and the foundation of future transformation.

HISTORICAL CHALLENGES

I want to acknowledge in closing that while I emphasize momentum, I am not ignoring the unfinished feminist agendas concerning sexuality, the body, and violence, as well as economic and political rights. I recognize, for example, that as market economies expand globally, they draw women from rural areas into the world of urban sexual commerce (including prostitution and pornography). At the same time, the freedom of choice within industrialized and recently democratized societies incorporates a sexualized consumer culture that remains fixated largely on representations of female anatomy and that exports those images internationally, often replete with racialized stereotypes. I think that feminist tensions over the right to choose sexual labor or to flaunt female sexual allure illustrate the dilemma of partial justice: without economic and political equality, when is sexual labor and allure a free choice and when is it implicitly coercive?

Nor am I ignoring the historical pattern that in every era in which women gain public authority, we face considerable backlash, from women as well as men. Opponents of change often appoint certain conservative spokeswomen to champion women's right to be supported in the home, while fundamentalist religious groups of all stripes insist that God has ordained women's obedience to men. Indeed, despite the predictive value implied by my title "No Turning Back," I am well aware that a feminist future is by no means inevitable. My argument about momentum rests upon a historical foundation of democratic longings combined with economic expansion. Where only one or neither of these conditions prevails, politics are particularly resistant to feminist critiques of gender hierarchy. Afghanistan under the Taliban represented an extreme case, but elsewhere, authoritarian states or ravished economies deepen patriarchal values. Women may continue to organize underground or in exile, as did the Revolutionary Association of the Women of Afghanistan by providing education and health care for refugees from the Taliban. But totalitarian regimes, war, and occupation undermine feminist momentum.

Even where feminism has been flourishing, it faces constant challenges. Religious fundamentalism represents one powerful international counterforce. Some Christian churches in the United States, for example, have revived an ideal of wifely obedience in the home. Throughout the world, a coalition of the religious right (including Catholics, Muslims, fundamentalist Protestants, and ultra-Orthodox Jews) mobilizes to restrict reproductive rights, including the withholding of state funding and international aid for family-planning programs. The political right also effectively deploys gender nostalgia to win votes and, once elected, tries to reverse feminist gains. For example, in 2002, the highly popular right-wing French presidential candidate Jean-Marie LePen promised that if elected, he would repeal the electoral reform of *parité*.

Furthermore, in both academic and popular culture, we now witness a resurgence of deterministic biological theories, which consider gender difference and male dominance natural. Sociobiologists have revived ideas about "human nature," updating the Enlightenment notion of "natural sex" to emphasize woman as reproducer and, in some cases, man as natural sexual predator. These views not only deny the full humanity of both women and men but also threaten the feminist political project, which is deeply grounded in the social and historical rather than merely biological construction of gender and, indeed, is deeply rooted in politically utopian rather than deterministic values.

All of these caveats and complications considered, I still believe that the historical momentum for achieving full economic and political citizenship for women is extremely powerful as long as it remains connected to broader campaigns for democratization and social justice and continues to be malleable. In the past, feminism has survived and gained momentum by combining old and new political strategies. The maternalist legacy, for example, survives within groups such as Las Madres del Plaza de Mayo (The Mothers of the Plaza de Mayo), who demonstrated against the disappearance of their children under the military dictatorship in Argentina, and the Mothers of East Los Angeles, who organize to oppose prison construction in the United States. With the liberal feminist goal of suffrage almost universally achieved, women now mobilize to increase their political representation by backing female candidates for office.

At the same time, NGOs proliferate to address women's local needs in regions only recently affected by democratic politics or market economies. In the former Soviet Union, for example, the GAIA Women's Center in Moscow provides a forum for consciousness raising, social services, job training, and political lobbying, while the Feminist League in Kazakstan supports feminist education and tries to eliminate sexism in the mass media. In the 1990s, the Chinese Women's Research Institute created the first national hotline for women, with trained volunteers responding to legal, economic, sexual, and health questions. This hotline legitimated public discussion of issues once considered too private to address. Though they often must struggle to survive, these groups represent a vast global underground that seeks to redress inequalities rooted in patriarchal practices.

Despite widespread discomfort with the term and repeated media proclamations of its death, feminism has persisted to become central to contemporary politics. Although it is resisted and contested, it will likely be critical to political histories of the next century, especially if human rights expand rather than contract, if caregiving and breadwinning tasks can be disentangled from gender, and if the legacies of colonialism are vigilantly refused.

As Gertrude Mongella, secretary-general of the Fourth World Conference on Women, told the gathering in Beijing: "A revolution has begun and there is no going back. There will be no unraveling of commitments — not today's commitments, not last year's commitments, and not the last decade's commitments. This revolution is too just, too important, and too long overdue."[16] In my view, the historical record supports her prediction.

Part Two | Sexual Boundaries

6 | The Historical Construction of Homosexuality in the United States

The treatment of the history of homosexuality in Intimate Matters: A History of Sexuality in America *illustrates the social-constructionist interpretation of sexuality. The book, which I coauthored with John D'Emilio, draws upon a materialist or Marxist-feminist framework and interweaves the topic of same-sex relations throughout the narrative to support broader arguments about the importance of sexuality in American history, the separation of sexuality and reproduction, the commercialization of sex, and the politicization of sexual identities. Since the publication of* Intimate Matters, *the study of lesbian and gay history in the United States has expanded to explore regional and racial diversity, discursive as well as materialist constructions of sexuality, and the implications of transgender politics. As the closing section of this essay states, I think we need to acknowledge the diversity of past sexual practices and identities and to see them in their historical contexts rather than to include them all under the modern rubric of homosexuality.*

THE CONCEPT OF the social construction of sexuality has become almost commonplace in academic writing and increasingly prevalent in political writing. Set in contrast to either biological or psychoanalytic determinism, which situates sexuality within the individual body or psyche, social construction suggests that every society creates or constructs a set of sexual ideals, rules, and possibilities that determine how individual sexual practices may be named and interpreted. These social constructs change over time and across cultures — they are subject to reconstruction given large historical forces, such as economic and demographic transformations. In short, what we consider "sexual" in our culture is not necessarily what we once considered "sexual" or what is considered "sexual" elsewhere. Thus, in contrast to scholars who assume an ahistorical or transhistorical homosexuality, my approach is based on the view that while individual same-sex

Previously published as Estelle B. Freedman, "The Historical Construction of Homosexuality in the U.S.," *Socialist Review* 25, no. 1 (1995): 31–46. Reprinted by permission of the publisher.

erotic desire may exist universally, homosexual identity is a relatively modern phenomenon.[1]

Recognizing the variability of sexual categories, however, raises some categorical problems of its own. For example, finding a historically accurate term to describe the various social constructs of same-sex desire presents a serious challenge. The term "homosexuality" did not exist until a little over a century ago, and individuals before that time did not think of themselves as lesbian, gay, or bisexual — nor do many whom we might so label today. I have found the rubric "same-sex love" useful in categorizing the overall subject, even though this term too has its pitfalls, for at times, lust, not love, is the subject.

When I refer to the historical construction of homosexuality, in this case in the United States, I mean the ways that inhabitants of this country have, since the colonial era, understood, practiced, and regulated sexual or romantic relations between members of the same gender. In this brief essay, my scope is ambitious — from the colonial era to the Stonewall riots of 1969 — and my purpose is to illustrate how sexuality in general is shaped and reshaped historically through the interaction of economic and social contexts and the behaviors of individuals and social groups.

Natives and Colonists

The cultural variability of same-sex desire and its labeling is evident from the era of European settlement. Before the arrival of Europeans, many Native American cultures incorporated a form of cross-gender identity and, in some cases, a form of same-sex marriage. In many tribes, a man who felt or dreamed that his true identity was that of a woman could take the female role, wear women's clothes, work at women's tasks, and marry a man. In a few tribes, a woman could take on a male identity and marry a woman. Europeans called this practice *berdache*, and they considered the Indians to be barbaric in their toleration of such relationships.

Historians and anthropologists disagree on whether these cross-gender individuals were simply tolerated or whether they were denigrated or in fact venerated by their tribes. In any case, certain groups — particularly tribes in which gender roles were relatively fluid in comparison to those among Europeans, in which religious beliefs did not denigrate carnal relations, and in which spiritual messages (such as dreams that decreed a gender reversal) carried great weight — provided a social space for a particular socially constructed identity, the cross-gender *berdache*. It is important to recognize, however, that gender identity, and not necessarily sexual desire, formed the core of this construct and that despite some contemporary efforts to claim those who engaged in the *berdache* as gay ancestors, the practice did not resemble modern homosexual identity, although it did include the opportunity for same-sex intimate relationships.[2]

The Europeans who pronounced the *berdache* so barbaric adhered to much more rigid gender roles. Their Judeo-Christian ethic also condemned all nonreproductive sexual relations. (They accepted that both women and men had sexual desire and the capacity for pleasure but insisted that lust be channeled into marriage.) Reproduction was especially important to the settlers who came to North America. America's scarcity of laborers and abundance of land encouraged a "high" reproductive strategy to populate the land. Indeed, natural increase largely accounted for the doubling of the European colonial population from the seventeenth to the eighteenth century; during this time, a married woman could expect to bear eight children.

Whether Puritans in New England or Anglicans in the southern colonies, the European settlers established firm laws to channel sexuality into marriage and reproduction, outlawing adultery, rape, and sodomy. Because they so clearly defied the norm of reproductive sexuality, the crimes of sodomy, buggery, and bestiality carried the death penalty.[3] As the founder of the Massachusetts Bay Colony, John Winthrop, explained in the case of a man who was executed for sodomy and corrupting youths "by masturbations," these acts were "dreadful" because they "tended to the frustrating of the ordinance of marriage and the hindering [of] the generation of mankind."

Execution was in fact rare, but men convicted of "sodomitical acts" such as "spending their seed upon one another" received severe and repeated whipping, burning with a hot iron, or banishment. Although the term "sodomy" was not applied to sexual relations between women, one colony, New Haven, listed women's acts "against nature" among its capital offenses. There were also cases of "lewd behavior" between women; in 1642, for example, a Massachusetts court severely whipped a servant and fined her for "unseemly practices betwixt her and another maid." The colonial crimes of sodomy or "unnatural acts" were not, however, equivalent to the modern concept of homosexuality. For one thing, sodomy referred to "unnatural" — that is, nonprocreative — sexual acts, which could be performed between two men, a man and an animal, or a man and a woman. In addition, unlike the Native Americans' attitude toward cross-gender *berdache*, British colonial society had no permanent cultural category for those who engaged in sexual relations with members of their own gender. Like other sinners, those who were punished for unnatural sexual acts did not acquire a lifetime identity as "homosexual" and could be reintegrated into the fold if sufficiently repentant.

Why colonial society had no social space for a modern concept of homosexual identity becomes clearer when we look beyond the legal record to the larger social and economic context of the period. In early America, sexual values and behaviors were almost fully contained within family life and organized around reproduction. In New England, solitary living was often outlawed. Although individual men and women might experience sexual desire for members of their own gender and, in some cases, act to satisfy that desire, it was economically impossible for men and women to leave their families and pursue what we would now call a "lifestyle" of homosexuality. Same-sex desire might result in an act, called sodomy, but it did not lead to a social role or identity that would conflict with the formation and maintenance of reproductive families. That transformation in meaning did not occur until the late nineteenth century, and understanding it requires an overview of the changing meanings of reproduction, sexuality, and love over the course of that century.

Instability and Transformation: The Nineteenth Century

The reproductive society began to erode in the late eighteenth century as a result of the decrease in abundant land for children to inherit, the greater social and political instability of the revolutionary era, and, eventually, the social transformations wrought by industrialization. From the late eighteenth through the early nineteenth century, a new familial and sexual order emerged, one that would remain powerful until the early twentieth century. In this period, along with duty and the need to procreate, passion became a more powerful component of sexual life.

The shift from procreation to passion as a central sexual meaning occurred within a particular social and economic context. For the emerging white middle-class family living in the nineteenth century, the growth of a market economy in both agriculture and industry transformed life in two important ways. First, the commercial and industrial economy encouraged a new reproductive strategy of family limitation since children were becoming an economic liability rather than an asset. Second, white men increasingly entered a public world of paid labor and trade, while white women ideally remained in a separate domestic sphere, nurturing children and husbands.[4]

As a consequence of these economic and social changes, sexual meanings began to shift in subtle and important ways. A key indicator of change in marital relations was the declining white marital fertility rate, which dropped by 50 percent over the course of the nineteenth century (from over seven children in 1800 to under four in 1900; African American rates dropped as well, but later in the century). While some white couples limited family size by managing their sexual lives through periodic continence, many couples began to use contraception or, when contraception failed, abortion. Thus, for both men and women, marital sex became less associated with reproduction and more important as a form of personal intimacy, especially within courtship and marriage. For example, letters and diaries reveal a new emphasis on the emotional and erotic meanings of marital sexuality, for both middle-class and working-class couples.

As many Americans adopted a more romantic attitude toward marital sexuality, elaborating a new, *nonreproductive* meaning of sex, they unwittingly created greater opportunity for nonreproductive, passionate same-gender love. Within the working class, men and women who began to live outside traditional families formed same-gender partnerships for economic or sexual reasons or both. Within the middle class, romantic friendships fostered both spiritual and physical intimacy that might become sexual. For men more than for women, same-gender relationships often crossed class boundaries. For both sexes, these relationships formed unself-consciously. Not until the last quarter of the century did those who engaged in same-sex relationships find it necessary to hide or deny their passionate attachments.

Same-gender relationships outside the familial model were most readily available to white, wage-earning men. The industrializing economy offered these men opportunities to explore sexuality outside marriage, whether on city streets or in the separate sphere of all-male activity. The ability to purchase goods and services allowed men to live beyond familial controls, while the city provided anonymity for their actions. Wage-earning men who lived in urban boardinghouses could bring other men to their rooms for the night or longer. For instance, one legal case involved two men in New York City who met in church and lived together for three months, engaging nightly in "carnal intercourse." During the 1860s, Walt Whitman frequently brought home young, working-class men whom he met in East Coast cities.

These relationships were not confined to cities; whenever young, single men congregated — as soldiers, prisoners, or cowboys — the possibility for same-gender relationships increased. During the Civil War, for example, when Whitman served as a nurse, he formed deep attachments to the young Union and Confederate soldiers he tended. The West also provided extensive opportunities for male-male intimacy. A territorial court case reveals that cowboys attempted to hire younger men to spend the night with them. At Fort Meade in the Dakota Territory, a "Mrs. Nash" first married a soldier, then married another man after her first husband was transferred. After her death, Mrs. Nash's identity as a man was discovered by the local community.

Working-class women also found that adopting the identity of the opposite sex could expand their opportunities. Most women did not share men's ability to support themselves outside the family. Thus, when working-class women sought to establish same-gender relationships, they often did so by adopting men's clothing and "passing" as men in order to earn wages and marry other women. In the 1850s, for example, Lucy Ann Lobdell left her husband in upstate New York and passed as a man in order to support herself. "I made up my mind to dress in men's attire to seek labor" and to earn "men's wages," she explained. Later, she became Reverend Joseph Lobdell and set up house with Maria Perry. The couple lived for ten years as man and wife.

Within the middle class, a different kind of same-sex relationship formed in the separate spheres of men and women, where romantic friendship was an acceptable part of social life. Many women formed close attachments that could rival marital relationships in their personal intensity. Women's socialization, at home or in boarding schools, encouraged them to form bonds with other women, and many chose a special female friend in whom to confide. These youthful friendships often turned into lifelong relationships that survived both marriage and geographical separation. Among women who attended college in the 1860s and 1870s, many formed intensely romantic relationships that paralleled heterosexual courtship.

In the early nineteenth century, few Americans associated women's physical closeness with sexuality because female sexuality at that time was still closely linked with reproduction. Gradually, however, the separation of sexuality and reproduction made Americans more conscious of the erotic element of these friendships. In 1875, the anonymous author of *Satan in Society* claimed that at schools for young ladies "the most intimate *liaisons* are formed under this specious pretext; the same bed often receives two friends." Women themselves clearly discovered the erotic possibilities between loving friends. In 1865, for example, a married woman wrote to her friend, the feminist orator Anna Dickinson, "I want to look into your eyes and squeeze your 'lily white hand,' and pinch your ears *all*, for love of you darling."

Through much of the nineteenth century, romantic friendships could be erotic in part because they were assumed to be sexually innocent. However, by the end of the century, loving friends had begun to question whether their physical intimacies marked them as deviant. Around this time, American doctors, following the lead of Europeans, began to define same-sex relationships as perverse, and they debated methods for treating "homosexuality" — a term coined in Germany in the 1860s and imported to the United States in the 1890s — as a diseased mental state. This shift in attitudes is evident in the case of Lucy Ann Lobdell, the passing woman from upstate New York. In 1855, Lobdell openly acknowledged her cross-dressing when she published a brief narrative of her life as "the female hunter." By 1883, however, she had become the subject of a medical account of "sexual perversion." Lobdell spent the last decade of her life in an insane asylum, where Dr. P. M. Wise categorized her as a "Lesbian."

By the time the medical discourse on sexual perversion emerged at the end of the century, the possibilities for same-gender love had already expanded greatly. Wage labor, the ability to live apart from families, and the sociability of the separate sexual spheres had fostered romantic, spiritual, homoerotic, and sexual unions. The medical labeling of same-sex intimacy as perverse, however, conflated an entire range of relationships and stigmatized all of them as a single, sexually deviant personal identity. Same-gender relationships thus lost the innocence they had enjoyed during most of the nineteenth century. Nonetheless, the opportunities for intimacy and sexuality apart from reproduction and the family continued to expand. In the late nineteenth and early twentieth centuries, more men and women would engage in same-sex relations but with greater self-consciousness about their sexual component. Thus, from both expanding opportunities and medical labeling, a new category of sexual behavior — homosexuality — emerged in American social history, supplementing earlier, more isolated cases of same-sex desire.

For at least two important historical reasons, same-gender relationships continued to flourish despite medical stigmatization. One was the increasing movement of women from the home to the public sphere — through higher education, social-reform movements, and wage labor. The other was the growth of a leisure culture that increasingly commercialized recreation, moving personal relationships further from the family to the marketplace. In short, the very forces that encouraged greater heterosexual self-consciousness created homosexual opportunities as well.[5]

College education and the ability to be self-supporting without marrying encouraged women's partnerships at the turn of the century. Indeed, so many educated women paired off in one city that the phenomenon gained the name "Boston marriage," referring to two women who lived together, owned property together, traveled together, shared holidays and family celebrations with each other, and usually slept in the same bed. The love letters these women wrote reveal an extraordinary emotional intensity. Take, for example, the letters between Evangeline Marrs Simpson and Rose Elizabeth Cleveland, the sister of U.S. president Grover Cleveland. At one point, Simpson sent some photos of herself to Cleveland, and the latter wrote back as she looked at them, "My Eve looks into my eyes with brief bright glances, with long rapturous embraces. . . . Her sweet life breath and her warm enfolding arms appease my hunger, and . . . carry my body in one to the summit of joy, the end of search, the goal of love! Here is no beyond!" After many years of correspondence and two marriages for Simpson, Cleveland's passion was fully requited; in 1910, the two women sailed together to Italy, where they lived until Cleveland's death eight years later.

"Boston marriages" were complex relationships, not merely sexual ones. As one businesswoman, born in the 1880s, explained, "I have [a] woman friend whom I love and admire above everyone in the world. . . . The physical factor is only one minor factor in the friendship." Substantial evidence suggests that overtly sexual relationships among unmarried college-educated women were not uncommon. In the 1920s, when Katharine B. Davis surveyed 1,200 unmarried college graduates, she found that 28 percent of the women's college graduates and 20 percent of those from coed schools had experienced intense ties with other women that included a physical component recognized as sexual. In addition, almost equal numbers had enjoyed intense emotional attachments that involved kissing and hugging.

Besides women's partnerships, which remained invisible in the privacy of the home, public leisure culture in major cities expanded social opportunities for both men and women, especially within the working class, which included large numbers of immigrants. Dancehalls, nickelodeons, and amusement parks all brought courtship into a public marketplace. Alongside a heterosocial youth culture, a public homosexual culture emerged between the 1880s and World War I. Meeting places proliferated. In 1890, a medical student found that "perverts of both sexes maintained a sort of social set-up in New York City, had their places of meeting, and the advantage of police protections." In many cities, men openly solicited one another on certain streets and other spots well-known as "cruising" areas—like the Young Men's Christian Association (YMCA) in Newport, Rhode Island, or Washington, D.C.'s, Lafayette Square and certain "smart clubs" in Boston, Chicago, St. Louis, and New Orleans. In San Francisco, the area surrounding the Presidio military base had become recognized by the 1890s as "a regular visiting place" for men seeking sex with men.

The furnished-room districts of large cities provided a setting where working women might form relationships with each other, and descriptions of the red-light districts suggest that some prostitutes formed lesbian attachments. In Harlem after World War I, the cross-dressing lesbian Gladys Bentley performed in men's attire and served as a magnet for other lesbians and male homosexuals, both blacks and whites.[6]

This nascent subculture, however, remained hidden and difficult to find, especially for middle-class women. A woman of twenty in the mid-1880s, Mary Casal felt isolated, writing that "I was the only girl who had the sex desire for woman." Also, for most men and women, the threat of punishment and social ostracism kept sexuality carefully guarded. As Francis Matthiessen, soon to become a renowned literary critic, wrote to his male lover in the early 1920s, "We would be pariahs, outlaws, degenerates" if the world were to know of their relationship.

Expansion and Resistance: The Twentieth Century

Increasingly, however, during the twentieth century, the world did learn about same-gender relations, moving an underground world into greater public consciousness. The willingness of popular culture to deal with sexuality, along with the growing influence of psychology and the experience of World War II, hastened the trend. In the 1920s, for example, a Broadway play, *The Captive*, dealt with lesbian relations. Novels such as *The Well of Loneliness* created fictional lesbian characters, while black entertainers addressed same-sex attraction in songs like "Sissy Man," "Fairey Blues," and "Bull-Dagger Woman," popular tunes on the so-called race records of the interwar years. The infiltration of psychiatric and psychoanalytic concepts into popular culture contributed to the labeling of homosexual desire, even as it cast a shadow over homosexuality. For example, with the onset of World War II, psychiatrists were incorporated into the nation's military effort, screening inductees for evidence of mental instability and, in the process, asking millions of young men questions about homosexual desire.

World War II did more than propagate psychiatric definitions of homosexuality; it also created substantively new erotic opportunities that prompted the articulation of a gay identity and the rapid growth of a gay subculture.[7] The war pulled millions of American men and women away from the social controls of their families, small towns, and ethnic neighborhoods in large cities and deposited them in a variety of sex-segregated, nonfamilial institutions. For men, this meant service in the armed forces; for many women, it meant migrating to cities for war jobs and socializing in often all-female environments. For a generation of young Americans, the war created a setting in which to experience same-gender love, affection, and sexuality and to participate in the group life of lesbians and gay men — terms that had begun to circulate within the homosexual subculture. As a teenager in Iowa, for example, Pat Bond had felt "forever alone" in her attraction to women; when she entered the Women's Army Corps, she found that "everybody was going with someone or had a crush on someone."

When young men and women left home to find employment, they escaped family surveillance and found space for sexual exploration. Thus, Donald Vining moved from southern New Jersey to New York City, where, living at the YMCA, he wrote in his diary, "The war is a tragedy to my mind and soul, but to my physical being, it is a memorable experience." Like many gay men and lesbians, Vining did not return to prewar patterns. After the war, he stayed in New York to participate in the gay life of the city. Pat Bond settled in San Francisco, where she patronized the lesbian bars that had opened during the war. Throughout the postwar era, a bar subculture spread and stabilized, relieving somewhat the isolation of an earlier generation and, by the 1950s, integrating black and white lesbian subcultures.[8]

The expanding possibilities for gay men and lesbians to meet did not pass without a response. The postwar years bred fears about the ability of American institutions to withstand subversion from real and imagined enemies. Political leaders mobilized the public to support a global commitment to contain communism. The ensuing Cold War left Americans prone to hunt for scapegoats to explain how the fruits of victory in World War II could sour so quickly. In an atmosphere of such anxiety, homosexuals suddenly found themselves labeled as a threat to national security and the target of widespread witch hunts. In June 1950, the U.S. Senate authorized a formal inquiry into the employment of "homosexuals and other moral perverts" in government. Dismissals from civilian posts increased twelvefold over the pre-1950 rate. In April 1953, the recently inaugurated President Dwight Eisenhower issued an executive order barring gay men and lesbians from all federal jobs. The Federal Bureau of Investigation initiated a widespread system of surveillance to keep homosexuals off the federal payroll. The armed forces sharply stepped up its purges of homosexual men and women; yearly discharges doubled in the 1950s and rose another 50 percent in the early 1960s. Throughout the 1950s and well into the 1960s, gay men and lesbians were subjected to unpredictable, often brutal crackdowns. In Washington, D.C., for example, arrests topped 1,000 per year during the early 1950s. Newspaper editors often printed the names, addresses, and places of employment of those arrested in bar raids.

Thus, hand in hand with the expansion of gay identity and subculture came official resistance to its emergence through policies that in fact may have further encouraged gay community formation. Just as the earlier medical labeling of same-gender love as "deviant" had not suppressed but may have encouraged the construction of gay identity, the antigay hysteria of the postwar era raised the political consciousness of a small group of lesbians and gay men who founded a "homophile movement," organized to improve their status as a minority group and to fight state suppression. In San Francisco, for example, the DOB — the Daughters of Bilitis — founded by Del Martin and Phyllis Lyon, began publishing *The Ladder*, a long-lived lesbian political and literary magazine. DOB organized chapters throughout the country to defend the basic human rights of lesbians. Once the social upheavals of the 1960s unleashed the energy and language of liberation movements — as civil rights turned to Black Power and women's rights to women's liberation — the historical stage was ripe for a "gay" liberation movement to build on the foundations of the defensive homophile-rights organizations of the 1950s.

The precise origin of a mass movement was Friday, 27 June 1969, when a group of Manhattan police officers set out to close the Stonewall Inn, a bar in the heart of Greenwich Village frequented by black and Latino gay youths. For the first time, lesbians and gay men — visibly led by drag queens — resisted arrest and attacked the police. Rioting continued far into the night as crowds of angry homosexuals battled the police up and down the streets. The following day, graffiti proclaiming "Gay Power" was scribbled on walls and pavements in the area. The rioting that lasted throughout the weekend signaled the start of a major social movement. As word of the Stonewall riots circulated among radical youths who were gay as well as among other disaffected homosexuals, the liberation impulse took root across the country.

How and why did gay liberation arise so rapidly in the 1970s? Throughout the 1950s and 1960s, a gay subculture had been growing, providing the setting in which homosexuals might develop a group consciousness. In the 1960s, the weakening of taboos against the public discussion of sexuality in general, the pervasive police harassment of the era, and the persistent work of a small coterie of pre-Stonewall activists — in the DOB and other groups — combined to make many lesbians and gay men receptive to the message of "Gay Power."

It was in this context that coming out of the closet became a key tactic of the movement, suggesting the extent of transformation in the meaning of same-gender love over the centuries. Coming out became basic to assumptions about being gay. It represented the adoption of an identity in which the erotic became emblematic of the person rather than an isolated act and in which identity was chosen rather than imposed as a medical label of deviance. The self-affirmation of coming out was, of course, part of a larger national obsession with the centrality of the erotic in American life. As radical as gay liberation may have seemed, it was, in a sense, the logical extension of the sexual liberalism that had been transforming American sexual attitudes — toward contraception, abortion, and premarital heterosexual relations. Like others in the 1960s and 1970s, lesbians and gay men were embracing the claims of psychological experts concerning the importance of sexual expression for personal well-being; by the 1970s, gay male subculture was paralleling the consumerist values that had already made sex a highly marketable commodity. In a sense, gay identity, gay communities, and gay politics emerged as much in tandem with as in opposition to mainstream American sexual history.

Over the past twenty-five years, a homosexual identity has found a place in the American social and political landscape, not just in isolated medical journals or an urban underworld. How are we to interpret this sweeping history of change? One way to encapsulate this past would be to see the emergence of gay identity and politics as a kind of progressive "success" story, from repression to liberation, from an unnamed category to a central form of identity and the basis for a mass political movement. An alternative interpretation, emphasizing the social construction of sexuality, suggests that economic, social, and intellectual forces have shaped and reshaped sexuality — in this case, same-gender love — in uneven patterns. Not everyone in this society experiences historical forces in the same way or at the same time. Thus, there is no unitary experience, and at any given time, there are in fact a variety of social constructions of sexuality, including the cross-gender *berdache*; romantic friendships; urban, anonymous sex; longtime companions and Boston marriages; bar culture; and gay identity and political consciousness.

I would argue that all of these social constructs can coexist at any given time as long as the material support for them continues. Thus, today we can still find cross-gender males, "passing women," celibate passionate friends, and monogamous homosexual partners. We can also find anonymous or "stranger" sex, along with a variety of other behaviors, such as married, heterosexual men and women who also seek same-gender sexual partners, whether they identify as bisexual or not. Increasingly, the gay movement has tended to claim all of the above under the single rubric of homosexuality —and more recently, through the redemption of the once stigmatizing term "queer." In many ways, this broad claim to the contents of the label "gay" is an astute political strategy, for it brings the largest number of constituents into one's camp. But the homogenizing label can mask the reality that not everyone experiences his or her "homosexuality" in the same way.[9] Whether "gay" identity will remain a stable feature of our socially constructed sexuality or whether further historical changes will reshape yet again how we think of ourselves remains to be seen.

In the meantime, in looking at the historical construction of homosexuality, it is worth remembering that the best way to understand the various behaviors described above may not come from asking the question "Were they 'gay?'"—that is, did they have modern, late-twentieth-century sexual identity. Rather, we need to ask how women and men in the past understood and experienced their own sexuality. Asking this question allows us to have a "gay history" that illuminates our own contemporary experience but at the same time remains respectful of those who, in the past, lived within a differently constructed sexuality than our own.

7 | Uncontrolled Desires | The Response to the Sexual Psychopath, 1920 – 1960

As I began to compare the response to male and female deviance in twentieth-century America, I kept encountering medical, legal, and popular references to the sexual psychopath. In this essay, I interpret the psychopath scare of the 1930s through the 1950s not simply as an expression of psychiatric authority but as a popular, discursive construction of male sexual boundaries in response to the sexualization of women and children and the greater visibility of homosexuality. Because it focuses on discourse, the article only hints at how the psychopath laws were enforced. Although those who promoted the segregation of sexual psychopaths may have conflated homosexuality and pedophilia, most of the men incarcerated under the new laws were heterosexual. I would now place the early-twentieth-century psychopath scare within a longer history of periodic outrage over the sexual abuse of children, from late-nineteenth-century child-savers to contemporary exposés of abusive teachers and priests.

IN THE 1931 German film *M*, Peter Lorre portrayed a former mental patient who stalked innocent schoolgirls, lured them with candy and balloons, and then, offscreen, murdered them in order to satiate his abnormal erotic desires. Two years later, when the film opened in the United States, the *New York Times* criticized director Fritz Lang for wasting his talents on a crime "too hideous to contemplate." Despite the reviewer's distaste for the public discussion of sexual crimes, the American media soon began to cater to a growing popular interest in stories of violent, sexual murders committed by men like "M." In 1937, the *New York Times* itself created a new index category, "Sex Crimes," to encompass the 143 articles it published on the subject that year. Cleveland, Detroit, and Los Angeles newspapers also ran stories about sexual criminals, while national magazines published articles by legal and psychiatric authorities who debated whether a "sex-crime wave" had hit America.[1]

Previously published as Estelle B. Freedman, "'Uncontrolled Desires': The Response to the Sexual Psychopath, 1920 – 1960," *Journal of American History* 74, no. 1 (June 1987): 83 – 106. Reprinted by permission of the publisher.

The sex crime panic soon extended beyond the media and into the realm of politics and law. Between 1935 and 1965, city, state, and federal officials established commissions to investigate sexual crime, passed statutes to transfer authority over sex offenders from courts to psychiatrists, and funded specialized institutions for the treatment of sex offenders. As a result, in most states, a man accused of rape, sodomy, child molestation, indecent exposure, or corrupting the morals of a minor — if diagnosed as a "sexual psychopath" — could receive an indeterminate sentence to a psychiatric, rather than a penal, institution. The laws defined the sexual psychopath as someone whose "utter lack of power to control his sexual impulses" made him "likely to attack . . . the objects of his uncontrolled and uncontrollable desires."[2]

A close look at the sex crime panics that began in the mid-1930s, declined during World War II, and revived in the postwar decade reveals that those episodes were not necessarily related to any increase in the actual incidence of violent, sexually related crimes. Although arrest rates for sexual offenses in general rose throughout the period, the vast majority of arrests were for minor offenses rather than for the violent acts portrayed in the media. Moreover, when arrest rates accelerated sharply during World War II, the popular discourse on sex crimes quieted, and no new psychopath laws were enacted.[3] The historical evidence also prohibits a conspiratorial interpretation in which power-hungry psychiatrists manipulated the public and politicians to create a sex crime panic and psychiatric solutions to it.[4] Most psychiatrists remained skeptical about psychopath laws. Rather, the media, law enforcement agencies, and private citizens' groups took the lead in demanding state action to prevent sex crimes. In the process, they not only augmented the authority of psychiatrists but also provoked a redefinition of normal sexual behavior.

The new image of aggressive male sexual deviance that emerged from the psychiatric and political response to sex crimes provided a focus for a complex redefinition of sexual boundaries in modern America. For one thing, public outrage over rare, serious sexual crimes facilitated the establishment of legal and psychiatric mechanisms that were then used to regulate much less serious but socially disturbing behaviors. The response to the sexual psychopath, however, was not merely the expansion of social control over sexuality by psychiatry and the state. Rather, by stigmatizing extreme acts of violence, the discourse on the psychopath ultimately helped legitimize nonviolent but nonprocreative sexual acts, inside or outside marriage. At the same time, psychiatric and political attention to the psychopath heightened public awareness of sexuality in general and sexual abnormality in particular between 1935 and 1960.

Thus, the response to the sexual psychopath must be understood in the context of the history of sexuality, for it evidenced a significant departure from the nineteenth-century emphasis on maintaining female purity and a movement toward a modern concern about controlling male violence. In the nineteenth century, the ideal of female purity had served symbolically to control male lust and to channel sexual impulses into marital, reproductive relationships. In practice, of course, individuals deviated from the ideal, and periodic sexual reform movements — such as moral reform, social purity, and antiprostitution — attempted to uphold female purity and restore the deviant to the fold. Antebellum sexual reformers typically employed moral suasion and social sanctions, but by the early twentieth century, reformers had increasingly turned to the state to enforce their vision of moral order. During the Progressive Era, for example, city and state governments investigated white slavery, Congress passed the Mann Act to prohibit the interstate transportation of women for immoral purposes, and during World War I, the U.S. Army mobilized against prostitution, incarcerating suspected prostitutes found in the vicinity of military training camps.[5]

By the 1920s, the Victorian ideal of innate female purity had disintegrated. Stimulated by Freudian ideas, a critique of "civilized morality" infiltrated American culture. Meanwhile, working-class youths, blacks, immigrants, and white bohemians had created visible urban alternatives to the old sexual order. They engaged in a sexually explicit nightlife, used birth control, and accepted sexuality outside marriage. Even for the middle classes, a recognition of female sexual desire and the legitimacy of its satisfaction — preferably in marriage but not necessarily for procreation — came to dominate sexual advice literature by the 1920s. As birth control, companionate marriage, and female sexual desire became more acceptable, female purity lost its symbolic power to regulate sexual behavior. Not surprisingly, by the 1930s, calls to wipe out prostitution could no longer mobilize a social movement. Reformers now had to base their arguments more on "social hygiene" — the prevention of venereal disease — than on the defense of female virtue.[6]

If the Victorian ideal divided women into the pure and the impure, modern ideas about sexuality blurred boundaries in ways that made all women more vulnerable to the risks once experienced primarily by prostitutes. "If woman in fact should be a sexual creature," Victorian scholar Carol Christ has asked, "what kind of beast should man himself become?" One response to her query was heralded in England during the 1880s by the crimes of Jack the Ripper, whose sexual murders of prostitutes, Judith R. Walkowitz has argued, created a powerful cultural myth associating sex with "violence, male dominance and female passivity."[7] In twentieth-century America, the image of the sexual psychopath further specified both the "kind of beast" man might become and the kind of victim he now sought. The sexual psychopath represented man unbounded by the controls of female purity, a violent threat not only to women but to children as well. But violence against women and children was not the underlying concern of the sex crime panics. Rather, the concept of the sexual psychopath provided a boundary within which Americans renegotiated the definitions of sexual normality. Ultimately, the response to the sexual psychopath helped legitimize less violent but previously taboo sexual acts while it stigmatized unmanly rather than unwomanly behavior as the most serious threat to sexual order.

To understand how and why this controversial psychiatric diagnosis attracted so much public attention and found its way into American criminal law requires analysis of three factors: psychiatric ideas, political mobilization, and sexual boundaries. Taken together, they reveal a complex relationship between psychiatry, social change, and sexuality. Psychiatrists, journalists, and politicians all helped create the sexual psychopath, but a public concerned with changing gender relationships seized upon the threat of "uncontrolled desires" to help redefine sexual normality and deviance in modern America.

When it first appeared in Europe in the late nineteenth century, the diagnosis of psychopathy did not refer exclusively either to sexual abnormality or to men. Akin to the concept of moral insanity, it was applied to habitual criminals who had normal mentality but exhibited abnormal social behavior.[8] The German psychiatrist Emil Kraepelin used the term "psychopathic personality" in his influential 1904 textbook to refer primarily to criminals with unstable personalities, vagabonds, liars, and beggars, although he also listed prostitutes and homosexuals. In 1905, Adolf Meyer introduced the concept of the psychopath into the United States, where sexual crime remained synonymous with female immorality.[9] William Healy's pathbreaking study, *The Individual Delinquent* (1915), mentioned female hypersexuality and described psychopaths as egocentric, selfish, irritable, antisocial, nervous, and weak willed, but Healy refused to discuss male sexual abnormality and recommended that most readers "leave the unpleasant subject alone." Until the 1920s, American psychiatrists who diagnosed mental patients as psychopaths typically applied the term to either unemployed men or "hypersexual" women.[10]

The transformation of the psychopath into a violent, male, sexual criminal occurred gradually as a result of three convergent trends. First, as courts and prisons became important arenas into which American psychiatry expanded beyond its earlier base in state mental hospitals, the recently established specialization of forensic psychiatry sought new explanations for criminal behavior. Second, the social stresses of the depression drew attention to the problems of male deviance. Third, the social scientific study of sexuality became respectable, and the influence of psychoanalytic theories on American psychiatry during the 1930s provided an intellectual base for a sexual theory of crime.

American criminologists began to use the psychopathic diagnosis during the 1920s partly because of weaknesses in the dominant theory that low mentality ("mental defect" or "feeblemindedness"), if not the cause of crime, was highly correlated with it. During the Progressive Era, several states had established separate institutions for the indeterminate commitment of mentally defective prisoners. In practice, however, many of the suspected "defective delinquents" turned out to have normal IQs. With the influx of psychiatrists into courts and prisons after 1915, criminologists increasingly turned to psychiatric diagnoses, such as "constitutional psychopath," to help explain these troublesome prisoners.[11] In 1921, the Massachusetts legislature enacted the Briggs Law, which required psychiatric evaluation of recidivist felons and those convicted of capital offenses. Many of those prisoners who could not be diagnosed as insane or mentally defective were eventually labeled "psychopathic." Such redefinitions expanded the category of insanity and helped create a new deviant population, the psychopath. In 1918, for example, psychiatrist Bernard Glueck diagnosed almost 20 percent of the inmates at New York's Sing Sing prison as "constitutional inferior, or psychopathic" and recommended the creation of a new state institution to house psychopathic and defective delinquents. Between 1919 and 1926, the percentage of inmates classified as psychopaths at one men's reformatory in New York rose from 11.6 to 50.8, while diagnoses of mental defect declined sharply.[12]

Despite increased use of the psychopathic diagnosis, male sexual crimes rarely received the attention of psychiatrists and criminologists during the 1920s. When sexuality and psychopathy were linked at that time, women, not men, remained the likely subjects. Indeed, the first specialized institution for psychopathic criminals, a hospital operated at the Bedford Hills Reformatory for Women between 1916 and 1918, had been established because of John D. Rockefeller Jr.'s interest in eliminating prostitution. Glueck's Sing Sing study did note an absence of sexual morality among psychopathic male inmates, 10 percent of whom had committed sexual crimes. However, his characterization of the psychopath emphasized recidivism, drug and alcohol use, and unstable work patterns rather than abnormal sexual impulses. Even when sexual crimes against children first became the focus of governmental reports in the 1920s, the psychopath was not associated with such offenses. Nevertheless, the malleable diagnostic category of psychopath had become more widely applied and would soon take on new meanings.[13]

The sexualization of the male psychopath occurred during the 1930s, when American criminologists became increasingly interested in sexual abnormality and male sexual crime. The disruption of traditional family life during the depression, when record numbers of men lost their status as breadwinners, triggered concerns about masculinity. Psychologist Joseph Pleck has argued that during the 1930s psychologists elaborated on sex differences and investigated sexual deviance in order to shore up the psychological basis of masculinity at a time when social and economic support for the traditional male role seemed to be eroding. In the process, the male sexual deviant became the subject of special attention, particularly if he was inadequately masculine (the effeminate homosexual) or hypermasculine (the sexual psychopath). Both categories of deviant males were thought to attack children, thus simultaneously threatening sexual innocence, gender roles, and the social order.[14] The psychopath neatly fit these concerns. From the origin of the concept, the psychopath had been perceived as a drifter, an unemployed man who lived beyond the boundaries of familial and social controls. Unemployed men and vagabonds populated the depression-era landscape, signaling actual family dissolution and symbolizing potential social and political disruption. Like the compulsive child murderer "M," the psychopath could represent the threat of anarchy, of the individual unbound by either social rules or individual conscience. The apparent "sexualization" of the drifter reflected, in part, a merging of economic and psychological identities in modern America.

In this social context, Americans embarked on the serious study of human sexuality, measuring normality and defining deviance. During the 1920s and 1930s, classic texts by European sexologists such as Richard von Krafft-Ebing, Havelock Ellis, and Magnus Hirschfeld became more widely available. A growing number of American researchers, including Katharine Bement Davis and Robert Latou Dickinson, conducted survey and case studies of sexual practices.[15] Within criminology, older biological theories combined with the recent identification of sex hormones to stimulate studies of the mentality of homosexuals, the impact of castration on rapists, and the levels of endocrines in senile sex offenders. New funding sources supported the investigation of sexuality. In 1931, the Rockefeller Foundation helped establish the National Research Council Committee for Research on Problems of Sex, which later supported the work of Alfred Kinsey. The Committee for the Study of Sex Variants, founded in 1935 and chaired by Eugen Kahn (an authority on the psychopath), sponsored a pioneering two-volume study of homosexuality by psychiatrist George Henry.[16]

A second intellectual current helps account for psychiatric interest in sex criminals in general and the sexual component of psychopathic personality in particular. In the 1920s, Freudian concepts of psychosexual development had begun to filter through the fields of psychiatry and criminology, a process that accelerated after the immigration of European analysts to this country. In the early 1930s, a few discussions of the psychopath — such as Kahn's important text, translated into English in 1931 — referred to infantile sexuality and to arrested sexual development. In the same year, psychiatrist Franz Alexander elaborated on the contribution to criminality of the Oedipal complex and of anal and oral eroticism. A 1937 article in the *Psychoanalytic Review* indicated the new direction in psychiatric interpretations when it characterized the psychopath as "the phallic man," fixated at an infantile stage of boundless bisexual energy. By the late 1930s, most discussions of the psychopath included at least a section on sexual types, such as "overt homosexuals, exhibitionists, sadists, masochists, and voyeurs." Some authors explicitly linked such deviants to the commission of sexual crimes.[17]

The most prolific advocate of the psychosexual interpretation of psychopathic behavior was Benjamin Karpman, chief psychotherapist at St. Elizabeth's Hospital in Washington, D.C.[18] In voluminous case studies of criminals, Karpman attributed most habitual criminality to arrested sexual development and identified psychopaths by their incapacity to repress or sublimate their overly active sexual impulses. The typical sexual psychopath was, he believed, "all instinct and impulse." Karpman once claimed, for example, that the psychopath was "always on the go for sexual satisfaction . . . like a cancer patient who is always hungry no matter how much he is fed." Later investigators would attribute sexual psychopathy to underdeveloped rather than overdeveloped libido, but Karpman held firmly to his belief that sexual psychopaths always had insatiable and uncontrollable desires.[19] Although his views were extreme among psychiatrists, Karpman's vision of the psychopath as emotionally primitive and sexually ravenous resonated with popular stereotypes that harked back to the theory of the born criminal. Thus, an older, hereditarian tradition merged with new psychiatric concepts to produce a crude model of the psychopath as oversexed, uninhibited, and compulsive. It was this image that found its way into the popular press and ultimately into the law.

THE INCORPORATION of the sexual psychopath into American criminal law began in the late 1930s in the wake of the first of two waves of popular concern about violent sexual crimes. Three constituencies — the media, citizens' groups, and law enforcement agencies — created the sex crime panic and demanded that politicians offer solutions to the problems of rape and sexual murder of children. Politicians, in turn, labeled sexual psychopaths as the villains in the sex crime drama and psychiatrists as the heroes who might rid society of the danger they posed.

Each of the two major sex crime panics — roughly from 1937 to 1940 and from 1949 to 1955 — originated when, after a series of brutal and apparently sexually motivated child murders, major urban newspapers expanded and, in some cases, sensationalized their coverage of child molestation and rape. Between 1937 and 1940 and again during the postwar decade, the *New York Times*, previously silent on the subject, averaged over forty articles per year on sex crimes.[20] In 1937, magazines ranging from *Science* and the *Christian Century* to the *Nation* and the *New Masses* reported on the sex crime panic. After World War II, news and family magazines, including *Time*, *Newsweek*, and *Parents' Magazine*, carried articles titled "Queer People," "Sex Psychopaths," and "What Shall We Do about Sex Offenders?" In its 1950 series "Terror in Our Cities," *Collier's* magazine summarized the newspaper headlines in St. Louis ("The City That DOES Something about Sex Crimes") in a representative composite:

KINDERGARTEN GIRL ACCOSTED BY MAN — CLERK ACCUSED OF MOLESTING 2 GIRLS IN MOVIE — MAN ACCUSED BY 8-YEAR-OLD BOY OF MOLESTING HIM IN THEATRE — 6-YEAR-OLD GIRL AT ASHLAND SCHOOL MOLESTED — LABORER ARRESTED FOR RAPE OF 10-YEAR-OLD GIRL — FINED FOR MOLESTING 2 BOYS, AGED 8 AND 10 — ARRESTED ON SUSPICION OF MOLESTING 4-YEAR-OLD GIRL — YOUTH WHO MOLESTED BOY 4, IS FINED $500 — 9 CHARGES AGAINST MOLESTER OF GIRLS.[21]

Despite the lack of evidence that the incidence of rape, child murder, and minor sex offenses had increased, public awareness of individual acts of sexual brutality led to demands that the state crack down on sex crimes. In 1937, after two child murders had occurred in New York City, residents of Ridgewood, Queens, held a protest meeting and demanded that police be given more power to "take suspicious characters in hand before they commit the crimes."[22] In Chicago, after the rape-murder of two nurses, a police squad was formed to "round up attackers." When a Philadelphia man confessed to attacks on both male and female children, that city's mayor recommended sterilization of sex offenders. In New Jersey, when six men were indicted for assaulting girls, the New Jersey Parents and Teachers Congress urged denial of parole to those convicted of sex crimes. In 1937, a mob in Inglewood, California, threatened lynching while the police sought the murderers of three local girls. In 1950, a Connecticut mob attempted to lynch a suspected sex criminal, and the national American Legion called for life sentences without parole for sex offenders.[23]

Federal Bureau of Investigation director J. Edgar Hoover played an important role in fueling the national hysteria and channeling it into support for stronger law enforcement. In 1937, Hoover called for a "War on the Sex Criminal" and charged that "the sex fiend, most loathsome of all the vast army of crime, has become a sinister threat to the safety of American childhood and womanhood." In a popular magazine article published in 1947, Hoover claimed that "the most rapidly increasing type of crime is that perpetrated by degenerate sex offenders." Implying that this threat to social order required total mobilization, Hoover continued: "Should wild beasts break out of circus cages, a whole city would be mobilized instantly. But depraved human beings, more savage than beasts, are permitted to rove America almost at will."[24]

In response to the sex crime panic, police roundups of "perverts" became common, especially in the wake of highly publicized assaults on children. The targets of the crackdowns were often minor offenders, such as male homosexuals. A rare glimpse of the reaction of "perverts" to such roundups appeared in a letter written in 1946 by one homosexual male to another after a brutal child murder in Chicago: "I suppose you read about the kidnapping and killing of the little girl in Chicago—I noticed tonight that they 'thought' (in their damn self righteous way) that perhaps a pervert had done it they rounded up all the females [male homosexuals]—they blame us for everything and incidentally it is more and more in the limelight everyday — why they don't round us all up and kill us I don't know." In this case and others, police justified increased surveillance of all deviant sexual behavior, whether violent or not, by emphasizing the need to protect women and children from sexual violence.[25]

While some politicians supported the call for law and order, others turned to psychiatrists for solutions to the sex crime problem. In the 1930s, the New York State legislature called on institutional psychiatrists to explain how to prevent sex crimes. New York City mayor Fiorello LaGuardia appointed psychiatrists, lawyers, and criminologists to a Mayor's Committee for the Study of Sex Offenses. In a move that foreshadowed the national political response to sex crimes, LaGuardia also instituted an emergency program that transferred accused and convicted sex criminals from city penitentiaries to Bellevue Hospital for medical observation.[26]

Some psychiatrists expressed discomfort about the sex crime panic. Karl Bowman, then director of the psychiatric division at Bellevue, observed that most of the men transferred there were minor offenders who did not belong in a mental hospital. At a 1938 symposium, "The Challenge of Sex Offenders," sponsored by the National Committee on Mental Hygiene, psychiatrists argued that no sudden increase in sex crime had occurred and cautioned against new legislation that would establish either castration or prolonged imprisonment for sex offenders. Bowman and other panelists called for more frank, rational discussions of sexuality and claimed that sexual repression caused sex offenses. Other psychiatrists, such as Ira Wile, wrote articles opposing prolonged imprisonment or castration for sex offenders. They recommended instead hospital care, psychiatric exams, and research on sex crimes.[27]

Despite psychiatric ambivalence about proposed legislation that would incorporate the psychopathic diagnosis into the law and strong criticism of such statutes within the legal profession, five states — Michigan, Illinois, Minnesota, Ohio, and California — passed "sex psychopath" laws between 1935 and 1939. The fact that not simply psychiatric leadership but the public mobilization to combat the alleged sex crime wave explains their passage is evident in the case of Ohio. In 1934, psychiatrists in that state's mental hospitals had failed to convince the legislature to fund separate treatment for psychopathic criminals. In 1938, however, after the *Cleveland Plain Dealer* ran a series of articles on sex offenders, civic groups created sufficient pressure to achieve quick passage of the Ascherman Act, which permitted the indefinite commitment of psychopaths to the state mental hospital.[28]

Although the psychopath laws were avowedly enacted to protect women and children, they were the product of men's political efforts, not women's. Several women's clubs publicly favored stronger criminal penalties for sex crimes, and male politicians frequently called on representatives of conservative women's organizations to testify on behalf of psychopath legislation.[29] However, in contrast to earlier movements for moral reform and social purity in which organizations such as the Woman's Christian Temperance Union had played a major part, the campaign for sexual psychopath laws had little female, and no feminist, leadership.

The hiatus in the sex crime panic during the early 1940s further suggests that its central concern was men, not women. The legitimization of male aggression during World War II and the shift of national attention toward external enemies combined to reduce the focus on violent sexual crimes. Although arrest rates remained high during the war, both newspaper and magazine coverage of sex crimes tapered off markedly, and only one state — Vermont — enacted a psychopath law. The wartime entry of men into the military and of women into jobs formerly held by men restored the "hypersexual" woman to the foreground. Social workers and government agencies condemned the phenomenon of "victory girls" — young women who willingly had sex with soldiers and sailors — and antiprostitution campaigns revived briefly in the name of protecting soldiers from venereal disease.[30]

The postwar years, however, provided a climate conducive to the reemergence of the male sexual psychopath as a target of social concern. The war had greatly increased the authority of psychiatrists, who had been drafted to screen recruits and to diagnose military offenders. Postwar psychiatric and social welfare literature stressed the adjustment problems of returning servicemen, some of whom, it was feared, might "snap" into psychopathic states. In addition, demobilization and reconversion to a peacetime economy stimulated concerted efforts to reestablish traditional family life. Returning male veterans needed jobs that had been held by women, who were now encouraged to marry, bear children, and purchase domestic products. Moreover, the onset of the Cold War, with its emphasis on cultural conformity, intensified efforts to control deviant behavior. Nonconformity — whether political, social, or sexual — became associated with threats to national security. Amid the pressures for social and sexual stability, Alfred Kinsey published his study of male sexual behavior, igniting unprecedented public debate about normal and abnormal sexuality.[31]

During the postwar decade, the sex crime panic gathered renewed momentum, peaking in the mid-1950s. As if to signal — or to enforce — the return of prewar gender relations, sex crimes once again became a subject of media attention and political action. Although arrests for rape and other sex offenses fell after the war, legislatures revised earlier sexual psychopath laws, and between 1947 and 1955, twenty-one additional states and the District of Columbia enacted new psychopath laws. In the early 1950s, arrest rates returned to prewar levels, but only after the second phase of the sex crime panic had begun.[32]

The sexual psychopath laws enacted during the two periods of panic operated alongside older penal codes that punished crimes such as rape and murder with incarceration in state penitentiaries or execution. Most sex offenders continued to be processed under the older codes. During the early 1950s, for example, California superior courts sentenced only 35 percent of convicted sex offenders to mental institutions as psychopaths; 54 percent went to prisons, and 11 percent to the youth authority. Prior to 1953, annual commitments of psychopaths averaged thirty-seven in each state with a special law. Revised laws and new facilities in the 1950s increased commitments in several states; Michigan and Maryland, for example, each averaged one hundred per year. Few of those committed, however, were the homicidal sex maniacs on whom the sex crime panic had originally focused. They tended to be white men, often professionals or skilled workers, who were overrepresented among those convicted of the crime of having sexual relations with children and minor sexual offenses. Black men, who continued to be overrepresented among those convicted of rape, were more likely to be imprisoned or executed than to be treated in mental institutions. In short, white men who committed sexual crimes were considered mentally ill; black men who committed sexual crimes were believed to be guilty of willful violence.[33]

The sexual psychopath laws did not necessarily name specific criminal acts, nor did they differentiate between violent and nonviolent or consensual and nonconsensual behaviors. Rather, they targeted a kind of personality or an identity that could be discovered only by trained psychiatrists. Whether convicted of exhibitionism, sodomy, child molestation, or rape, sexual psychopaths could be transferred to state mental hospitals or psychiatric wards of prisons for an indefinite period, until the institutional psychiatrists declared them cured. The laws rested on the premise that even minor offenders (such as exhibitionists), if psychopaths, posed the threat of potential sexual violence. Indefinite institutionalization of sex offenders would protect society from the threat of violent sexual crimes, and psychiatric care would be more humane than castration, life imprisonment, or execution.[34]

In addition to passing laws, elected officials in ten states appointed special commissions to investigate the nature of sexual offenders, the problem of sex crimes, and the legislative means to prevent them. The documents published by such commissions varied in depth and tone from superficial accounts of popular attitudes to serious discussions of the psychiatric, legal, and ethical issues raised by sex-offender legislation. In general, the state reports echoed themes raised by the earlier New York City Mayor's Committee. They found little evidence of increases in local sex crime rates, bemoaned the vagueness of the classification "sexual psychopath," called for scientific study of these mysterious offenders, and recommended new or revised psychopath laws that would, unlike many of the earlier statutes, require conviction of a crime before institutionalization. The preventive measures suggested by state commissions took two forms: specialized psychiatric institutions for men convicted of sex crimes and preventive measures such as psychiatric screening of potential psychopaths at schools or behavior clinics and sex education to promote a healthy family life.[35]

Whatever ambivalence psychiatrists may have had about incorporating the psychopathic diagnosis into law, the postwar response to sexual crimes helped to solidify psychiatric authority within the criminal justice system in two important ways. Following state commission recommendations for more research, a half dozen states provided funding for psychiatric studies of sex offenders. In California, for example, the sex crime panic enabled Karl Bowman, director of the Langley Porter Psychiatric Clinic of the University of California, to obtain funds from the state legislature for programs on sexual deviates, although his previous requests for state funding had been denied. The New Jersey Sex Offender Acts of 1949 and 1950 established the New Jersey Diagnostic Center for the study of juvenile and adult offenders, and New York State's Sex Delinquency Research Project funded studies of sex offenders at Sing Sing prison.[36]

The second means by which the state expanded both its own and psychiatrists' authority was the establishment of specialized institutions to treat sexual offenders. Under the initial sexual psychopath statutes, men committed for sexual offenses served their indeterminate sentences either in mental wards of prisons or in criminal wards of mental hospitals, such as Howard Hall at St. Elizabeth's Hospital. In 1949, the Ohio legislature appropriated over $1,000,000 to build a specialized facility for mentally defective and psychopathic criminals at the Lima State Hospital. Maryland legislators authorized funding for the maximum-security Patuxent Institution, which opened in 1951, for the psychiatric treatment of habitual offenders, mental defectives, and sexual criminals. In 1954, California transferred the men who had been sentenced as psychopaths from state mental hospitals to the newly completed, $10,000,000 Atascadero State Hospital. Once institution-alized, the psychopath received treatments in accord with the therapeutic trends of the era: Metrazol, insulin shock, or electroshock treatments; hormonal injections; sterilization; group therapy; and, in some cases, frontal lobotomy. According to the clinical literature, none of these proved effective in reducing "uncontrolled desires."[37]

The sexual psychopath laws, always controversial among psychiatrists and lawyers, came under renewed criticism in the 1950s and 1960s. In 1949, the Committee on Forensic Psychiatry of the liberal Group for the Advancement of Psychiatry issued a report that argued that the concept of the psychopath was too vague and controversial to be written into law. The following year, in the New Jersey State report on sex offenders, sociologist Paul Tappan attempted to refute the myth of escalation from minor to violent sex crimes, noting that sex offenders had the lowest recidivism rates of all criminals.[38] Legal scholars stepped up their critique of the sexual psychopath laws, and during the 1960s, a "due process revolution" in mental health inspired constitutional challenges to sexual psychopath laws on the grounds that they denied both due process and equal protection to accused sex offenders. By 1968, when Michigan repealed the first of the original state psychopath laws and abolished the legal category of "criminal sexual psychopath," an experiment in psychiatric criminology seemed to have come full circle.[39]

AS THEY DEBATED the treatment of the sexual psychopath, psychiatrists and politicians spoke to deeper social concerns about the meaning of sexuality. At a time when the standards of sexual behavior for both women and men were changing rapidly, the psychopath became a malleable symbol for popular fears about the consequences of new sexual values. A close reading of the popular, legal, and psychiatric literature related to the sex crime panics and the psychopath laws reveals at least three ways in which the concept of the sexual psychopath served to create or to clarify boundaries between normal and abnormal behavior. First, the discussion of the sexual psychopath influenced the redefinition of rape as not only a male psychological aberration but also an act in which both women and children contributed to their own victimization. Second, it drew a strict boundary between heterosexual and homosexual males, labeling the latter as violent child molesters. Finally, the creation of the psychopath as an extreme deviant figure helped Americans adjust to a sexual system in which nonprocreative acts were no longer considered abnormal.

Unlike the Progressive Era antiprostitution crusade, the sex crime panic of the 1930s, 1940s, and 1950s virtually ignored women as perpetrators, while redirecting concern about victims to include not only women but especially children of both sexes. Child molestation, like rape, clearly predated the sex crime panics, but for the first time, the sexual victimization of children became a subject of popular concern. The gradual acceptance of female sexual desire helped focus attention on children, for if women now actively sought sexual fulfillment, they were less accessible as symbolic victims, while childhood innocence remained a powerful image. In the film *M*, for example, a real-life rapist of women was transformed into a child murderer, as if rape alone were not enough to horrify the modern audience. At the same time, Freudian ideas about childhood sexuality and Oedipal desire raised the specter of children's participation in sexual acts. Finally, just as the continued entry of women into the paid labor force evoked fears about unattended children becoming juvenile delinquents, it may have also heightened fears of children's susceptibility to the sexual advances of strangers.

A close investigation of the psychopath literature suggests that women — and to some extent children — were paying a high price for the modern recognition of their sexual desire and the removal of female purity as a restraint on male sexuality. Female victims were often portrayed as willing participants in the acts men were accused of committing. For example, the New York City Mayor's Committee for the Study of Sex Offenses explained that "in most sex crimes, the fact that a particular girl is a victim of a sex assault is no accident. Generally there is to be found something in the personality, the environmental background, or the family situation of the victim . . . which predisposes her to participation in sex delinquency." The theme that victims were in some way delinquent themselves recurred during the 1950s in the work of relatively liberal critics of the laws, such as Bowman and Bernice Engle, of the influential California Sex Deviate Research Project, and Morris Ploscowe, a lawyer and judge who championed liberalization of laws regulating sexuality. These critics reiterated doubts that a woman could be raped without some predisposition. The legal reforms that they recommended to improve the treatment of the psychopath included corroboration of rape charges by witnesses, investigation of victims' past sexual activity, and proof of "complete sexual penetration" — in short, the very legal mechanisms that feminists would seek to dismantle a decade later. Moreover, in a major study of child sexual abuse and incest conducted at California's Langley Porter Clinic, the authors described the majority of the victims (80 percent of whom were female) as "seductive," "flirtatious," and sexually precocious. They labeled those for whom abuse persisted over time as "participating victims." Thus, in a movement allegedly based upon the urgent need to protect women and children, the victims were ultimately as stigmatized as the perpetrators. As in the case of the southern rape complex, in which black men lived in fear of accusation and white women lived in fear of assault, the threat of the sexual psychopath served to regulate sexual behavior not only for "deviant" men but also for women.[40]

The image of the rapist in the psychopath literature further attests to the marginal influence of women's interests on the response to the sexual psychopath. The laws rested on the premise that most rapists were "sick" men, suggesting that rape was an isolated act committed by crazed strangers. In fact, recent scholarship has shown that sexual assault is a common experience for women, its perpetrators as likely to be family members or acquaintances as strangers. Even more interesting is a shift in the psychiatric and legal interpretations that occurred by the 1950s. Critics of the psychopath laws increasingly suggested that, in the words of one state report, "aggression is a normal component of the sexual impulse in all males." By this logic, as long as he did not mutilate or murder his victim, the rapist might be considered almost normal and certainly more "natural" than men who committed less violent, and even consensual, sexual acts such as sodomy and pedophilia. Accordingly, men diagnosed as psychopaths were more likely to be accused of pedophilia and homosexuality than of rape or murder.[41]

The response to the sexual psychopath was not, then, a movement to protect female purity; its central concern was male sexuality and the fear that without the guardianship of women, either men's most beastlike, violent sexual desires might run amok or men might turn their sexual energies away from women entirely. Adult women were now suitable objects for "normal" male sexual desire, even normal male aggression, but the discourse on the psychopath mapped out two new forbidden boundaries for men: sex with children and sex with other men. The literature frequently played on fears of child molestation, and a significant minority of psychopaths were charged with male homosexual acts, with either children or adults. This fact and the frequent overlap in use of the terms "sex criminal," "pervert," "psychopath," and "homosexual" raise the question of whether "psychopath" served in part as a code for "homosexual" at a time of heightened public consciousness of homosexuality.

Social historians have recently identified the 1940s as a critical period in the formation of a public homosexual world in the United States. Although homosexual subcultures had begun to form in American cities as early as the 1890s, it was not until the 1930s that literature and the theater drew national attention to the existence of homosexuals in this country. The war years provided new opportunities for young men and women to discover homosexuality as they left their families and hometowns to enter the military or defense industries. During the 1940s, both homosexual men and lesbians created visible social institutions, including bars, social clubs, and political organizations. By 1950, the early homophile rights movement, the forerunner of gay liberation, was articulating a positive view of homosexuals as a cultural minority group. However, society as a whole remained strongly homophobic. As Barbara Ehrenreich has argued, during the 1950s, "fear of homosexuality kept heterosexual men in line as husbands and breadwinners."[42] Despite efforts to remove the stigma from homosexuality, the American Psychiatric Association categorized it as a mental disease until 1973. Moreover, in the 1950s, the federal government launched a campaign to remove homosexuals from government jobs.[43]

The psychopath literature did reinforce the fear of male homosexuality. At times, it appeared that a major motive of the psychopath laws was to prevent the contagion of homosexuality from spreading from adults to youths. Such contagion might corrupt the entire community and ultimately result in violent death. For example, a 1948 article in the *American Journal of Psychiatry* argued that when adults indulged in homosexual acts with minors, "the minors in turn corrupted other minors until the whole community was involved." As evidence, the authors cited "the recent killing of a 7-year-old boy by a 13-year-old because he [the younger child] would not perform the act of fellatio." Furthermore, the beliefs that homosexuals actively recruited among youths and that seduction in youth or childhood was the "commonest single environmental factor" explaining homosexuality were both used to support psychopath legislation. Dr. J. Paul de River, a crude popularizer of theories of sexual psychopathy, stated the case for vigilance in his book *The Sexual Criminal*: "All too often we lose sight of the fact that the homosexual is an inveterate seducer of the young of both sexes, and that he presents a social problem because he is not content with being degenerate himself; he must have degenerate companions and is ever seeking for younger victims." Thus, homosexuality was increasingly linked to violence and, especially, to the allegedly coercive recruitment of minors for illicit sexual activity.[44]

The panic over the sexual psychopath, however, did not merely shore up traditional sanctions against male homosexuality by associating it with violence. Rather, even the seemingly repressive aspects of the campaign promoted a new, more open, public discourse on nonmarital, nonprocreative sexuality. The literature on the sexual psychopath helped break down older taboos simply by discussing sexual deviance. At the same time, the literature encouraged a reevaluation of heterosexual behavior during a time of rapid flux in sexual standards. At a basic level, the psychopath literature helped disseminate information about sexual practices that had previously been outside the bounds of proper discourse. Now, in the name of preventing children from either becoming or succumbing to sexual psychopaths, professionals began to argue that sex education should not ignore such practices as oral and anal sex. The state commissions on sex crimes took an especially active part in this educational campaign, holding extensive public hearings and conducting attitudinal surveys on sexual abnormality. For example, the Michigan Governor's Study Commission distributed "A Citizens' Handbook of Sexual Abnormalities and the Mental Hygiene Approach to Their Prevention." An Oregon social hygiene council published a fourteen-page "Introduction to the Problem of the Sex Deviate." The city of Long Beach, California, distributed a cartoon-illustrated booklet for children as its "answer to sex fiends." Like the antimasturbation literature of the nineteenth century, the sexual perversion literature of the postwar era was, no doubt, as educative as it was preventive.[45]

In commenting on the widespread concern about psychopaths, many writers pointed to the influence of Kinsey's study of male sexuality, published in 1948, which revealed the extensive practice of nonprocreative sexual acts, inside and outside marriage. An editor of the *American Journal of Psychiatry* even argued that Kinsey's evidence of a "gap between cultural mores and private behavior" might have set off a "reaction formation against anxiety and guilt" that had led, in turn, to the scapegoating of extreme sexual offenders. Liberal critics of the psychopath laws also referred to Kinsey's study, citing his results to argue that sexual variations were now so common among "normal" couples that they should be excluded from the psychopath laws. For example, Bowman and Engle attempted to differentiate between the dangerous acts of the psychopath and the newly acceptable practices of masturbation, premarital petting, and "unnatural acts" (that is, oral and anal sex) performed in private between consenting adults. Thus, they assured the public that "serious" perversions did require psychiatric treatment but that healthy sexuality might include nonprocreative heterosexual acts. In this way, the discourse on the psychopath helped redefine the boundaries of normal sexuality and may well have contributed to the sexual liberalism of the 1960s.[46]

FROM THE 1930S through the 1950s, the sexual psychopath provided the focus for public discussions of sexual normality and abnormality, while the state played an increasingly important role in defining sexual deviance and prescribing psychiatric treatment. The debates on the psychopath statutes did more than expand the legal authority of psychiatry. The critics of the laws ultimately helped to legitimize nonprocreative heterosexual acts; the media and national commissions helped educate the public about both "natural" and "perverse" sexual behaviors. At the same time, the psychopath literature tended to stigmatize female and child victims of sexual assault and to draw a firm sexual boundary proscribing all homosexual activity and linking it with extreme violence, especially against youths.

It is difficult to assign any simple meaning to the response to the sexual psychopath. Like "M," or his later American counterpart in Alfred Hitchcock's film *Psycho*, the image of the sexual psychopath revealed a deep discomfort with the potential violence of male sexuality unconstrained by female purity — or "uncontrolled desires." The response to the sexual psychopath also confirms that, as in the case of lynching, the fear of sexual violence can provide an extremely powerful tool for mobilizing political support against nonconforming individuals. The ultimate historical legacy of the response to the sexual psychopath, however, was to expand the public discourse on sexuality, focus attention on male violence, and heighten the importance of sexuality as a component of modern identity. In so doing, the response to the sexual psychopath helped redefine the boundaries of acceptable sexual behavior in modern America.

8 | The Prison Lesbian | Race, Class, and the Construction of the Aggressive Female Homosexual, 1915 – 1965

I first encountered references to lesbianism in women's prisons during my dissertation research in the 1970s, but when I later uncovered rich accounts of sexual relations between prisoners in the papers of Miriam Van Waters, I decided to look more closely at this phenomenon. The prison lesbian, like the male psychopath, seemed to supplant the prostitute as a threat to social order during a period when the white female chastity ideal was declining. The psychopath remained a racially stable diagnosis applied to white men, but the prison lesbian transformed from a primarily African American threat to include both white and black working-class women. New historical research on both women's prisons and homosexuality among incarcerated men in the twentieth century may help clarify the intriguing associations between race and gender roles in single-sex institutions.

IN THE MID-TWENTIETH century, the subject of lesbians in prison began to attract both scholarly and popular attention in the United States.[1] After World War II, criminologists depicted lesbian inmates as menacing social types. In popular culture as well, women's prisons became synonymous with lesbianism. The emergence of the prison lesbian as a dangerous sexual predator and the changing contours of this category over time provide a unique historical window on the social construction of homosexual identity.

The prison lesbian also reveals a complex reconfiguration of the class and racial meanings attached to sexuality in modern America. In the early twentieth century, most prison literature equated female sex crime almost entirely with prostitution and rarely inquired into the homosexual activities of delinquent women. As criminologist Charles A. Ford puzzled in 1929, despite widespread evidence of lesbian relationships within women's refor-

Previously published as Estelle B. Freedman, "The Prison Lesbian: Race, Class, and the Construction of the Aggressive Female Homosexual, 1915 – 1965," *Feminist Studies* 22, no. 2 (Summer 1996): 397 – 423. Reprinted by permission of Feminist Studies, Inc.

matories, very few studies had been written about the subject. When authors did mention homosexuality, they usually identified black women as lesbian aggressors and white women as temporary partners. By the 1960s, psychologists and criminologists had become intrigued with lesbianism in prison, publishing books and articles on the subject and suggesting that homosexuals "present the greatest sexual problem" in women's prisons. Unlike the earlier literature, the later studies extended the lesbian label to white women, emphasizing the threat of their aggressive homosexuality.[2]

The following exploration, first of the criminological literature and then of the records of the Massachusetts Reformatory for Women in Framingham, analyzes these simultaneous shifts in the conception of the prison lesbian. From an initial association with African American women, the image of the aggressive female homosexual extended after World War II to include white working-class prisoners as well. At the same time, greater public scrutiny of prison lesbianism and concern about its "contaminating" effect on the society at large intensified the process of labeling female homosexuality in women's prisons and beyond their walls.

A SMALL BODY OF historical literature provides a context for investigating the prison lesbian. Alongside earlier studies of middle-class women's romantic friendships and the medical reclassification of these relationships as perversion in the twentieth century, a rudimentary narrative of working-class lesbian identity and community is now emerging. In brief, it suggests that in industrializing America, economic necessity led some working-class women to "pass" as men and sometimes marry other women; in the early twentieth century, some single working-class women pooled their resources and lived together as couples in urban, furnished-room districts. For African American women, the Harlem Renaissance fostered a sexually experimental subculture that offered a measure of tolerance for homosexual relationships. During World War II, women's work force and military participation intensified a process of homosexual community formation. Even in the postwar decade, when the hostile Cold War climate condemned homosexuals as subversive, a public, working-class lesbian bar culture became increasingly visible.[3]

The prison system provides another location for understanding not only working-class lesbian history but also the importance of race and class relations within this history. By the 1920s, almost every state and the federal government had established a separate adult women's reformatory.[4] The majority of inmates came from working-class backgrounds and were often daughters of immigrants; only a small minority were African American.[5] Most of the reformatory inmates had been sentenced for "crimes against public order," including drunkenness, vagrancy, and a variety of prostitution-related offenses once labeled "crimes against chastity." Many of the educated and professional women who worked in the reformatories sought to "uplift" the sexual morality of female inmates. Until the 1940s, however, women's prison authorities concentrated on diverting inmates from heterosexual acts prohibited by law — especially prostitution. They rarely mentioned lesbianism as a problem, and most women's prison officials ignored evidence of homosexuality among inmates. This lack of interest contrasted with the approach of administrators of men's prisons, who frequently labeled and punished homosexuality.[6]

The one exception to the disavowal of lesbianism in women's prisons highlights the racial construction of the aggressive female homosexual in the early twentieth century. Beginning in 1913, criminologists, psychologists, and state officials denounced one form of lesbian relationship — romances between black and white inmates — for disrupting prison discipline. These accounts usually represented African American women prisoners as masculine or aggressive and their white lovers as "normal" feminine women who would return to heterosexual relations upon release from prison. The earliest criminological study of lesbianism in prison described the practice of "nigger loving" by young white women committed to reformatories. Author Margaret Otis explained that "the love of 'niggers'" had become a tradition in which black inmates sent courtship notes to incoming white inmates. The ensuing relationships ranged from casual to those of an "intensely sexual nature." Despite this intensity, Otis claimed, once released, the white women rarely had contact with "the colored race," nor, presumably, with women lovers.[7]

Observations of interracial lesbianism recurred within women's prisons over the following decades. An officer at the New York State Reformatory for Women at Bedford Hills testified in 1915 that "the colored girls are extremely attractive to certain white girls." Another official explained that these relationships had existed since the founding of the reformatory in the nineteenth century, but recent overcrowding had made them more frequent. Blaming unrest at the reformatory on these liaisons, an investigative committee recommended the segregation of black inmates at Bedford Hills. Their rationale echoed the sexual fears that underlay Jim Crow institutions in the South. The committee held that segregation was necessary not simply "because of the color line" but because "the most undesirable sex relations grow out of this mingling of the two races." Even though these homosexual relationships did not lead to the kind of amalgamation most feared by white supremacists — namely, mixed-race offspring — the thought that white women would reject heterosexuality entirely — and thus reject their racial duty to reproduce — was intolerable. Even segregation, however, did not discourage interracial homosexual unions or lessen the mythology surrounding black women's sexual aggression. Black-white relationships persisted noticeably in New York prisons, for example, fifteen years after the Bedford Hills investigation.[8]

In writing about interracial lesbian relationships, criminologists emphasized the ways that race substituted for gender in women's prisons. Black women took the role of "husbands," white women of "wives," in the New York reformatory Charles Ford studied in the 1920s. Samuel Kahn later quoted a New York City inmate who claimed that "there are more colored daddies and more white mamas" among women in the city jails. In 1943, one scholar reasoned that "Negroes" were sexually attractive to whites "because the White girls interpret the Negro aggression and dominance as 'maleness'" and because the blacks' "uninhibited emotional expressions and some of their physical characteristics (dark skin) seem to enhance the sex attraction of the Negro girls."[9] In a 1941 fictional portrayal of a segregated women's reformatory in the South, novelist Felice Swados incorporated the stereotype of black lesbian aggression. Inmate lore described "a cute blonde with dimples" who "got to going around with niggers." The woman wound up in the hospital after "a great big black" woman "got too hot. Went crazy. Just tore her insides out."[10]

Explanations of interracial attraction in terms of "male" aggression by black women mirrored in part the then-dominant theories of homosexuality as a form of gender inversion.[11] At the same time, assigning the male-aggressor role to black women and preserving a semblance of femininity for their white partners racialized the sexual pathology of inversion. In this interpretation, white women were not really lesbians because they were attracted to men, for whom black women temporarily substituted. Thus, the prison literature racialized both lesbianism and butch/femme roles, implicitly blaming black women for sexual aggression and, indeed, homosexuality by associating them with a male role.

Whether or not these explanations accurately reflected women inmates' own erotic systems, the official interpretations reinforced long-standing associations among race, sexuality, and gender roles. In the nineteenth century, for example, medical authorities had regarded African women's genitals as pathological, and according to Sander Gilman, they even associated "the concupiscence of the black" with "the sexuality of the lesbian." Because "lesbian" then connoted both maleness and a lack of feminine virtue, the label effectively denied gender privileges to black women. Like the cultural assignment of strong, even insatiable, sexual desire to African American women, the identification of black women as aggressive butch lesbians rested on a denial of their womanhood.[12]

Similarly, twentieth-century criminologists often correlated race, sexual deviance, and aggression. Theories of black women's greater criminality rested in part on a model of sexual inversion, in which black women more easily engaged in "male" aggressive behaviors. As one criminal psychiatrist explained in 1942, "colored females" predominated among aggressive women criminals because the "accepted ideological codes of Harlem" condoned violence on their part, especially if related to a love triangle. The writer identified one other category of aggressive female felonies, which he labeled "lesbian homicides." Presumably committed by black or white women, in these cases, "murder obviously afforded an unconscious destruction of the murderess' own homosexual cravings." Another study of working-class black women suggested that homosexuality was prevalent among black prostitutes because both prostitution and homosexuality stemmed from a "fundamental inability" to accept the "feminine role."[13]

White women clearly participated in lesbian relations in prisons, and no doubt they had white as well as black partners. Yet the early-twentieth-century criminological literature on white women's sexuality invariably discussed prostitution, not homosexuality. Even as psychoanalytic concepts filtered into American criminology, it was white women's heterosexual deviance that attracted attention. As historian Elizabeth Lunbeck has shown, in the early twentieth century, the new diagnosis of sexual psychopathy — a term implying uncontrollable libidinal instincts that would later become a code for male homosexuality — at first applied to heterosexually active white women. Because psychologists presumed that black women were naturally promiscuous, they did not label them as diseased psychopaths.[14] Throughout the 1920s and 1930s, the growing literature on psychopathic crime rarely addressed lesbianism. A 1934 study of psychopathic women, for example, found that only a few cases could be classified as homosexual. As late as 1941, one criminologist argued that juvenile homosexuality was more common among male than female offenders, while "heterosexual delinquency is by far the girl's premier offence." Even as a "lesbian taboo" in marital advice literature warned middle-class women to remain heterosexual or risk becoming abnormal deviants, few writers portrayed white lesbians as danger-ous criminals.[15]

The paucity of either scholarly or popular attention to lesbianism among women in prison did not necessarily reflect the extent of the practice between 1915 and 1940. The few criminologists who did observe women's relation-ships in prison documented a sexually active and often racially constructed lesbian subculture. In the New York City House of Detention, for example, women prisoners engaged in "bulldiking," and their love affairs included regular tribadism. At other institutions, "wives" and "husbands" found ways to send sexually explicit love letters to each other. "You can take my tie / You can take my collor / But I'll jazze you / Till you holier," one black "husband" wrote to "My dearest Wife Gloria," who responded, "Sugar dady if I could sleep with you for one little night, I would show you how much I hon[es]tly and truly I love you." Other inmates scratched their "friend's" initials on their skin and smuggled contraband presents in their bras. The administra-tor of one reform school recalled that white girls aggressively pursued black girls, a pattern rarely reported in the criminological literature.[16]

For the most part, women's prison administrators either tolerated these lesbian relationships or denied their existence. When physician Samuel Kahn published the first book-length study of prison homosexuality in 1937 (based on research conducted a decade earlier), he seemed dismayed to re-port that at the New York City Women's Workhouse, in contrast to the men's division, "the homosexuals have been unclassified and are not segregated . . . so that they all mingle freely with the other inmates." When Kahn sought out lesbians to interview, neither the woman warden nor the male priests at the workhouse were willing to identify inmates as homosexuals. In *Five Hundred Delinquent Women*, the classic 1934 study of women prisoners con-ducted at the Massachusetts women's reformatory, criminologists Sheldon Glueck and Eleanor Glueck never referred to lesbianism.[17]

Women's prison administrators may have been reluctant to call attention to the subject of homosexuality because many of them were single profes-sional women who maintained close personal bonds with other women and could be vulnerable to charges of lesbianism. According to the superinten-dent of several reform schools for girls, in the 1920s women's prison workers recognized the problem of homosexuality but never openly talked about it. One superintendent who lectured inmates of a girls' reformatory about the dangers of homosexuality was pressured into resigning in 1931, in part be-cause she addressed such an "embarrassing subject" and in part because she accused both staff members and local businesswomen of having "immoral relationships." In 1931, officials preferred to be silent about these possibilities of lesbianism rather than call attention to them.[18]

The disinclination to acknowledge lesbianism in prison lasted until the 1940s, when both prison administrators and criminologists began to express more concern about female homosexuality. The reasons for a gradual shift in awareness included increased arrests for prostitution during World War II and consequent prison overcrowding. Some prostitutes were also lesbians, and the doubling up of women in cells may have intensified lesbian activity. A growing lesbian subculture centered around predominantly white, working-class bars may have heightened lesbian identity for some women who wound up in jails and prisons. Aside from any actual increase in lesbian activity in prison, fears about the dangers of female sexual expression escalated during wartime, especially targeting white women as the purveyors of venereal disease to soldiers or as seductive saboteurs. It was in this context that female homosexuality in general and lesbianism among white women in prisons came under closer scrutiny.

A new consciousness about prison lesbianism appeared, for example, among the superintendents of women's institutions, who met annually to discuss common problems. Several of them had acknowledged black-white sexual liaisons in institutions previously, but for the most part, the superintendents had been concerned about heterosexual irregularities among inmates. Only during the 1940s did they introduce the topic of how to manage homosexual relationships in institutions. At one annual conference, for example, they questioned their guest speaker, Margaret Mead, about "how much we should worry about homosexuality." Although Mead advised them to "keep it down as much as possible," the anthropologist — who had herself been sexually involved with women — also argued that female homosexuality was much less socially dangerous than male homosexuality because women tended toward "more or less permanent relationship[s] in which one person looks after the welfare of the other, makes them silk underwear, etc. The male homosexuality, on the other hand, is exploitive and promiscuous — it is not a paired sexuality." Mead believed that women's relatively benign institutional homosexuality was a temporary substitute for heterosexual relations. Unlike earlier writers, however, she did not identify any racial patterns in lesbian role-playing. Her tolerant attitude, echoed by other speakers, counseled adequate recreation and social stimulation as diversions from homosexuality in prison.[19]

In the postwar decade, however, the relative tolerance that had characterized the treatment of prison lesbianism gradually gave way to greater surveillance and ultimately to condemnation. The shift from lack of interest to fascination with the prison lesbian can be seen within U.S. popular and political culture shortly after World War II. In the 1950s, *True Confessions* magazine sensationalized accounts of "love-starved girls in reform school," while pulp novels incorporated women's prison seduction scenes. Hollywood produced a series of women's prison films, replete with lesbian innuendo. In contrast to the earliest women's prison films, in which the lesbian was portrayed as comic and benign, a dangerously aggressive lesbian criminal now threatened the innocence of young women, as in the 1950 film *Caged*. At the same time, politicians began to target "aggressive female homosexuals" in prison as a serious threat to moral order. During the 1950s, they invoked images of lesbians in prison as part of a larger Cold War campaign to discredit liberal reformers for being soft on perversion, as on communism.[20] By the late 1950s, women who formed homosexual relationships in prison had become stock cultural characters associated with threats to sexual and social order. At the same time, black women ceased to be the primary suspects as prison lesbians. Class marking seemed to be replacing earlier race marking, making both black and white working-class women more vulnerable to charges of deviance, while still exempting middle-class women. By the 1960s, the criminological literature no longer relied on an exclusively racial definition of lesbians and emphasized the social threat of white lesbian activity.

These changes coincided with a larger cultural emphasis on both the power of female sexuality and the need to contain it within domestic relationships among white and middle-class Americans. Reflecting the rhetoric of Cold War America, which sought to identify internal enemies who threatened social order, the postwar clinical literature on lesbianism elaborated upon the image of the aggressive female homosexual, but it rarely targeted black women. The new stereotype drew upon earlier concepts of the male sexual psychopath, whose uncontrolled, often violent, sexuality threatened to disrupt social order. In contrast to earlier studies that had posited little relationship between psychopathy and lesbianism, writers now suggested "the possibly greater tendency of the [female] psychopaths to engage in sex acts with other girls." New psychoanalytic theories also contributed to the image of a dangerous, promiscuous lesbian. One writer, for example, differentiated between female homosexuals who simply preferred the company of women and a rarer group containing "the more dangerous type — the promiscuous Lesbian who passing quickly and lightly from affair to affair, usually with physical relations, may cause great harm and unhappiness." Just as the male psychopath was invariably portrayed as white and often middle class, the dangerous lesbian was no longer marked as a racial minority but appeared to be white, although usually working class.[21]

Along with serious psychological studies, pseudoscientific works of the 1950s conflated the lesbian and the woman criminal. In her study of postwar lesbian imagery, historian Donna Penn has summarized the portrayal of the lesbian found in popular works such as Frank Caprio's *Female Homosexuality* as the "promiscuous, oversexed, conquering, aggressive dyke who exercised masculine prerogative in the sexual arena." Like the prostitute, the lesbian now spread moral contagion. In Penn's view, the demonization of the sinister, working-class lesbian helped shift the meaning of female homosexuality away from the "Boston marriages" and innocent romantic friendships of middle-class women.[22]

The prison literature confirms Penn's analysis but suggests a racial, as well as class, realignment in the demonology of lesbianism. The dangerous lesbian was less identified with a racially specified aggressive invert. Even though interracial unions continued to characterize women's prison life, by the 1950s, it was the homosexuality of white women prisoners that became the object of intense scrutiny. Larger social trends contributed to this racial shift, including the gradual sexualization of white women in popular culture and the emergence of visible white, working-class lesbian institutions in the postwar period, such as the bar culture studied by Madeline Davis and Elizabeth Lapovsky Kennedy.[23] The prison lesbian now appeared not primarily as an African American but more typically as a white woman, albeit one who may have sexually crossed a racial boundary in the process of becoming homosexual. Of either race, she became the "unnatural woman" personified, a threat to other inmates and to women outside the prison. If earlier tolerance had rested on an assumption of the natural depravity or inherent sexual inversion of black women, it is not surprising that the revelation of white women's lesbianism in prison would sound an alert, a warning about the potential degeneration of theoretically "true" womanhood. Indeed, by the mid-1950s, institutional tolerance gave way to a call to "sort out the real homosexual" in prison through psychological testing and to "segregate those who show strong homosexual inclinations," with no reference to race.[24]

A good example of the new attitude toward prison lesbianism appeared in a popular 1956 book written by Katharine Sullivan, a conservative member of the Massachusetts parole board. According to Sullivan, "No age or race is immune to the temptations of homosexuality in prisons." Moreover, the prison lesbians she described had violent, almost animalistic, characters. Jealousies led to "hand-to-hand fights or even free-for-alls." If separated from a lover, Sullivan warned, the surviving partner "may suffer an acute attack of homosexual panic, with violent screaming and frothing at the mouth, followed by a period of wan anxiety."[25]

In contrast to earlier writers, Sullivan firmly believed that once a woman engaged in homosexual acts in prison, she quickly became "addicted" and built her life around the practice after release. In one example, a young, white parolee named Mary learned about the "doll racket" in prison and now wanted nothing to do with men. Visited on parole, she sported a new boyish haircut, no makeup, and boys' clothes, and, significantly, had set up a household with two black women. Unlike the "nigger lovers" described by Otis in 1913 who rejected interracial relations after release, Mary continued to associate with black women on the outside. She even adopted a butch identity that had been racially specific to black women in the past. Earlier racial stereotypes continued to operate as well. Sullivan depicted Mary's black roommates as the antithesis of natural women: they were "large," "rangy," and sloppily dressed in jeans and T-shirts. Mary, she implied, had descended into an interracial netherworld from which she would emerge an addicted lesbian. Indeed, Mary declared that when she turned twenty-one, she intended to "leave home and go to live permanently in one of the big cities in America, where Lesbians flourish." Sullivan clearly wished to prevent white women like Mary from being exposed to homosexuality in prison; she seemed much less concerned about the black women who adopted male styles.[26]

By the time the prison lesbian became the subject of extensive academic inquiry in the 1960s, race had practically disappeared from the scholarly research agenda. Sociological accounts of the "problem" of the prison lesbian described widespread homosexuality in women's institutions and focused on the butch-femme role system that organized prison life, but like other supposedly "race-blind" works of the period, they evaded race, even when it influenced their findings.[27] The two classic case studies that appeared in the 1960s — David A. Ward and Gene G. Kassebaum's *Women's Prison: Sex and Social Structure* and Rose Giallombardo's *Society of Women: A Study of a Women's Prison* — avoid mentioning race in their descriptions of prison social life and sexual roles. Giallombardo's discussion of fictive marriage patterns among women prisoners never referred to race, even though her kinship diagrams, read closely, reveal that the majority of "marriages" were interracial.[28] In short, race may have continued to play a role in the erotic life of prisoners, but observers presented a lesbian world that, lacking racial markers, appeared to be entirely white.[29]

The racial shift in the construction of the prison lesbian, taken together with other evidence of postwar moral panics, suggests deep-seated cultural anxieties about the instability of white heterosexuality. Although focused on working-class women who wound up in prison and those who were forming a lesbian subculture in various cities, the discourse reached a broader public. Literary critic Lynda Hart has argued that the historical construction of the lesbian has often projected a "secret" sexual identity onto working-class women, as well as women of color, while it simultaneously speaks loudly to fears about the sexuality of middle- and upper-class white women. In postwar America, as popular and commercial culture elaborated upon white women's sexual availability and effective medical treatment of venereal disease made prostitutes seem less threatening than in the past, several new boundaries appeared to help shore up white, marital heterosexuality. The outlaws included the frigid career woman, the black welfare mother, and the prison lesbian.[30]

A CASE STUDY of the Massachusetts Reformatory for Women further illustrates both the changing racial construction of the aggressive female homosexual and the shift from a period of institutional denial or tolerance to one of labeling and strict surveillance. The reformatory, founded in 1877, typically housed between 300 and 400 adult female prisoners, the vast majority of whom served two- to five-year terms for minor offenses against public order, such as drunkenness and prostitution (often coded as vagrancy or "lewdness"). As in most northern reformatories, until the 1960s, the population was overwhelmingly white. The institution had a scattered history of liberal administrations aimed at uplifting so-called fallen women. Miriam Van Waters, who became the reformatory superintendent in 1932, expanded upon this mission by providing education, social welfare services, psychiatric counseling, and work opportunities outside prison.

As in other institutions, the earliest references to lesbian relations at the Massachusetts reformatory noted attractions between white and black inmates. In the 1930s, when Van Waters detected "black-white manifestation of homosexuality," she followed the advice of writers such as Charles Ford and attempted to divert the black inmates by "stressing their prestige in Dramatics, Spirituals, [and] Orchestra." Other staff members also learned of romantic liaisons between inmates during the 1930s. One officer informed

Van Waters of inmate gossip about the "doll" situation — the prison code for lesbians — and noted "the fuss the white girls make over the colored girls." A few years later, when Van Waters commented that she observed no "overt white-white" relationships, she identified several interracial couples.[31]

Van Waters and her staff distinguished between true homosexuality and temporary attractions. They believed the former could be detected by the Rorschach test; in the absence of such "positive evidence," they assumed that the boredom of prison routine stimulated unnatural interest in same-sex relationships. By offering an active program of classes and clubs, they attempted to channel the energies of both black and white prisoners into what the staff considered healthier recreations. Nonetheless, underground homosexual unions survived. Newcomers quickly learned about "dolls," and love letters circulated among inmates. In 1938, for example, when an inmate tried to use her fear of sexual advances to convince the parole board to release her from the reformatory, she submitted love letters from other women to support her case. In addition, officers occasionally discovered two women in bed together, a problem that escalated during World War II, when increased prison commitments led to overcrowding.[32]

Prison records also reveal contradictory attitudes toward lesbian relationships on the part of reformatory and court officials. The former were reluctant to label women as homosexuals, while the latter were willing to impose harsh penalties for openly lesbian relationships. The case of Marie LeBlanc, a white woman of French Canadian background, illustrates psychiatric tolerance within the institution and the punitive response of parole boards and courts.[33] LeBlanc had become sexually involved with Eleanor Harris, another white inmate. The prison psychiatrist who "treated" her saw no reason not to recommend her for parole. When parole agents learned that, after release, LeBlanc had been sleeping with Harris and her husband, they revoked LeBlanc's parole "for the best interests of herself and the community." She returned to prison for a year, then left on parole again. This time, she reportedly became involved with another former inmate, Jane MacGregor. The court convicted LeBlanc of "Open and Gross Lewdness" and sentenced her to another two years in the reformatory because of her lesbian relationship.[34]

Jane MacGregor's records further highlight the conflicting policies toward lesbianism. According to a reformatory psychiatrist, MacGregor had "no preference" between "hetero- and homosexual experience." Because she was "not the aggressive one" in the latter, the psychiatrist did not consider her a true lesbian. Even after officers discovered MacGregor in bed with another inmate, the psychiatrist emphasized her need for motherly love and recommended that "it is far better to have some of these intense feelings directed toward an officer where the activity can be controlled than toward another student [inmate]." Only after MacGregor was repeatedly found in bed with other women did prison officials fear that she was "in danger of becoming a true homosexual." Despite efforts to divert her interest in women into athletics and the care of animals (to "help take care of her need to demonstrate affection"), the psychiatrist eventually concluded that MacGregor was in fact "strongly homosexual." Nonetheless, he supported her request for parole. The more conservative parole board revoked her release, however, explaining that she "engaged in homosexual activities to such an extent that she is unable to adjust in employment."[35]

The inmates clearly knew that reformatory officials were reluctant to label same-sex relations, as the case of Barbara Jones illustrates. A white woman, Jones had been committed to prison for idle and disorderly conduct, which may have meant prostitution. At the reformatory, she tended to pair off with a "colored inmate," laboring to maintain the relationship by "coveting favor with small gifts." The staff tried to discourage the pairing by transferring Jones to a housing unit apart from her friend. Annoyed by the move, Jones wrote to a staff member with the expectation of tolerance and understanding. "You told me one time if I didn't want people to complain to you about my actions I shouldn't make them so obvious," she explained. "I didn't this time. It was purely what people thought. True, I was carrying on an affair, but I certainly wasn't loud about it."[36]

The relative tolerance toward homosexuality among the staff at the Massachusetts Reformatory for Women could not survive long after World War II. Just as the psychological and popular literature began to emphasize a sinister, even predatory, lesbian, conservative Massachusetts politicians seized on the prison lesbian to discredit the unusually liberal reformatory administration. The investigation of an inmate suicide in 1947 led to reports of a "doll racket" at the reformatory, giving the Massachusetts Department of Corrections an opportunity to launch a series of probes of Superintendent Van Waters's administration. Among their complaints, they charged that "many of the inmates receiving special favors are 'known' homosexuals or dangerous psychopaths." Although Van Waters denied the charges, the politicians exploited them in the press, using prison lesbianism as a sensationalistic wedge with which to expose Van Waters's liberal attitudes toward rehabilitation.

Like the federal officials who soon outlawed the employment of homosexuals on the grounds that they spread corruption in the government, Massachusetts officials claimed that homosexuals corrupted the young women of the state. Instead of prostitution, which had so disturbed an earlier generation of Americans, homosexuality now represented the great destroyer of young women's virtue. As Senator Michael LoPresti told the press, "Supt. Van Waters' administration of the Women's Reformatory has been more damaging to the morals and mental health of young girls than has the operation of White Slavery in all New England over the same period of time."[37] In 1949, when the commissioner of corrections dismissed Van Waters from office, he charged that she had "known of and failed to prevent the continuance of, or failed to know and recognize that an unwholesome relationship has existed between inmates of the Reformatory for Women which is called the 'doll racket' by inmates and some officer personnel; the terms 'stud' and 'queen' are used with implied meanings, and such association has resulted in 'crushes,' 'courtships,' and homosexual practises [sic] among the inmates in the Reformatory."[38] Although the grounds for dismissal included Van Waters's allowing inmates to work for pay outside the institution and hiring former inmates on the reformatory staff, the homosexual motif ran throughout the charges, fueling sensational newspaper coverage of the issue.

During several months of public hearings, Van Waters successfully defended her policies, in part by minimizing the existence of homosexuality at the reformatory, and in part by deferring to psychiatric authorities when asked about homosexual tendencies among inmates. Typical of her strategic evasion was this response to hostile interrogation about whether certain acts or personal styles revealed homosexual tendencies: "That, sir, is so distinctly a medical and technical question that I would not presume to answer it. One of the first things we are taught is that a homosexual tendency must be distinguished from a homosexual act. A homosexual tendency may be completely repressed and turned into a variety of other expressions, including a great aversion to emotion." By invoking the power of psychiatry, Van Waters acknowledged the shifting meaning of homosexuality from an act to an identity and from a crime to a mental disorder. At the same time, she tried to avoid a labeling process that would mark close friends, mannish women, and those who had crushes on other inmates as confirmed homosexuals. Responding to further questions, she explained that a woman's mannish dress and preference for men's jobs resulted from early childhood neglect, not homosexual desire.[39]

Whether consciously or not, Van Waters's testimony represented a form of resistance to the use of accusations of homosexuality to discredit nonconforming women. Rather than sacrifice some "mannish" women or close female friends by calling them homosexuals, latent homosexuals, or women with homosexual tendencies, she firmly opposed labeling. At the same time, like psychologists of the period, she did so by accepting a definition of true homosexuality as a pathology.

When the superintendent evaded the labeling of homosexuality, she also sidestepped implicit questions about her own sexual identity. In her personal life, Van Waters had refused to label her love for a woman as a form of homosexuality, despite her long-term romantic partnership with Geraldine Thompson, who was known publicly only as a wealthy benefactor and a supporter of Van Waters's reforms. Thus, she hesitated to assume that other women who appeared to fit the definition really were homosexuals, a term she reserved for women's pathological, although curable, sexual aggression toward other women.[40]

In March 1949, a special panel appointed by the governor exonerated Van Waters of all charges and reinstated her as superintendent. During the two years of publicity concerning the "doll racket" at Framingham, however, the image of the homosexual woman criminal had been widely disseminated by both local and national media coverage of the Van Waters hearings. In the aftermath of the Van Waters case, prison lesbianism came under greater scrutiny, with white as well as black women subject to the charge. A few months after the hearings, for instance, the Massachusetts parole board taunted a white woman they suspected of homosexuality by asking whether she ought to have a sex-change operation because of her "boyish swagger."[41] In addition, popular media further stereotyped inmates as lesbians. The Van Waters case directly inspired *Caged*, the prototypical women's prison film, in which older, aggressive lesbians compete for access to an innocent young inmate. The lurid *True Confessions* tales of reform school lesbians also followed in the wake of the Van Waters case.

The image of the "aggressive homosexual," along with greater surveillance by the Massachusetts Department of Corrections and the public, helped erode the earlier tolerance toward prison lesbianism among the Framingham staff. In the 1950s, despite Superintendent Van Waters's continuing belief that healthy recreation could divert women from situational homosexuality, the reformatory capitulated to the antihomosexual climate by attempting to transfer lesbians out of the institution. Previously, even evidence of homosexual relations did not disqualify an inmate as a candidate for parole. Now, however, when a white woman on parole "made a connection with a married woman with the result that the woman left her husband," Van Waters's staff refused to keep her at the reformatory. Labeled "hard-core," these women were now transferred to county jails to serve their additional terms without benefit of reformatory programs.[42]

These efforts to weed out hard-core lesbians did not protect the Massachusetts Reformatory for Women from further political scrutiny. In July 1957, an escapee fighting extradition claimed that alcohol, drugs, and homosexuality made her afraid to return to the reformatory. Newspapers had a field day with the ensuing investigation. "Charge Sex Fiends, Boozers Run Wild in Women's Prison" and "Girl Inmates 'Wed' in Mock Prison Rites," the headlines read. A committee chaired by a conservative woman legislator accused "aggressive homosexuals" of "escaping, assaulting officers and practicing unnatural acts!" The committee recommended greater security as well as the segregation of "aggressive homosexuals and belligerent nonconformists." Even though such activity was "not rampant" at the reformatory, the legislators argued that the "real factor to be considered here" was "not the extent but the fact that it appears to have been overlooked." They stated that "there have been mock marriages; there have been unnatural acts witnessed and reported by members of the staff, and there have been numerous indications of parolees carrying this type of activity outside the institution in association with others who had never participated in such actions before."[43]

Because these lesbians — significantly unidentified by race — were believed to corrupt other inmates and spread homosexual contagion into the broader society, officials now called for sexual, rather than racial, segregation. By 1959, after Van Waters had retired, the Massachusetts Reformatory for Women instituted a lecture on sexuality for young inmates in which a psychiatrist warned them about experimenting with lesbianism because "it is a sick way of life" and one that could never lead to happiness.[44]

AS IN THE LARGER society, in which McCarthy era campaigns identified homosexuals as the source of communist subversion and moral ruin, in the microcosm of the women's prison, the lesbian became a scapegoat for the demise of institutional order and gender propriety. The very term "women's prison" would long evoke an image of lesbian aggression. The association of lesbianism and criminality may have served as a warning to women who might be tempted to acknowledge their homosexual desires. To do so meant to lose both class and, for white women, race privilege, to descend into a criminal underworld vulnerable to the control of police and parole agents.

The prison lesbian thus represented an inverse of the ideal white woman of the 1950s, the "reprivatized" suburban housewife who served rather than challenged men.[45]

The shifting racial construction of the prison lesbian, in which the role of sexual aggressor extended from black to all working-class inmates, raises larger historical questions about race and sexuality. Although the sources reveal little about how either black or white lesbians constructed their own identities or about racial distinctions in the treatment of lesbians in prison, they do point toward a fluidity in the racial construction of sexual boundaries. After the 1940s, prostitution and promiscuity seemed less problematic for white working-class women than they had before; white unwed mothers, for example, could now be forgiven and "cured." In contrast, homosexuality among white working-class women loomed larger as a threat to social order, as evidenced by the negative portrayals of bar dykes, lesbian athletes, and prison lesbians. At the same time, for working-class black women, homosexual aggression now attracted less attention than did the newly emergent image of the black unwed mother on welfare. The literature on deviance reacted against both white women's rejection of reproductive heterosexuality (lesbianism) and black women's "excessive" reproductive activity (illegitimacy).[46]

Specific historical contexts in the postwar period can help explain this shift, including the development of penicillin, which lessened fears about prostitutes, and the increased social costs of out-of-wedlock births in light of the establishment of government aid to dependent children. The pattern of reaction, however, can be found much earlier in American history, especially during the race suicide scare at the turn of the twentieth century, when mass immigration triggered admonitions to middle-class white women to bear children lest the foreign-born dominate American society. Similarly, the shifting sexual and racial demonizations during the 1940s responded in part to the continued northern migration of blacks. In addition, wartime economic opportunities may have contributed to fears about women usurping male prerogatives, so that the aggressive white lesbian became a symbol of excessive female independence.

The representation of the prison lesbian also suggests how class became a clearer marker of sexual identity. Middle-class women who resisted the labeling of lesbianism — as did Miriam Van Waters — may have avoided social stigma for themselves and protected some of the women under their supervision. Nonetheless, the image of the aggressive female homosexual made these reformers vulnerable to political attacks that eventually weakened their moral authority and lessened their ability to protect working-class lesbians in prison. At the same time, the emergence of the malignant image of the criminal lesbian widened the class gulfs among women. Many white women who loved other women gladly claimed their race and class privilege by disassociating themselves from a category that included bar lesbians and criminals. In the process, these middle-class women often denied their own desires or insured their own social isolation. For those who did acknowledge their lesbianism, maintaining middle-class status meant rejecting any affiliation with working-class lesbians and the butch-femme roles that had been pathologized by the 1950s.[47]

It was the prison lesbian, however, who paid the highest price for the greater cultural recognition of women's sexual desires and the weakening of middle-class women's public authority. Once ignored or tolerated, the prison lesbian became a symbol of social disorder, not unlike the prostitute of an earlier period. Even as subsequent generations of middle-class women first rejected the models of criminality and sickness in favor of lesbian feminism and more recently have elaborated a subversive "outlaw" identity, women in prison have continued to suffer from the older cultural construction. Prison lesbians, a 1987 study proclaimed, are "more criminalistic, more feministic and more aggressive" than other prisoners. These stereotypes help explain why lesbians serve longer terms than nonlesbians and why prison officials continue to treat lesbians more harshly than other women. The greater vulnerability of prison lesbians is suggested, as well, by the fact that implications of lesbianism have been part of the prosecution strategy in 40 percent of the cases of women currently awaiting execution in the United States.[48] The serious consequences of the persistent conflation of lesbianism and aggressive criminality are rarely addressed by either contemporary feminists or penologists because working-class women in prison remain largely invisible in critiques of sexual injustice. Ignoring the historical construction of the aggressive female homosexual, however, allows the specter of the prison lesbian to continue to police class and sexual boundaries, both inside and outside prison walls.

9 | The Burning of Letters Continues |
Elusive Identities and the Historical Construction of Sexuality

The story behind Miriam Van Waters's burning of her personal correspondence illus-
trates the problem of interpreting sexual identities historically. Like the working-class
lesbians in prison, the administrators and staff of women's reformatories were vulner-
able to charges of sexual deviance. Long before I became her biographer, I had heard
rumors about Van Waters's personal life, so the question "Was she a lesbian?" lurked
in the background as I wrote. Each discovery of new sources contributed to my analy-
sis. When I finished the book, I wrote this essay to retrace my interpretive process. I
wanted to show not only what the evidence revealed about Van Waters but also how I
came to reframe the question of lesbian identity by breaking it into historically useful
components. This essay, more than my earlier work, acknowledges the inseparable
layers of subjective, discursive, and social meanings that constitute sexuality.

ON A CLEAR June morning in 1948, the controversial prison reformer Miriam Van Waters made a painful and momentous decision. For months, she
had been embroiled in a political struggle with conservative state officials
who wished to dismiss her as the liberal superintendent of the Massachusetts Reformatory for Women. Local newspapers headlined the claims that
Van Waters coddled prisoners, hired ex-inmates, and condoned homosexual
behavior in prison. Investigators from the Department of Corrections inter-
rogated her staff and seized inmate files as evidence.

As she sat before a glowing fireplace in her home that June morning, Van
Waters fueled the blaze with some of her most precious possessions. "The
Burning of Letters continues," she wrote in her journal that day. "One can
have no personal 'life' in this battle, so I have destroyed many letters of over

Previously published as Estelle B. Freedman, "'The Burning of Letters Continues': Elusive Identities and the Historical Construction of Sexuality," *Journal of Women's History*
9, no. 4 (Winter 1998): 181–200. © *Journal of Women's History*. Reprinted by permission
of The Johns Hopkins University Press.

22 years." Van Waters had met her patron and romantic partner, Geraldine Thompson, twenty-two years earlier. Since the late 1920s, they had corresponded almost daily, sharing their thoughts, their activities, and their love during the weeks between their regular visits with each other. All but a few of the daily letters Thompson had addressed to her "Old Sweet," her "Dearest Dearest Love," went up in flames that day. As she burned the letters, Van Waters recorded her sense of loss: "They might have been inspiration, history, joy, style—to me in 'old age.'" Instead, she resolved to keep their message within herself: "The letters are bone and sinew now in my carnage. Doubtless my character has been formed by them."[1]

As Van Waters's biographer, I felt deeply mixed emotions when I read this passage in her journal.[2] On the one hand, my empathic pain for her loss quickly turned to anger at the politicians and the society whose condemnation of love between women forced her to destroy this personally meaningful correspondence—and, in the process, prevented me from reading this significant historical evidence. On the other hand, uncovering the revelation that she had destroyed the bulk of her correspondence from Thompson provided in itself an important clue in my quest to understand Van Waters's elusive sexual identity. "The Burning of Letters" passage offered a smoking gun of sorts to explain the absence of evidence documenting the intimacy of the Van Waters–Thompson relationship. Furthermore, that threats of political scandal had prompted the burning helped confirm my interpretation of Van Waters's ordeal as a precursor of the sexual surveillance of the McCarthy era.

Van Waters's decision to destroy the record of her intimate relationship with another woman was not unique among professional women of her generation. Born in the late nineteenth century, just as the modern concept of homosexuality emerged within European and American medical literature, educated women like Van Waters bridged two eras in the social construction of sexual identity. Although they came of age in a world that still valued female intimacy, over the course of their lifetimes, romantic friendships lost the sexual innocence they had once enjoyed.[3] That so many women in public life destroyed their correspondence with close female friends or partners indicates their awareness of the process of stigmatization that took place in the early twentieth century. As a result, self-censorship—apart from familial or historical suppression of evidence—has created historical silences that speak worlds about the relationships between such women as Miriam Van Waters and Geraldine Thompson, Alice Paul and Elsie Hill, Molly Dewson and Polly Porter, M. Carey Thomas and Mamie Gwinn, and Frieda Miller and Pauline Newman, to name a few who burned all or part of their personal papers.[4]

Van Waters's conscious effort to conceal her relationship with Thompson represents only one of the many challenges I faced as a feminist biographer committed to interpreting private as well as public life. Two related problems complicated this task: evasion and contradiction within existing historical sources and the weaknesses of my own preconceived historical categories.

These problems surfaced even before I became Van Waters's biographer. Years ago, a historian who knew of my interest in women's prisons suggested that I write about Miriam Van Waters. When I seemed uninterested, he added the tantalizing comment, "She was a lesbian, you know." Although I did not undertake a biography at the time, I did become intrigued a few years later when I looked up the heading "lesbian" in the Schlesinger Library card catalog and found a lone reference to files in the Van Waters Papers. Catalog drawer in hand, I walked into the archivists' office, mentioned that someone had once told me that Miriam Van Waters was a lesbian, and asked, rather naively, "Was she?" An archivist responded — I paraphrase slightly — "We don't say that about anyone without proof." The implication, in tone and words, was that I was making an unpleasant accusation.

In retrospect, I realize that my penchant for naming and the library's reluctance to do so were equally problematic. Each of us acted upon certain assumptions about lesbian identity. My modern "lesbian feminist" impulse sought to reject what Blanche Cook has called "the historical denial of lesbianism" in favor of restoring the lesbian element to women's history, without questioning the historical meaning of the term "lesbian." Or perhaps I was unconsciously adopting Adrienne Rich's concept of a lesbian continuum, which generously labeled a range of woman-centered behaviors as lesbian.[5] The archivist, it seemed to me, adopted a modern homophobic response, seeking to protect historical subjects from accusations of identities that might have offended them (or, I suspected, her). The library's policy, I later learned, was that only self-identified lesbians would be categorized as such.

Eventually, my simplistic question "Was she a lesbian?" would evolve into a more complex inquiry into Van Waters's sexual subjectivity. By the time I made the commitment to write a biography of Van Waters, I recognized the need to historicize my own inherited categories, particularly those — such as homosexuality — that derive from modern, Western notions of the self, identity, and politics. The very category of sexual identity often rests upon concepts of a unified self and describes the consciousness of a bourgeois (male) historical actor, for whom the taken-for-granted privileges of gender, class, and frequently race permit the foregrounding of sexual subjectivity. For many women, class, race, or ethnicity may be more salient than sexuality in the formation of modern identities. Moreover, as scholars such as Earl Lewis and Dana Takagi argue, for many women and people of color, multiplicities of identities are perpetually uncertain and in flux. Whether in the case of visible ethnicity or invisible sexuality, identity categories mask the complexity of incoherent identities. Recognizing this fact, however, does not preclude the need to understand the historical construction of identities, which in practice wields significant power on the levels of both individual and social relationships. Studies of sexuality thus face a dilemma similar to those that address ethnicity: should scholars and activists discard or claim social categories that we admit to be unstable?[6]

I BELIEVE that exploring the concept of sexual identity remains a critical task for historians, despite the difficulty of pinning down our subject. Let me briefly survey the historiographical landscape to contextualize my approach. While the historical denial of homosexuality has recently given way to extensive scholarly inquiry, competing theories continue to characterize the literature. At one extreme lie essentialist notions of a transcendent "gay" identity that disregard historical and cultural specificity. These theories range from the biological/hormonal/genetic to the historical argument that "gay" people have always existed, from the Greeks to the moderns, as a unique category. At the other extreme lies a postmodernist tendency to fragment identity into a category so fluid and unstable that it threatens to return, curiously enough, to the denial with which we began. In short, we cannot study lesbians in the past because the term is too modern and limiting, too falsely universalizing, and too much a figment of discursive imagination.[7]

A middle ground, where I am most comfortable, draws on the model of social construction first articulated by the British sociologist Mary McIntosh. This account of the historical transition from homosexual acts to homosexual identities emphasizes the impact of economic and social relations within Western industrial societies. John D'Emilio and I applied elements of this model to our survey of American sexual history, arguing implicitly against theories of the discursive creation of homosexual identity by modern medical and psychiatric authorities. Rather, we suggested, within an emerging capitalist society, the separation of reproduction and heterosexuality, along with the growth of wage labor, provided economic and social spaces for the emergence of self-conscious same-sex relationships, which were then labeled homosexual. The possibilities for these relationships, outside traditional family controls, in turn made possible, and likely, the formation of gay identity and eventually modern gay politics.[8]

As feminist scholarship reminds us, however, the timing and meaning of this transition differed by gender. Trying to fit women into the (traditional)-acts-to-(capitalist)-identity model raises problems, given women's continuing reproductive responsibilities and their economic dependence within both middle- and working-class families in the nineteenth century, when this transition was occurring. Nonetheless, distinct female constructions of same-sex relationships did emerge in response to new economic roles. These included but were not limited to women who passed as men and married other women, usually associated with the working class; romantic friendships, usually associated with middle-class women; and mutual households, known as "Boston marriages," largely associated with educated women but adopted by working women as well.[9]

Only in the twentieth century, however, as the U.S. consumer culture increasingly sexualized women of all classes, did an explicitly lesbian identity emerge, first within black and white working-class cultures and later among middle-class feminists. As I have suggested elsewhere, racial and class constructions of female sexuality deeply influenced this process. Given the sexual objectification of African American and working-class women and the denial of sexual agency to middle-class white women, the lesbian label was often applied to black and working-class women who were already associated with criminality and prostitution.[10] Despite their practices of same-sex love, white middle-class women rarely claimed lesbianism as an identity before the 1940s, with the notable exception of some artists, writers, and bohemians.[11]

This social-constructionist account of the emergence of lesbian identity remains, I feel, too abstract. Its very insistence on the social, as opposed to individual, meaning of sexuality risks overlooking the fact that identity formation is in fact as much an individual as a social phenomenon. Indeed, the two are often in conflict, especially in periods of transition, when individuals raised with the sexual categories of an earlier culture partake in the social changes that redefine their behaviors. Historians too rarely acknowledge either the complications of contradictory and competing identities in their subjects or the dilemmas we face in handling elusive identities.[12]

In the interest of becoming more explicit about how historians grapple with the elusive subject of sexual identity, I want to reflect on my own process of research and interpretation by recalling three kinds of evidence that combined to shape my understanding of Miriam Van Waters's sexuality: first, what her professional writings reveal about her intellectual categories—that is, the authoritative discourses she encountered and may have internalized or modified; second, how personal sources such as letters and diaries provide clues to her subjective experience of sexuality; and third, how rumors, accusations, and assumptions enter the historical record and influence the historian. Together, these sources help explain why the burning of letters continued in Van Waters's lifetime and what it meant for her identity.

Discourses

In the early twentieth century, highly educated women such as Miriam Van Waters might have been exposed to published literature that clearly named both male and female homosexuality. Only a generation earlier, even romantic female friends and women who passed as men perceived their experiences within frameworks largely devoid of sexual references. The "female world of love and ritual" mapped by historian Carroll Smith-Rosenberg allowed same-sex attractions to "pass" as sexually innocent, whether they were or not. Beginning in the late nineteenth century, a modern conception of homosexuality emerged, articulated first as a form of gender inversion and later as an expression of erotic desire.[13] Gradually, an explicitly sexual language characterized the literature on same-sex relationships. Helen Horowitz's insightful interpretation of M. Carey Thomas provides a good example of the transition. In the 1870s, Thomas's reading of romantic and pre-Raphaelite poets afforded her an initial and asexual framework for understanding passion between women; after the 1890s, however, the Oscar Wilde trial and the availability of works by sexologists such as Richard von Krafft-Ebing allowed Thomas to name sexual acts between women. Similarly, Lisa Duggan's analysis of the Alice Mitchell trial suggests that during the 1890s the popular press helped create a complex—and contested—erotic lesbian subject, associated in part with insanity and crime.[14]

As a graduate student at Clark University between 1910 and 1913, Van Waters easily discovered the scholarly literature on sexuality. She read Havelock Ellis, Krafft-Ebing, and some Sigmund Freud, as well as the work of her adviser, psychologist G. Stanley Hall. Her own writing recognized the power of sexuality and stressed the importance of sex education and the strategy of channeling youthful energies into recreation and social service. She also became curious about gender identity and same-sex relationships, as a questionnaire she designed reveals. The survey of adolescent girls asked, for example, "Did you wish to be a boy?" and "[Was your first] love for some one you knew closely, or for some distant person . . . or for some older woman or girl friend?" A separate questionnaire for teachers asked if "crushes" between girls were "based on mutuality of interest and inclination; or are they more likely to exist between 'masculine,' and excessively 'feminine' types?"[15] The questions suggest Van Waters's interest in whether same-sex attractions correlated with gender identity, an inquiry prompted in part by Ellis's notion of sexual inversion, which associated "mannish" women with lesbianism.

Although Van Waters never conducted this survey, her intellectual curiosity about gender nonconformity and its relationship to homosexuality recurred in her doctoral dissertation, "The Adolescent Girl among Primitive People." At this time, she consciously rejected Freudian interpretations of sexuality and adopted Ellis's language of inversion — albeit without the pathological notions of deviant sexuality. Her views also reflected the cultural relativism of Franz Boas. After describing institutionalized gender-crossing among North American Indians, for example, Van Waters concluded that "among primitive peoples, a useful and appropriate life-role is commonly furnished the inverted individual. . . . It is quite possible that modern policy could profitably go to school to the primitive in this regard."[16] Similarly, in an appendix on contemporary American approaches to adolescent delinquents, Van Waters analyzed the case of a cross-dressing young woman accused of being a "white slaver" because she brought girls to her rooms at night. Reluctant to label the girl a "true homosexual," she reported that "it is impossible for her to earn an honest and adequate living while dressed as a woman" and claimed that sympathy for women of the underworld rather than sexual proclivities accounted for her behavior.[17]

During her subsequent career working in juvenile and adult female reformatories, Van Waters retained a liberal tolerance for homosexuality, even as she increasingly incorporated Freudian views of sexual psychopathology. When she discussed the management of " 'crushes' and sentimental attachment" among reformatory inmates in her 1925 book, *Youth in Conflict*, she advised that a trained social worker should draw out the girl and replace unhealthy attachments with healthy ones through a beneficial "transference." A harsher passage reflected conservative medical views of sex and gender when she labeled as the most perverse juvenile case she had encountered a narcissistic girl whose "emotional life will be self-centered or flow toward those of her own sex" and who would "never wish to live the biologically normal life."[18]

Despite these published critiques of unhealthy homosexual attachments, as superintendent of the Massachusetts Reformatory for Women in Framingham from 1932 to 1957, Miriam Van Waters consistently resisted the labeling of prison relationships as homosexual. Her liberal administration emphasized education, social welfare services, psychiatric counseling, and work opportunities outside prison for the 300 to 400 women inmates, the large majority of whom were young, white, Catholic, and working class. Although the criminological literature at the time identified black women in prison as the aggressors in interracial sexual relationships, Van Waters and her staff did not draw a racial line around prison homosexuality. Even when staff discovered two women in bed together — of any racial combination — they hesitated to label them as homosexual.

Van Waters's tolerance of prison homosexual liaisons contributed to the conservative assault on her administration in the 1940s. The commissioner of corrections who dismissed her from office charged that she had failed to recognize or prevent the "unwholesome relationship" he called the "doll racket."[19] Van Waters evaded the charge, invoking psychiatric authority to draw a distinction between a homosexual act and a possibly repressed homosexual tendency.[20] Thus, she protected the mannish women and female friends in prison without directly questioning the view of homosexuality as pathology.

In the 1950s, partly in response to her reading of the Kinsey reports and partly in the wake of accusations about prison lesbianism during her dismissal hearings, Van Waters's public lectures urged greater tolerance. Homosexuality, she explained, could be "found in all levels of society," in all types of people. Her emphasis, however, was on treatment. Once revealed through use of the Rorschach test, she believed, homosexual tendencies could be reversed with the aid of psychiatry.[21]

In short, for Miriam Van Waters, lesbianism was a curable social problem not unlike alcoholism. Although she initially encountered lesbianism among working-class, immigrant, and black reformatory inmates, she recognized that it occurred within other groups as well. Rather than emphasizing a heterosexual solution, Van Waters placed great faith in "healthy" female bonding as an alternative to lesbianism. In this sense, whether or not she had internalized modern medical categories, she strategically invoked an earlier discourse of sexually innocent and nurturing female friendships as a corrective to the increasing stigmatization of women's love for women as a form of perversion.

Evidence of Subjectivity

When Superintendent Van Waters evaded the labeling of homosexuality during her dismissal hearings, she also sidestepped implicit questions about her own sexual identity. Just as she had refused to label her long-term romantic partnership with New Jersey philanthropist Geraldine Thompson, Van Waters avoided applying the term "lesbian" to other women. She reserved the homosexual label to refer to women's pathological, though curable, sexual aggression toward other women.[22]

What of her internal consciousness of her own sexuality? The private story of Miriam Van Waters's own relationships with women both parallels and contradicts her public pronouncements. Beginning in adolescence, she fell deeply in love with other women and, for the most part, preferred their company to the attentions of male suitors. Never a sexual prude, Van Waters recognized the importance of the erotic, especially in the poetry and fiction she wrote in her late twenties. But she also placed great stock in the power of sublimation for harnessing erotic energy into expression as art, spirituality, or public service. Thus, upon reading Radclyffe Hall's *The Well of Loneliness* in 1929, Van Waters commented in her journal that had Stephen Gordon's parents been more loving, instead of becoming a lesbian, Gordon might have "run a girls camp," become a high school counselor, or supervised a juvenile protective agency, all activities remarkably similar to those Van Waters chose.[23]

The detailed introspective journals Van Waters kept as an adult provide further clues about her subjective experience of sexuality, despite the frequently coded and intentionally obscure nature of her writing.[24] Tantalizing passages in Van Waters's journals made little sense to me until late into my research, when I gained access to a cache of personal papers that had not been deposited in the archives. Literally locked away in a rusting trunk and forgotten in an attic, that cache included passionate letters from two of Van Waters's ardent admirers: one set was from Hans Weiss, a young Swiss social worker who wished to marry Van Waters; the other, a year's worth of daily letters from Geraldine Thompson, the older, wealthy, married philanthropist whose subsequent correspondence Van Waters burned in 1948. Working with both the journals and the "courtship letters," as I called them, I learned how Van Waters struggled to balance the erotic, the emotional, and the spiritual in each of these relationships.

Despite significant differences between the Weiss and Thompson correspondence — his letters were more erotic, hers more spiritual; he was more emotionally demanding, she longed to be of service to her beloved — I was struck by the consistency in Van Waters's response to her male and female suitors. In each case, she remained publicly silent, restrained in her responses to passion, and conflicted about making any lifelong commitment. The two relationships did present separate challenges to Van Waters's sexuality. The younger, less established Weiss frequently articulated his erotic longings; in response, Van Waters struggled to incorporate physical passion while subsuming it to her ideal of a spiritualized romantic friendship. The older, wealthier, and more powerful Thompson longed for "the Justice of the Peace and church bells" to signify their commitment; in response, Van Waters feared the dependency that could result from their union.[25]

In both cases, the management of passion was a recurrent theme for Miriam Van Waters. Although her journals were characteristically obscure about sexual experiences, one passage written after a visit with Weiss alluded to an unidentified young "Beloved" with whom she had experienced both a spiritual epiphany and a "yielding to love." In one entry, she recalled a candlelit scene in which her "hands were flung up by a strong clasp of young hands on my wrists — and with another soul — I plunged down a glittering waterfall immeasurably high, and sunk at last — into a pool — where two floated in weariness and content."[26] More typical, however, was her insistence on limiting their intimacy. "As a lover I yield to no one in sustained worship," she wrote in her journal. To Weiss, she explained that their spiritual union transcended the need for physical proximity, suggesting that unrequited love could yield the "deepest spiritual gain."[27] By 1930, she had successfully encouraged Weiss to wed someone else and had informed him of another unnamed attraction.

The Thompson courtship, begun during the late 1920s, overlapped with the waning of Van Waters's intimacy with Weiss. Both women valued romantic and spiritual intimacy, and neither wrote explicitly about their sexual experiences. Yet Van Waters left hints about her consciousness of lesbianism and her continuing management of erotic impulses. In 1930, she read an article about Katharine B. Davis's 1929 study of female sexuality, which found that a quarter of unmarried women college graduates acknowledged a sexual component in their intense emotional relationships with other women. Van Waters placed a star next to the statement that these were normal, not pathological, women, as if to differentiate her experience from the perversions she had earlier identified among juvenile delinquents.[28] As in her relationship with Weiss, however, Van Waters continued to place limits on erotic expression. Thus, when Thompson expressed a desire "to 'catch your soul's breath' in kisses," Van Waters questioned the impulse in her journal: "What one calls appetite — satisfaction of warmth needs — hunger needs — is not just that. . . . In maturity some times in some circumstances — to feed hunger fully — is to lose hunger. There are other ways of quenching the fire — and all must be escaped." Professionally, she had recommended channeling youthful sexual energies, whether heterosexual or homosexual. But her personal ideal suggested that desire should not only be sublimated but also could be maintained best by leaving it largely unfulfilled. While staying at Thompson's home, she again alluded to the value of control: "The secret of life is manifested in hunger — it can't safely be quenched — neither by denial, nor complete feeding, nor running away, nor escape — but by a new way."[29]

Whether or not she discovered this "new way" of managing desire, by the time she and Thompson pledged their love at the end of 1930, Van Waters recognized that she had crossed some line. "The object which arouses love — cannot be foreseen or controlled," she wrote in her journal. "All we know is — that same force which engulfs us, and makes us ready for service to husband and children — some times — to some persons — flows out to a man, woman, child, animal, 'cause,' idea." Van Waters did not, however, acknowledge her love publicly nor claim a lesbian identity. When Geraldine longed to "shout about" their love so that her family would "know what life through you is giving me," Miriam counseled discretion.[30] Similarly, when an acquaintance who lived openly with another woman later asked Van Waters in public about the ring she wore — a gift from Thompson — Van Waters seethed at the impudence of this inquiry into her private life. Perhaps her status as a civil service employee and as the guardian and later adoptive mother of a child made Van Waters more cautious than her independently wealthy partner, Thompson. Equally likely, Van Waters struggled to reconcile her passion with the psychological construction of lesbianism she had already formed.

Another cryptic journal entry suggests how powerfully that psychological construction influenced her. In a dream, she wrote, she had enjoyed a feeling of "Understanding" that derived in part from "the recent Rorshak [sic] and integration." Van Waters used the Rorschach test to detect "innate homosexuality" among inmates; in 1938, a trusted friend administered the test to her, and the results made Van Waters feel confident and optimistic. One line in this passage was crossed out heavily in pencil, especially over someone's name, but the entry continued, "Geraldine and I shall learn together."[31] In my reading, the Rorschach test proved to Van Waters that she was not an innate homosexual, thus freeing her of the deviant label and, ironically, granting her permission to integrate her love for Thompson without adopting a lesbian identity.

Rumors

Why, then, the burning of letters? Even if Van Waters did not consider herself a lesbian, the world around her was not as thoroughly convinced. Although her close associates insisted to me that the relationship was much too spiritual to have been homosexual, Van Waters's partnership with Thompson made her increasingly vulnerable to the insinuations of her political opponents.

In the conformist atmosphere after World War II, accusations of communism, often conflated with homosexuality, fueled an attack on liberalism. Thus, in 1948, claims that Van Waters tolerated homosexuality at the Massachusetts women's reformatory facilitated her dismissal from office. Aside from the widely publicized claims about the "doll racket" among inmates, rumors about Van Waters's sexuality circulated underground, though never in print. For example, Eleanor Roosevelt — a friend of Thompson's and supporter of Van Waters — learned of the whispering campaign when she received several "vile" letters that were so disturbing that she destroyed most of them. Similarly, a hostile postcard sent to supporters referred to Van Waters as "supt. (or Chief Pervert)" of the reformatory.[32] It was at this time that Van Waters burned most of Thompson's correspondence, carefully locking away only that one year of "courtship" letters.

Despite the private insinuations that led her to burn Thompson's letters, Van Waters survived the attempt to fire her. The publicity surrounding prison lesbianism during her hearings, however, contributed to a national preoccupation with homosexuality and to the naming of lesbianism as a social threat. No matter how confident Van Waters may have been that she was not a lesbian, outside observers often assumed that she was. Late in my research, after years of waiting to receive Van Waters's FBI file, I found a 1954 document that seemed to place an official government seal upon Van Waters's identity. While carrying out surveillance on Helen Bryan, a suspected communist sympathizer with whom Van Waters had a romantic friendship later in life, a local FBI informant read the correspondence between the two women. Shocked by the "unusual" nature of the letters, which contained "numerous repeated terms of endearment and other statements," he came to "the definite opinion that Dr. VAN WATERS and BRYAN are Lesbians."[33] It was to prevent just such a conclusion from being drawn that Van Waters had earlier burned Thompson's letters.

That identity formation is often a social as much as an individual phenomenon is further revealed by a final anecdote from my research on Van Waters, a coda of sorts that brings the story into the 1990s. My book completed, I turned to the task of acquiring permission to quote from sources, including Geraldine Thompson's courtship letters. With trepidation, I sent a permission form to Thompson's eldest surviving granddaughter, who soon called to discuss the request. Her initial words, "I will not grant permission," struck further terror in me, until I absorbed the rest of her sentence: "I will not grant permission to repeat any lies; I want the truth." Too much had been concealed in her family, she explained, too much smoothed over. By the end of our conversation, she had told me with confidence that her grandmother had been a lesbian and that she was sure that Thompson and Van Waters were lovers because they had shared a bed during family vacations. "Do you know what we grandchildren called Miriam when she came to visit'?" she asked. "Grammy Thompson's yum-yum." She gladly granted permission to quote when I seemed willing to reveal "the truth."[34]

I WOULD LIKE to close this retrospective account of my construction of Miriam Van Waters's sexuality with several reflections on the burning of letters. My research affirms the insights of such historians as Blanche Cook and Leila Rupp who claim that we cannot depend on either labels or direct evidence of sexual behavior to locate the subjects of lesbian history. At the same time, however, we need to be historically specific about the meaning of sexual identity. For many middle-class women of Van Waters's generation, lesbianism connoted a psychopathology that did not resonate with their experience of loving women. Rejecting the label did not mean rejecting the practice, but it did mean distancing themselves from other women — notably the working-class and African American women who were forging an explicitly erotic lesbian community in the postwar era. Class and race privilege thus took precedence over sexuality as a source of identity, especially for women in public office. Ultimately, however, even Van Waters's resistance to labeling could not prevent the public discourse on homosexuality from imposing an identity on her that seemed to be at odds with her self-understanding.

Social-construction theory emphasizes how either medical, legal, and literary discourses or economic and familial relationships create the possibilities within which individuals can act out and interpret their sexuality. One weakness of social-construction theory, however, is that as a collective argument it tends to flatten individual differences and does not account well for individual agency. Writing a biography of Miriam Van Waters allowed me to explore an individual case study of identity formed both in tandem and in conflict with the social construction of sexuality.

Van Waters came of age at a transitional moment when the social possibilities for romantic and sexual love between women increased but also when medical labeling pathologized these relationships. As an educated, professional woman exposed to such sexologists as Ellis and Freud, she was both conscious of the erotic and aware of the psychopathic label then attached to same-sex relationships. At the same time, Van Waters was attracted to women; she was able to live outside heterosexual institutions; and she could and did take advantage of the opportunity to establish a partnership with another woman, even as she fiercely resisted lesbian identification.

Perhaps the fear of losing her job and her social standing kept Van Waters from identifying as a lesbian. But her rejection of lesbianism as an identity was not merely self-serving because she just as fiercely resisted the labeling of working-class prison inmates as lesbians, and during her dismissal hearings in 1949, she more or less placed her class and race privilege on the line to defend these women from such charges. In the end, it was Van Waters's privileges —combined with her distinguished career of service and her upper-class political connections—that protected her from public disgrace. The working-class women she tried to protect would forge their own public lesbian identity, one that equally rejected the pathological discourse of the early twentieth century.

I suspect that Miriam Van Waters would have liked to live in a world that no longer existed, one in which neither labels nor stigma surrounded women's passionate relationships. To contemporary feminists who value our own historically constructed ideal of the openly lesbian sexual subject, Van Waters seems anything but progressive. Yet if we are serious about the feminist scholarly enterprise of recognizing women's historical agency, we have to be willing to accept beliefs, and possibly behaviors, that go against the grain of a "progressive" narrative that embraces categories we have claimed for ourselves. And we must keep in mind that this narrative rests heavily upon a highly class- and race-specific lesbian identity constructed since the 1960s, one that depathologized white middle-class women's love for women but simultaneously failed to recognize a range of other sources of identity.

For complex reasons, then, I think that historians must be careful not to impose upon the past identities constructed in our own times. Rather, we must read for past constructions and consider where they originated, how they changed, and how multiple layers of meaning — intellectual, emotional, and political — could influence individual identity. Miriam Van Waters's case suggests the ways that some women could simultaneously internalize, resist, manipulate, and ignore the cultural constructions of sexuality in their times. Above all, her story reminds us to look beyond our sources, to read both silences and speech, and, at times, to accept the historical integrity of elusive personal identities.

10 | When Historical Interpretation Meets Legal Advocacy | Abortion, Sodomy, and Same-Sex Marriage

On several occasions, I have been asked to speak at historical meetings about contemporary legal cases related to my scholarship on sexuality. At the American Historical Association meeting in 1989, I participated on a panel on reproductive rights entitled "Women's History in the Policy Arena"; in 2004, while the Massachusetts state legislature was deliberating gay marriage, I was asked by the Organization of American Historians to provide historical context for same-sex unions at a public session on "The Peculiar Institution of Marriage."[1] At both panels, I questioned the search for historical precedents to justify contemporary policies. In this essay, I have revised my earlier talks, along with comments on a landmark sodomy case, to rethink the role of historical interpretation in legal advocacy.

WHEN HISTORIANS craft interpretations of the past, our usual audience consists of other scholars, students, and a few interested lay readers. In the past few decades, historical expertise has attracted an expanding legal audience as well. To guide their decisions, American judges frequently invoke the phrase "history and traditions," implying that the past is critical to constitutional interpretation. To influence judicial opinions, lawyers have turned to our profession to help strengthen the historical foundations for their arguments. At least since the 1954 school desegregation case *Brown v. Board of Education*, lawyers have incorporated historians' research, and judges have increasingly used the past to elucidate constitutional meanings. As a result, historians have weighed in on a range of cases concerning contested public policies, including Native American land claims, sex discrimination in the workplace, and welfare reform.[2] In this essay, I reflect upon my own experience of collaborating with other scholars and lawyers in legal cases concerning reproductive and sexual rights.

Historians' contributions to legal advocacy take several forms. When scholars provide paid expert testimony at trials, they instruct the judge or jury on historical points relevant to the case and are subject to cross-examination by the opposing legal team. In the 1980s, for example, women's historians testified in the sex discrimination suit brought by the Equal Economic Opportunity Commission against the retailer Sears Roebuck. As that case illustrated, historical experts can serve on both sides.[3] Some historians submit affidavits, declarations, or an "offer of proof" that summarizes research relevant to a case without necessarily testifying in person. Another form of historical interpretation applied to the legal process is the friend of the court, or amicus curiae, brief filed at the appellate level. Professional and advocacy groups, such as the American Bar Association, the National Association for the Advancement of Colored People, and the American Civil Liberties Union, have submitted these briefs since the early twentieth century. Multiple amicus briefs have become common in Supreme Court cases in the past decades, including those written by academics in association with lawyers.[4] In contrast to the interrogatory format of expert testimony given by an individual witness, historians' amicus curiae briefs resemble scholarly papers, but they also depart from typical patterns of historical writing. Produced collaboratively in a short period of time, the briefs apply historical research to support particular legal claims, necessarily leaving out much of the context and complexity so valued in our craft.

As a participant in drafting several amicus briefs related to the history of sexuality, I have noticed a recurrent tension between turning to the past as precedent and interpreting the dynamics of social change. This tension reflects a broader debate among legal scholars over the merits of stressing "originalism" — the intent of the framers of the Constitution — as opposed to reinterpreting the law over time.[5] Recent legal cases concerning the right to abortion, the decriminalization of sodomy, and the legality of gay marriage illustrate these distinctions. These subjects raise questions about whether certain reproductive or sexual acts, such as abortion or homosexuality, were tolerated at the time the Constitution was written; when and why each act was criminalized; and what the implications of this history offer us as we shape current social policies. At the outset, I want to be clear that I personally support both reproductive and gay rights; the effectiveness of arguments for those rights, however, depends on maintaining a delicate balance between the use of historical precedents and the recognition of historical change.

I initially attributed the tension I noticed between arguments based primarily on precedent and those emphasizing change over time to an inherent conflict between the goals of legal advocacy and the practice of historical interpretation. I feared that historical complexity would be lost in the process of fitting evidence to legal arguments. After further collaborations on amicus briefs, I came to recognize that both lawyers and historians struggle to balance past precedents and changing historical contexts. I now believe that historians can engage in legal advocacy without oversimplifying the past, but we need to be careful about the ways we apply our interpretive tools. As I hope this essay will illustrate, our profession has a great deal to offer in elucidating the different meanings of "history and traditions," a phrase that too often treats these distinct terms as if they were identical. When historical interpretation meets legal advocacy, static interpretations of "tradition" can be enriched by exploring historical silences, contingencies, and exceptions to apply the dynamics of social change to legal arguments.

Reproductive Rights and Original Intent

The politics of abortion illustrate well the dilemmas faced by historians who engage in legal advocacy. Ever since the Supreme Court established a limited national right to abortion in *Roe v. Wade* (1973), a battle over reproductive policies has intensified in American politics. In the courts, lawyers have repeatedly turned to historical research to establish either a right to abortion or grounds for its criminalization. In the landmark 1973 decision, Justice Harry Blackmun's opinion in support of abortion rights drew on the available "medical and medical-legal history" to determine "what that history reveals about man's attitudes toward the abortion procedure."[6] Since that decision, the historical literature on abortion in America has expanded, as have legal challenges to *Roe* and the use of history in legal advocacy.

In an effort to limit the effects of *Roe*, conservative state and federal legislators imposed restrictions ranging from laws requiring parental consent for minors seeking abortions, to mandatory waiting periods, to limitations on state funding for the procedure. In the 1980s, for example, Missouri legislators banned non-life-saving abortions in public hospitals (regardless of the patient's ability to pay). In response to this law and as part of a broader legal strategy to defend *Roe*, advocates of reproductive rights challenged the constitutionality of the Missouri statute, and they turned to historians at the appellate level to support their case in *Webster v. Reproductive Health Services*.

A key actor in bringing historical research to reproductive policy, Sylvia Law, had become aware of the Supreme Court's use of history in civil rights cases. A feminist and professor of law at New York University, Law conceived of a historians' amicus brief urging the Court to reject the Missouri ban in 1988. Realizing that the government's case against abortion cited recent historical research by James Mohr, Law hoped to counter the misuse of his work. In early 1989, she convened a group of scholars with expertise on reproduction, sexuality, and social policy to help draft a brief. Once the Court agreed to hear *Webster*, a larger group of about a dozen scholars commented on successive versions of a document drafted by Law and attorneys Clyde Spillenger and Jane Larson.[7] Within two months, they produced a thirty-page brief that carefully recounted the legal status of abortion in the American colonies, the social context for its criminalization in the late nineteenth century, and the relatively recent appearance of anti-abortion arguments concerning fetal life. The brief circulated among historians, and by the time of the decision, over 400 scholars had signed it.[8]

In 1989, the Supreme Court ruled in *Webster v. Reproductive Health Services*, by a five to four vote, to uphold the Missouri law limiting access to abortion. They failed to overturn *Roe*, however, in part because Associate Justice Sandra Day O'Connor, who issued a separate concurring decision, did not join the decisions of the four other justices voting in the majority, which would have taken the case further to reconsider the issue of state protection of the fetus.[9] Although the ruling upheld restrictions on abortion, Sylvia Law concluded that the historians' brief had succeeded in "having precluded the Court from using history in a shallow and deterministic way."[10] It also set a precedent for collaborations between lawyers and historians to influence the Court.

The apparent unity of purpose among the hundreds of historians who opposed *Webster* did not necessarily imply a unity of historical interpretation. Reading the successive drafts of the brief, I often disagreed with particular arguments.[11] When I voiced my criticisms to Professor Law, she treated them with the greatest respect and incorporated most of them into revisions of the draft. While I felt satisfied enough to sign the brief and to urge others to do so, I remained intellectually frustrated by the need to simplify and the intense time deadline, which precluded careful historical debate. (The revision process seems even more impressive in retrospect since we were communicating through the mailing or faxing of hard copies rather than by e-mail.)

I had no qualms with the major argument in the historians' brief that prohibitions on abortion had been enacted only since the late nineteenth century. My chief reservations concerned the opening section of the document, which tried to establish "original intent." It is important to keep in mind the context for this approach, namely, the political and legal culture of the

1980s, when conservatives insisted on a strict originalism as a constitutional standard. Attorney General Edwin Meese, among others, was insisting that "the original intention of those who framed it would be the judicial standard in giving effect to the Constitution."[12] Even though the Constitution never mentioned abortion, opponents of the procedure argued in defense of the Missouri statute — and with an eye to overturning *Roe* — that the original intent of those who wrote the Constitution was to outlaw it. In response, those advocating the right to abortion held that the Constitution had incorporated a tolerance for abortion. In large part, they based their defense of abortion on the constitutional right to privacy and the Ninth Amendment's assurance that individuals retained all rights not specifically enumerated in the Constitution. In addition, the lawyers working on the *Webster* brief sought historical evidence to show that an implicit right to abortion existed in America at the time the Constitution was written.

It seemed to me both possible and reasonable to show that abortion before "quickening" — when a woman first felt the fetus move — had not been illegal at the time of the writing of the Constitution and had remained legal during much of the nineteenth century. I had qualms, however, about maintaining that eighteenth-century legal thought incorporated an implicit right to abortion. More generally, I worried about seeking an eighteenth-century constitutional justification for twentieth-century social needs. For one thing, I felt that historical studies, building on modern constitutional theory, should illuminate the ways in which the law has responded to historical change, not simply the ways that historical precedents justify a particular legal interpretation. The original-intent argument, however, was a strategic response to the static argument of opponents of *Roe* that "unmitigated hostility" to abortion ran throughout our history. Although that statement was deeply flawed, I remained uncomfortable about refuting one static historical interpretation with another. Having to rely on less than definitive evidence — such as the silence about abortion in the Constitution and assumptions about its use in the eighteenth century — in order to make a case for either unmitigated tolerance or unmitigated hostility meant overlooking more nuanced interpretations of the changing meaning of family limitation over the course of U.S. history.

In *Webster*, the original-intent argument appeared most boldly in the first draft of the historians' brief. The title of Argument II read, "For the original constitutional framers abortion was an unremarkable and legitimate part of the fabric of ordinary social life." During the drafting of the amicus brief, I took issue with that statement, and the revised title read, "At the time the federal constitution was adopted, abortion was known and not illegal." Nonetheless, the text claimed that "abortion was not uncommon in colonial America." As evidence, the brief called midwives' prescriptions of abortifacients "routine." It also stated that in the 1780s, "at the same time our founders drafted the Constitution, including the Ninth Amendment's guarantee [of unenumerated rights] . . . the use of birth control and abortion increased" (8).

Despite evidence about the use of abortifacients in the colonial era, I would hesitate to argue that abortion was "not uncommon," given the strong economic and religious motives for childbearing within families. In the colonial era, most families relied on neither contraception nor abortion because they hoped to procreate, whether for economic or religious reasons. Moreover, both sermons and court cases condemned not only nonprocreative sexual practices (such as masturbation, bestiality, and sodomy) but also efforts to destroy the fruits of sexual intercourse. The most widely used means to do so, according to court cases, was infanticide, probably more effective than the herbal abortifacients used at the time. Single rather than married women had the strongest reasons for resorting to infanticide. Despite individual efforts to avoid pregnancy, however, the high fertility rates of over eight children per married woman suggest that in seventeenth- and eighteenth-century America, women did not rely on abortion to limit family size. Yet the brief juxtaposed the falling birth rates in the 1780s with the statement that "at the same time our founders drafted the Constitution, including the Ninth Amendment's guarantee that the enumeration of certain rights 'shall not be construed to deny or disparage others retained by the people,' the use of birth control and abortion increased" (7–8).

Behind that statement lies a more complex history. The demographic record reveals that even though pre- and extramarital sexual activity did increase in the late eighteenth century, the rise of both "early marriages" (bridal pregnancies) and illegitimate births suggests — by the very nature of the evidence — that sexually active unmarried couples did *not* use abortion. They married precisely because of pregnancy. At the end of the eighteenth century, marital fertility rates did begin their long-term decline, but it was too limited at the time of the constitutional convention to indicate any widespread use of abortion. In short, at the time of the framing of the Constitution, abortion was not subject to public debate in large part because economic and social conditions — particularly the centrality of reproductive family life — discouraged its use. Given this history, the founders may well have ignored, rather than accepted, abortion.

Over time, however, these conditions would change, making abortion more widespread and increasingly controversial. As the historians' brief explained, in the nineteenth century, a growing commercial and industrial economy encouraged smaller family size, which necessitated greater efforts to limit births. Along with contraceptive use, reliance on abortions increased, especially, James Mohr has shown, among married women.[13] By 1900, average marital fertility rates fell to around four children (although the decline occurred later and more slowly among rural, immigrant, and African American families). The brief synthesized historians' arguments that the criminalization of abortion in the late nineteenth century represented, along with a consolidation of medical authority, a response to a constellation of fears about white middle-class women's rejection of motherhood. By the next century, fears about racially imbalanced birth rates contributed to the charge of "race suicide" leveled at elite white women.

During the century of criminalization, contraception and abortion did not disappear; they largely went underground, often at great personal risk to women and to some providers. Both practices would resurface in public view because of historical changes in the nature of work and family. Over the twentieth century, family limitation became more widespread, abetted by the birth control movement and necessitated by married women of all races entering the wage labor force. Women's reproductive and economic choices went hand in hand. By the 1960s, the growth of dual wage-earning families who desired to limit and space births paralleled a shift in medical and legal support for decriminalizing abortion. Women's changing roles as workers and mothers thus help explain the road to *Roe*; they also framed the initial opposition. Early anti-abortion activists mobilized women whose identities remained rooted in motherhood. Long before they employed claims about the personhood of the fetus, critics of abortion echoed nineteenth-century rhetoric about the value of maternity to American cultural stability.[14]

Given this historical framework, I wanted the *Webster* brief to argue more centrally that women needed reproductive choice in the late twentieth century not because of similarities with women in the eighteenth century but precisely because our lives differ from those of our forerunners, despite our shared reproductive vulnerability. The brief did in fact document the changing context of abortion law, and I agreed with those sections of it. I nonetheless questioned the overall strategy of relying so heavily on historic rights because this approach did not represent the full range of historical or political arguments. Aside from my qualms about the representation of late-eighteenth-century practices, it seemed evasive to claim abortion as an implicit original right without acknowledging, as Linda Gordon's scholarship has shown, that late-nineteenth-century women's rights advocates condemned the practice. For them, abortion symbolized an undue burden on women, who alone paid the price of unwanted pregnancies. Although the brief cited Gordon's analysis of "voluntary motherhood," it ignored the feminist opposition to abortion. Recently, however, this history has been used by some opponents of abortion as a precedent for their cause. In invoking this history, they adopt a static interpretation of feminism, ignoring the economic and political disparities that led earlier activists to insist on the fusion of reproduction and sexuality.[15]

A related political weakness in seeking original, implicit rights to abortion is highlighted by contemporary feminist critiques of reliance on a language of rights that reinforces individual, as opposed to social, responsibility for reproduction in order to defend reproductive choice. By accepting this "right," we overlook the reasons why women need access to abortion, including inadequate contraceptive methods and research, unequal economic opportunities, and the lack of social services for mothers and children. All of these gender-based inequalities make childbearing and economic self-sufficiency incompatible for women. By arguing for abortion on the grounds of the right to privacy, I felt, the historians' amicus brief in *Webster* necessarily oversimplified a range of theoretical (and practical) justifications for abortion and neglected a range of related political issues. It had to adopt a liberal feminist politics, emphasizing rights without reconsidering the historical changes, such as wage earning, that have made reproductive choices even more problematic than in the past for many women.[16]

Working on this brief complicated my notion of a usable past. Citing historical research to justify a legal interpretation can imply that past practice is more salient than current needs. This privileging of the past can be and often has been used for conservative ends, and the reverse — that change is more salient than historical precedent — may also be the case. Some elements of abortion history do provide telling precedents for current politics, though often as negative rather than positive models. For example, the history of abortion law illustrates how sex and reproduction have been manipulated politically, as both Mohr and Gordon have shown — whether to advance the authority of medical professionals or to justify state-sponsored eugenic projects that targeted African Americans, Native Americans, and Mexican Americans as well as the disabled. Learning from this history of sexual politics cautions us to be more careful as we reformulate reproductive rights. We should seek to make our policies undermine rather than reinforce hierarchies of class, race, and gender. Along with such critical explorations of past practice, I felt strongly after the *Webster* brief, we need to foreground the changing social contexts in which we adjudicate the regulation of sexuality and reproduction.

Sodomy Laws, Tradition, and Social Change

My concerns about the role of historical interpretation in legal advocacy resurfaced in later court cases concerning homosexuality. Just as the opponents of abortion had claimed long-standing hostility to the practice, the Supreme Court in *Bowers v. Hardwick* (1986) based its support for state antisodomy laws on the "ancient roots" of state regulation of homosexual conduct. That decision, which helped justify a range of discriminatory practices against homosexuals, stood until 2003, when the Court heard the case of *Lawrence v. Texas*, which challenged a state prohibition on sodomy for homosexual but not heterosexual acts. *Lawrence* provided a critical opportunity for the Supreme Court to reconsider *Bowers*, and once again, a group of historians collaborated to produce an amicus brief.

In this case, a historian, University of Chicago professor George Chauncey, drafted the document at the request of Lambda Legal Defense, a gay rights organization, and in collaboration with several private attorneys working pro bono. The deadline was even tighter than with *Webster*. Within two weeks, Chauncey prepared at least three full drafts, circulating each to a small group of scholars. Six of us offered substantive revisions and contributed historical evidence, and nine scholars signed the final brief.[17] As with *Webster*, I raised questions about the framing of the argument and the use of evidence, and Chauncey incorporated into the brief most of my suggestions and those of other signers. Successive drafts refined the central arguments about the relation of the modern concept of homosexual identity to the historical enforcement of sodomy laws. Some of my concerns — such as introducing the broader context of the regulation of sexuality — could not be fully addressed in the thirty-page brief. Chauncey shared my concern, but as he explained at the time, "it gets really complicated when we try to boil this sort of argument down for this short and consequential a brief."[18] After reading the drafts of amicus briefs being prepared by the Cato Institute and the American Civil Liberties Union, which addressed more fully the history of sodomy law, I felt reassured about our decision to focus more heavily on the history of homosexual identity.

As in the *Webster* case, the historians' brief in *Lawrence* had to take into account both legal precedents concerning homosexuality and changing social attitudes. For the most part, in response to the static historical logic in *Bowers*, the historians emphasized change over time rather than tradition. It would have been a much harder task to claim implicit sexual rights than in the *Webster* case, given the explicit antisodomy laws in early America. Rather, the historians' brief in *Lawrence* highlighted changing constructions of and attitudes toward homosexuality. Distilling a generation of scholarship, the brief explained that although a range of nonprocreative sodomitic acts—between men and women, men and men, and humans and animals—had been proscribed in colonial America, these laws had not singled out "homosexual sodomy." Indeed, the term "homosexuality," referring to a distinct identity, did not appear until the late nineteenth century.

But the document also created its own version of originalism when it presented an alternative legal tradition to counter the "unmitigated hostility" claimed in *Bowers*, which had held that "homosexual conduct" had been subject to state regulation "throughout the history of Western civilization." To show that there had been no continuous tradition of singling out gay sex as illegitimate, the *Lawrence* brief cited biblical and medieval texts that applied the terms "sodomy" and "unnatural acts" "inconsistently to a diverse group of nonprocreative sexual practices" that could include sex "in the wrong position or with contraceptive intent" (5). For colonial and nineteenth-century America, the brief used legal sources to document an early focus on bestiality, buggery, and other nonprocreative acts rather than "homosexual conduct." The Texas ban on homosexual sodomy, it argued, could not be justified in terms of long-term historical precedent.

The brief went on to show that laws specifically penalizing homosexuals—as opposed to a broader category of nonreproductive sexual acts—were largely a product of the late twentieth century and not the original intent of the framers of the Constitution. Rejecting the logic of *Bowers*, the brief proclaimed that "the specification of 'homosexual sodomy' as a criminal offense does not carry the pedigree of the ages but is almost exclusively an invention of the recent past" (4). In short, the broad proscription on all nonprocreative acts that dominated colonial laws eventually narrowed to target a relatively new class of individuals—homosexuals. The brief thus applied a version of original intent in reference not to the framers of the Constitution but to the popular construction of sexual categories in early America. Homosexuality per se had not been condemned in the eighteenth century, it argued, since it had not yet been constructed as a sexual category. Rather than claiming an implicit "right" or even a degree of tolerance, the brief suggested a "relative indifference" to sodomy among authorities in the early republic.

Despite this reliance on tradition, a dominant interpretation in this brief concerned the changing historical applications of sodomy laws, which had "varied in content over time." In response to the growing visibility of lesbian and gay subcultures in the twentieth century, the discriminatory impact of these laws had intensified. As a generation of scholars has shown, heightened state prosecution accompanied this new visibility, particularly from the 1930s through the 1960s. That era of "public hysteria," however, should not be read backward ahistorically as a static hostility that could be used to justify laws directed solely at homosexual behavior.

The brief in *Lawrence* emphasized historical change in other ways as well. It showed how the movement of women into the wage labor force and full citizenship contributed to undermining older medical views of lesbians in the early twentieth century. The brief documented an important shift from a period of escalating persecution of homosexuals after World War II to one of growing public tolerance in media and law since the 1970s. These contexts helped explain why the psychiatric profession eventually removed homosexuality from its diagnostic list of pathologies. In sum, change over time rather than original intent required the removal of discriminatory statutes such as the Texas law at issue in this case.

In the process of revising successive drafts of the brief and despite extremely tight time constraints, our dialogue over sources and interpretations was greatly facilitated by e-mail, which had not been available during the *Webster* case. As in that earlier brief, however, time and space constraints meant that it was not possible to do justice to all of the perspectives that historical writing would consider. For example, in documenting the era of intensified prosecution, we could only allude to the broader historical context of American sex panics, which periodically targeted groups such as prostitutes and homosexuals in antivice crusades. Another theme that we could only suggest but that influenced the Court's decision concerned the changing application of sodomy laws: Had they initially been used primarily to prosecute *nonconsensual* sexual relations, either between men and men or between men and boys, since rape laws explicitly covered only heterosexual relations?[19] If so, the application of sodomy laws may have broadened in the twentieth century, effectively criminalizing once-tolerated same-sex consensual relations.

Finally, in pointing to a decline in hostility toward homosexuality since the 1970s, the historians' brief may have been overly sanguine. To claim that "in the last decade, the acceptance of lesbian and gay men as full and equal members of our society has become commonplace" (26) certainly resonates with the experience of living in San Francisco, Los Angeles, or New York. The marketing of queer and lesbian subjects in the national media notwithstanding, I suspect that on the subject of homosexual rights, the battle for public opinion will continue for some time into the future. The brief did acknowledge the persistence of discriminatory laws — the Texas statute among them — but it concluded that such laws "hold no legitimate place in our Nation's traditions" (29). It may be formulaic to invoke tradition in these constitutional cases, but in *Lawrence*, perhaps more so than in *Webster*, historians had to counterbalance arguments based on "tradition" with a reliance on social change in order to justify a decision that would overturn discriminatory laws against gay sexual practices.

On 26 June 2003, by a six to three majority, the Supreme Court ruled that the Texas statute against homosexual sodomy violated the due process clause and was thus unconstitutional.[20] The decision, which overturned *Bowers*, stated that the Constitution provides individuals, including homosexuals, the right to choose their personal relationships "without being punished as criminals" (2) and to engage in consensual sexual practices "without intervention of the government" (18). One section of the decision drew directly from the historians' brief to correct the erroneous interpretation of the "ancient roots" of hostility to homosexuality. The majority opinion, written by Associate Justice Anthony Kennedy, stated, for example, that "there is no longstanding history in this country of laws directed at homosexual conduct as a distinct matter" (7). Quoting *Intimate Matters*, it affirmed that "the modern terms *homosexuality* and *heterosexuality* do not apply to an era that had not yet articulated these distinctions" (8).

I could not have been more pleased with this use of historical interpretations and of my own work to support legal change. I also felt that the decision as a whole endorsed historical process over precedent. In the closing paragraph of the decision, Justice Kennedy commented on those who had written and ratified the due process clause in the Fifth and Fourteenth Amendments: "They knew times can blind us to certain truths and later generations can see that laws once thought necessary and proper in fact serve only to oppress. As the Constitution endures, persons in every generation can invoke its principles in their own search for greater freedom" (18). It is this principle that can make historical interpretation so central to the process of legal change.

Gay Marriage: Precedents, Alternatives, and Politics

In his dissent from the *Lawrence* decision, Associate Justice Antonin Scalia predicted that overturning *Bowers* left "shaky grounds" for state opposition to same-sex marriage. At the time, I doubted that Scalia's fears about gay marriage would soon materialize. Thus, the speed with which same-sex marriage gathered momentum in the United States surprised me. Marriage in Canada or Denmark or civil unions in France all seemed far more predictable. In November 2003, however, when the Supreme Judicial Court of Massachusetts in *Goodridge v. Department of Public Health* ruled in favor of same-sex couples seeking to marry, its decision unleashed long-pent-up demands for state recognition of same-sex unions, and not merely in the guise of the civil unions instituted in Vermont in 2002. Although the Massachusetts court gave the state legislature six months to respond to the decision, lesbians, gay men, and their straight allies on both coasts acted in advance of the law. Even in my progressive hometown of San Francisco, I had never expected to witness thousands of couples seeking marriage licenses, accompanied by dozens of city officials, all willing to engage in civil disobedience to facilitate the gay and lesbian weddings that took place in early 2004.

Political battle lines over gay marriage soon formed, and as with abortion and sodomy law, historical research contributed to the ensuing legal cases. Dozens of historians testified, consulted with lawyers, and signed amicus briefs in cases in New York, New Jersey, Oregon, Washington, and California. Historians of marriage such as Nancy Cott have been deeply involved in drafting some of the arguments, and I have signed several of these briefs.[21] While I both support and seek the extension of full legal rights to lesbians and gay men, I want to acknowledge that my personal response to the exuberance about same-sex marriage parallels my ambivalence about the legitimation of homosexuals in the military — that is, I oppose legal exclusion of gays and lesbians from these institutions, but I would also resist compulsory enlistment in either of them, whether through informal social pressures to marry or a formal military draft. For the historian, though, the gay-marriage cases provide another window on how to balance tradition and social change when legal advocates turn to the past.

Both precedent and change in American history can inform the legal debates about gay marriage. From the standpoint of precedent, even though religion, law, and public opinion have long defined marriage as a heterosexual institution, we can find social-historical examples to support an alternative tradition of same-sex unions. However, seeking one kind of precedent can obscure other traditions, including opposition to marriage itself. A second and stronger use of historical research asks what social changes have enabled gay marriage to become a possibility at this time in our history.

The arguments from past precedents, while exceptional, attest to historical variations in family forms. Long before the current wave of civil unions and weddings, Americans formed same-sex, extralegal partnerships that included common domicile, financial interdependence, sexual relations, and sometimes parenting. In one manifestation, men and women who crossed genders might live with same-sex partners. For example, some Native American men who felt or dreamed that their true identity was female could wear women's clothes, work at women's tasks, and become the wives of men. Among the Mohave, women who crossed genders could acquire wives themselves, establish households, and raise children (either adopted or from a wife's previous union).[22] Although not culturally institutionalized, gender crossing sometimes occurred among Anglo settlers in the nineteenth-century West, such as "Mrs. Nash," a man who married several soldiers. In the nineteenth century, as well, newspapers frequently published reports of women who passed as men, often to earn wages, and some of whom married women. In upstate New York, Lucy Ann Lobdell became Reverend Joseph Lobdell and lived for a decade with his wife, Maria Perry. In the twentieth century, some women continued to adopt male identity and to create families with other women. Thus, midwestern jazz musician Billy Tipton, born a woman, married several times and raised children who did not know until his death that their father was a woman.[23]

Men and women who retained their gender identity also established marriagelike relationships in the era before homosexual identity. They exchanged rings or set up common domicile, such as the "Boston marriages" named for the city in which many educated women paired off at the turn of the twentieth century. These women often owned property jointly, planned their travels together, shared family celebrations, and usually slept in the same bed.[24] Cultural assumptions of asexuality tended to protect respectable female couples from scandal. In the early twentieth century, however, male lifelong companions, such as Harvard professor F. O. Matthiessen and his lover Russell Cheney, could not escape the increasing stigma associated with homosexuality; Matthiessen eventually committed suicide. As gay and lesbian subcultures formed in large cities in the twentieth century, opportunities for same-sex unions expanded along with explicit sexual identities.

Among lesbians, working-class "butch-femme" couples often paired off and at least some "married." In Harlem during the 1920s, African American lesbians staged large weddings, complete with bridesmaids and even marriage licenses (after a gay man applied at City Hall as the surrogate for a lesbian "groom").[25] By the 1950s, a growing gay bar culture in American cities provided public space for butch-femme couples to meet, and many of them subsequently lived together.

Invoking these precedents of same-sex unions, however, raises serious historical problems for legal advocates of gay marriage. For one thing, while these practices imitated marriage, most Americans who acknowledged same-sex erotic desires could not participate in them. Aside from being exceptional, these precedents tend to conflate a range of practices over time under the rubric of "marriage." In contrast to the strategy in the *Lawrence* brief, which distinguished between earlier and contemporary constructions, the search for same-sex unions in the past blurs distinctions in order to emphasize continuities. Unlike the logic in the *Lawrence* brief, too, these precedents rely on an anachronistic, ahistorical definition of gay or homosexual, conflating distinctive identities for political purposes. Perhaps for these reasons, historians have not elaborated on precedents for same-sex unions in the amicus briefs concerning gay marriage.

Another problem with searching for precedents to support a tradition of gay unions is the risk of overlooking other precedents that complicate the meaning of marriage and challenge its historical hegemony. In the past, for example, some heterosexuals have ignored, resisted, or questioned marriage as an institution. Not all heterosexual couples formally married. During the nineteenth century, African American slaves who wished to wed could not do so legally. In the southern backcountry, informal marriage was common. For some urban working-class couples, common-law marriage sufficed.[26] Utopians living in communities such as John Humphrey Noyes's Oneida experimented with forms of group marriage. Free-love advocates, including Frances Wright, rejected state-sanctioned marriage on principle because it inhibited individuals. "Free love" referred not to sex with multiple partners but to the belief that love rather than marriage should be the precondition for sexual relations. In his 1852 tract, *Love vs. Marriage*, Marx Edgeworth Lazarus argued that just as the state thwarted the individual, the "legalized prostitution" of marriage oppressed women and suppressed love. Highly unpopular, free lovers risked arrest for expressing their beliefs. In 1887, for example, when Lillian Harmon "married" Edwin Walker without blessing of church or state, both were imprisoned in Kansas for violating the marriage act by living together as man and wife without having been legally married.[27]

Although they pioneered what would later become the practice of cohabitation, free lovers shared many values with their legally married contemporaries. They formed long-term committed relationships, and most of them condemned homosexual relations as unnatural. By the early twentieth century, anarchist and free lover Emma Goldman reversed the latter judgment by endorsing love in any form, but she still rejected church or state regulation. Even those bohemians and radicals who objected to monogamy often remained deeply rooted in the values of romantic unions, struggling with the jealousies that could erupt when they embraced open relationships. Despite this history of isolated efforts to circumvent marital laws, the institution of marriage has remained a widespread and privileged site for heterosexual unions.

The current historians' amicus briefs in support of gay marriage largely ignore precedents of past gay unions and prior challenges to state-sanctioned marriage. Instead, they concentrate on the historical transformation of marriage in American culture that has been well documented in recent scholarship. At least three measures illustrate this history. First, reproduction is no longer a primary function throughout the life of a marriage. Average marital fertility rates have fallen from almost eight births in 1800 to around two births in 2000; parents now live longer after children are grown; and many more couples choose to remain childless, even with the availability of technologically assisted reproduction. Second, as marriage has become a route to personal happiness and women have gained greater economic leverage, both partners feel freer to exit. Longer lives, fewer children, and the goal of happiness have all fueled the divorce rates; almost as many marriages end as survive. Rather than forming lifelong unions, most heterosexual couples now practice a form of serial monogamy. Third, the state's role in privileging marriage has expanded because federal benefits (social security, inheritance, immigration, taxes) flow through this institution.[28]

While opponents of gay marriage cite the tradition of heterosexual unions, the recent historians' amicus briefs counter by emphasizing the malleability of marriage over time. In particular, they note the shedding of many of the patriarchal trappings of wifely obedience in favor of a modern, companionate model of marriage. For example, the brief of history scholars in a 2005 Washington State gay-marriage case challenged the "traditional definition of marriage" by pointing out that "far from being a rigid institution with a fixed definition, marriage is, and has always been, evolving in response to social and cultural change."[29] Similarly, the "Brief of Professors of History and Family Law" in *Samuels et al. v. The New York State Department of Health*, a 2005 case before the New York State Supreme Court, described the history of marriage as "a history of change." To support the point that marriage law has never been static, both briefs recalled the decline of the principle of coverture in favor of a wife's independent legal identity in the nineteenth century; the latter brief also cited, among other legal changes, the rejection of the marital rape exemption in the 1980s.[30]

In addition to the shift from patriarchal to companionate marriage, the civil rights movement provides historical context for gay-marriage cases. Recent efforts to legalize same-sex unions parallel earlier claims made by members of minority groups who sought full citizenship through the transformation of marriage law, particularly by challenging prohibitions on interracial marriage. Overturning state "antimiscegenation" statutes took decades, with key decisions in California in 1948 (*Perez v. Sharp*) and by the U.S. Supreme Court in 1967 (*Loving v. Virginia*). In *Goodridge*, the Massachusetts Supreme Court cited this history:

> In this case, as in Perez and Loving, a statute deprives individuals of access to an institution of fundamental legal, personal, and social significance — the institution of marriage — because of a single trait: skin color in Perez and Loving, sexual orientation here. As it did in Perez and Loving, history must yield to a more fully developed understanding of the invidious quality of the discrimination.[31]

Similarly, the Washington State amicus brief addressed the relationship between racial equality and marital equality, noting that while "expanding the freedom to choose one's partner without regard to race was a fundamental change," the institution of marriage survived the demise of antimiscegenation statutes.[32]

By concentrating on arguments about what might be called a tradition of legal change, the historians' amicus briefs have not addressed several broader contexts that help explain the current demands for same-sex marriage. While heterosexual marriage has changed in law and practice, the campaign for gay marriage would not have gathered legal momentum without significant transformation in same-sex partnerships as well. Once relegated to a shadowy cultural margin, since the 1970s, gay communities have increasingly replaced the closet with public visibility. The sexualization of women in modern America, which removed the mask that once protected romantic friends, enabled the formation of openly lesbian partnerships. For men who could once pursue only anonymous, furtive sex, an openly gay culture led not only to the open celebration of pleasure but also to the search for life partners. For both women and men, webs of fictive kin relations help sustain gay identity and community, including former partners who become family and coparents who raise their nonbiological children with friends and lovers. As more lesbian and gay couples began to live together openly in committed relationships, they sought legal protection unavailable to unmarried partners.

The explosion of lesbian and gay social worlds, however, is not sufficient to explain the recent quest for marriage. Throughout the 1970s and 1980s, most lesbian and gay activists were more likely to criticize the institution for its patriarchal heritage than for its exclusivity. I would argue that since the 1980s, both the AIDS crisis and the expansion of gay parenting made legal marriage a more pressing issue. In the wake of the epidemic, political lines diverged over the critique of anonymous sex, with some activists defending an alternative sexual subculture and others calling for more committed marriagelike relationships. More important, life partners who served as caretakers encountered unacceptable limits on hospital visitation and authority to determine medical procedures; some could not inherit property they had helped purchase.

In the same era, gay parenting expanded. Since the 1960s, individual lesbians and gay men have appeared in courts to retain custody of or visitation rights to children born in prior heterosexual marriages. Increasingly, however, parenting in same-sex relationships has become a matter of choice, given the opportunities afforded by artificial insemination, surrogacy, and adoption. The resultant "gay-by boom" that began in the 1980s and has gathered force in the past decade has added another level of similarity between contemporary same-sex and opposite-sex families. Like the personal response to AIDS, parenting has unleashed a demand for greater legal protections, including second-partner adoption. Judicial victories by lesbian and gay parents have in turn paved the way for the gay-marriage movement.[33]

In short, marriage and homosexuality, once viewed as diametrically opposed, have increasingly converged in recent American history. Marriage is no longer the sole venue for caring, sexual, and reproductive partnerships, nor is it a lifelong or primarily reproductive institution for most Americans. Many heterosexuals still form permanent unions and raise children, but so do lesbians and gay men; the latter, however, do so without protections granted their heterosexual counterparts. Thus, since the 1970s, same-sex couples have appeared in state courts to obtain marital rights. Religious commitment ceremonies, "gay weddings," domestic partnerships, and, in recent years, civil unions and legally defiant marriage licenses are all responses to demands for public recognition and legal protection.[34]

So, too, the gay movement has had to respond. Although reluctant to support gay-marriage cases through the 1980s, groups such as Lambda Legal Defense have joined the quest for recognition. New organizations focus solely on the right to marry, buoyed by the decriminalization of sodomy in *Lawrence v. Texas* and the legalization of same-sex partnerships in parts of Europe and Canada. Even those who do not wish to marry have been forced to take a stand in solidarity with those who do, particularly in the face of legislation such as the Defense of Marriage Act (1996) and the proposed constitutional amendment to limit marriage to a man and a woman.[35]

In the rush to expand or contract access to marriage, however, we should not forget the radical critique launched by free lovers and anarchists and echoed by radical feminists, gay liberationists, and queer activists. Given conservative opposition to same-sex marriage, it has become politically awkward for liberals to question the importance of gay marriage. Yet some critics, such as historian Lisa Duggan, ask what alternatives we ignore by focusing solely on marriage. Why not establish social benefits for all forms of caring relations — or for all individuals — rather than privileging marital unions?[36] Members of the far left and the far right find some common ground in the concept of civil unions, albeit for slightly different political reasons. Radical critics recommend civil unions for all, separating the religious institution of marriage from state regulation. Some conservatives who desire to preserve for heterosexuals the symbolic sanctity of the term "marriage," along with at least some of its benefits, have begun to cede ground to once-radical civil unions, even as they seek to outlaw gay marriage federally.

Now that the first court-mandated same-sex marriages have taken place in Massachusetts, popular opinion, which continues to oppose legalized same-sex unions, may either polarize or adapt, depending in large part on how politicians exploit the issue (as the 2004 elections illustrated well). Historians do best explaining the past, not predicting the future. But it is tempting to extrapolate from the admittedly uneven comparison with race. Like the Supreme Court in *Brown*, which mandated integrated schools, and in *Loving*, which legalized interracial marriage, the Massachusetts court ruled in *Goodridge* to redress an inequality at a time when most Americans opposed the practice that the decision legalized. Just as civil rights leaders once hesitated to press for interracial marriage, many lesbians and gay men have mixed feelings about both marriage as a political priority and the costs of conservative backlash.[37] Nonetheless, these prior rulings did encourage gradual shifts in public opinion. And as in the civil rights movement, the sight of thousands of protesters — such as the same-sex couples lined up around San Francisco's City Hall — can affect national sentiment. In the end, far more than any precedents from the past, it will be couples like these who will determine the next chapter in the history of marriage.

In the meantime, historians continue to weigh in on the question of gay marriage, both as expert witnesses and in amicus briefs. What characterizes their contributions thus far is the interpretation that marriage has evolved as an institution, both socially and legally. One of the New York briefs, in distinguishing between "history as description and history as justification for discrimination," summarized well the limitations of legal tradition: "The history of the exclusion of same-sex couples from marriage describes but does not explain or justify the continuation of that rule."[38] At times, these arguments prevail, as when the San Francisco Superior Court ruled in 2005 that the California Family Code's definition of a valid marriage as a "union between a man and a woman" violated the state constitution because that document allowed that "the legislative embodiment of history, culture and tradition is constitutionally permissible" only when an "underlying rational basis" justifies the law. Just as the 1948 California Supreme Court decision in *Perez* overturned the state's ban on interracial marriage because of its irrational basis, and in light of the *Lawrence* ruling, the San Francisco court ruled that a tradition of past discrimination alone could not justify a ban on gay marriage.[39] Other courts, however, have overruled decisions based on these grounds, and the verdict is far from clear, even in liberal states like California and New York.

I HOPE THESE reflections on the role of historical interpretation in cases concerning sexuality and reproduction have complicated the meaning of "history and traditions" in legal advocacy. At times, historians have supplied precedents of past practices, from abortifacients to same-sex unions; at other times, historians have insisted on distinguishing between past and present constructions of sexuality, including the shift from sodomy to homosexual identity. Historians have balanced tradition and history differently in each of the legal issues I have reviewed. The *Webster* brief, submitted during the Reagan administration, relied more heavily on original intent, seeking precedents of original tolerance in support of reproductive rights, a strategy grounded in the absence of anti-abortion statutes at the time the

Constitution was written. In *Lawrence*, historians applied both precedent and change. While educating the Court about the changing definition of sodomy and the recent appearance of homosexuality as an identity, their brief, as was the case in *Webster*, appealed to a past marked by relative tolerance toward behaviors not yet specifically criminalized. Not surprisingly, given the weight of legal precedent in favor of opposite-sex unions, the current historical arguments in support of gay marriage foreground the past malleability of legal definitions of marriage.

In working on cases in which the history of sexuality can inform contemporary policies, historians clearly have more to offer to legal advocacy than mere precedents. We bring layers of interpretation, revealing how economic, demographic, and social changes require new public policies. Only some of these analyses may be useful within the parameters of specific legal arguments. But as historians continue to collaborate with lawyers, I hope we can challenge any static view of "history and traditions." Traditions may well guide us, whether in the form of legal precedents or social practices, but history is at heart a study of change. One of our most important jobs as historians may be to educate not only our students but also judges, juries, and policymakers about that dynamic process.

Notes

Introduction. Identities, Values, and Inquiries: A Personal History

1. Virginia Woolf, *Three Guineas* (1938; reprint, New York: Harcourt Brace Jovanovich, 1966), 66.

2. Linda K. Kerber, *Toward an Intellectual History of Women* (Chapel Hill: University of North Carolina Press, 1997), 12.

3. These essays later appeared as *Radical Feminism*, edited by Anne Koedt, Ellen Levine, and Anita Rapone (New York: Quadrangle, 1973).

4. Taking a noncredit course offered by Columbia University professor Seymour Melman on "The Peace Budget" deeply affected my political outlook and made me more receptive to the antiwar movement.

5. Estelle B. Freedman, "The New Woman: Changing Views of Women in the 1920s," *Journal of American History* 61 (September 1974): 372–93. I remain grateful to Professor John Garraty for recommending that I submit this seminar paper to the journal at a time when I knew nothing about publishing.

6. I first developed my analysis in "Their Sisters' Keepers: An Historical Perspective on Female Correctional Institutions in America, 1870–1900," *Feminist Studies* 2, no. 1 (1974): 77–95, and later published a revised version of my dissertation, *Their Sisters' Keepers: Women's Prison Reform in America, 1830–1930* (Ann Arbor: University of Michigan Press, 1981). The book manuscript won the 1978 Alice and Edith Hamilton publication prize in women's studies from the University of Michigan.

7. For example, Chandra Mohanty, "Under Western Eyes: Feminist Scholarship and Colonial Discourses," *Feminist Review* 30 (Autumn 1988): 61–85; Leila Rupp, *Worlds of Women: The Making of an International Women's Movement* (Princeton, N.J.: Princeton University Press, 1997); and Amrita Basu, ed., *The Challenge of Local Feminisms: Women's Movements in Global Perspective* (Boulder: Westview Press, 1995).

8. See Estelle B. Freedman and Barrie Thorne, "Introduction to 'The Sexuality Debates,'" *Signs: Journal of Women in Culture and Society* 10, no. 1 (Autumn 1984): 102–5.

9. The colleagues in these two study groups who most influenced my thinking included Allan Bérubé, Amber Hollibaugh, Shelly Rosaldo, Gayle Rubin, Mary Ryan, Judy Stacey, Barrie Thorne, and, during his California stays, John D'Emilio.

10. The video, based on research by Allan Bérubé, is distributed through Women Make Movies (‹http://www.wmm.com›). A short photo essay appears in *Hidden from History: Reclaiming the Gay and Lesbian Past*, edited by Martin Bauml Duberman, Martha Vicinus, and George Chauncey Jr. (New York: New American Library, 1989).

11. The essay appeared as "Sexuality in Nineteenth-Century America: Behavior, Ideology, and Politics," *Reviews in American History* 10 (December 1982): 196–215. Mary Ryan suggested expanding it into a book and helped me imagine how to do so.

12. In the Canadian case, *Tomen and Ontario Public School Teachers' Federation v. Federation of Women Teachers of Ontario et al.* (1987), 61 O.R. (2d) 489 (H.C.J.), over twenty academics submitted affidavits cited in the "Factum of the Respondent." For my commentary on the Thomas hearings, see "The Manipulation of History at the Clarence Thomas Hearings," *Southern California Law Review* 65, no. 3 (March 1992): 1361–65.

Chapter 1. Separatism as Strategy: Female Institution Building and American Feminism, 1870–1930

I would like to thank Irene Diamond for inspiring me to write about history and strategy; Mary Felstiner for the perceptive comments she and members of the graduate seminar in women's studies at San Francisco State University offered; the members of the women's faculty group at Stanford University and the members of the history of sexuality study group for forcing me to refine my thinking; and both Yolaida Durán and John D'Emilio for support and criticism as I rewrote this essay.

1. Gayle Rubin, "The Traffic in Women: Notes on the 'Political Economy' of Sex," in *Toward an Anthropology of Women*, edited by Rayna R. Reiter (New York: Monthly Review Press, 1975), 157–58.

2. Michelle Zimbalist Rosaldo, "Woman, Culture, and Society: A Theoretical Overview," in *Woman, Culture, and Society*, edited by Michelle Zimbalist Rosaldo and Louise Lamphere (Stanford, Calif.: Stanford University Press, 1974), 17–42. According to Rosaldo, "Women's status will be lowest in those societies where there is a firm differentiation between domestic and public spheres of activity and where women are isolated from one another and placed under a single man's authority in the home" (36). For a reconsideration of her views, see Michelle Zimbalist Rosaldo, "The Use and Abuse of Anthropology: Reflections on Feminism and Cross-Cultural Understanding," *Signs: Journal of Women in Culture and Society* 5, no. 3 (Spring 1980): 389–417.

3. Rosaldo, "Woman, Culture, and Society," 37–38. Rosaldo lists as a separate women's public sphere women's trading societies, church clubs, and "even political organizations" as well as Iroquois and West African societies in which "women have created fully articulated social hierarchies of their own." This strategy differs significantly from the argument that women's domestic sphere activities are a source of power. On the recent anthropological literature on the domestic and public spheres, see Rayna Rapp, "Review Essay: Anthropology," *Signs: Journal of Women in Culture and Society* 4, no. 3 (Spring 1979): 505, 508–13.

4. Carroll Smith-Rosenberg, "The Female World of Love and Ritual: Relations

between Women in Nineteenth-Century America," *Signs: Journal of Women in Culture and Society* 1, no. 1 (Autumn 1975): 1–29.

5. Nancy F. Cott, *The Bonds of Womanhood: "Women's Sphere" in New England, 1780–1835* (New Haven: Yale University Press, 1977).

6. Blanche Wiesen Cook, "Female Support Networks and Political Activism: Lillian Wald, Crystal Eastman, Emma Goldman," *Chrysalis* 3 (1977): 43–61; Nancy Sahli, "Smashing: Women's Relationships before the Fall," *Chrysalis* 8 (Summer 1979): 17–27.

7. Feminist historians need clear definitions of women's culture and women's politics to avoid such divisions between the personal and the political. Women's culture can exist at both private and public levels. Women's politics, too, can be personal (intrafamilial, through friendship and love, for example) as well as public (the traditional definition of politics). The question of when women's culture and politics are *feminist* has yet to be fully explored. At this time, I would suggest that any female-dominated activity that places a positive value on women's social contributions, provides personal support, and is not controlled by antifeminist leadership has feminist political potential. This is as true for the sewing circle, voluntary civic association, or women's bar as for the consciousness-raising group, coffeehouse, or women's center. Whether that potential is realized depends in part on historical circumstances, such as the overall political climate, the state of feminist ideology and leadership, and the strength of antifeminist forces. Women's culture can remain "prefeminist," as in the case of some nineteenth-century female reform associations that valued women's identity as moral guardians but did not criticize the status quo. When the group experience leads to insights about male domination, however, the reformers often become politicized as feminists. Women's culture can also become reactionary, for instance when women join together under the control of antifeminist leadership, as in the case of Nazi women's groups in prewar Germany or women in right-wing movements in America today. The more autonomous the group, the more likely it is to foster feminist political consciousness. Cott raises some of these questions for the early nineteenth century in her conclusion to *Bonds of Womanhood*. On moral reformers, see Carroll Smith-Rosenberg, "Beauty, the Beast, and the Militant Woman: A Case Study in Sex Roles and Social Status in Jacksonian America," *American Quarterly* 23 (October 1971): 562–84; and Mary P. Ryan, "The Power of Women's Networks: A Case Study of Female Moral Reform in Antebellum America," *Feminist Studies* 5, no. 1 (Spring 1979): 66–85. Jo Freeman's discussion of the communications network as a precondition for the rebirth of feminism in the twentieth century is also relevant. See Jo Freeman, *The Politics of Women's Liberation: A Case Study of an Emerging Social Movement and Its Relation to the Policy Process* (New York: McKay, 1975).

8. These theories are surveyed in Estelle B. Freedman, "The New Woman: Changing Views of Women in the 1920s," *Journal of American History* 61 (September 1974): 372–93.

9. Smith-Rosenberg, "Female World of Love and Ritual." On changing ideologies of womanhood, see Mary Ryan, *Womanhood in America: From Colonial Times to*

the Present (New York: Franklin Watts, 1979); and Gerda Lerner, "The Lady and the Mill Girl: Changes in the Status of Women in the Age of Jackson," *American Studies Journal* 10 (Spring 1968): 5 – 15.

10. See Ellen DuBois, "The Radicalism of the Woman Suffrage Movement: Notes toward the Reconstruction of Nineteenth-Century Feminism," *Feminist Studies* 3, nos. 1 – 2 (Fall 1975): 63 – 71. On opposition to women's rights from a "traditional" woman, see Kathryn Kish Sklar, *Catharine Beecher: A Study in American Domesticity* (New Haven: Yale University Press), 266 – 67.

11. *History of Woman Suffrage* (1881 – 1902), reprinted in *The Feminist Papers: From Adams to de Beauvoir*, edited by Alice Rossi (New York: Columbia University Press, 1973), 457 – 58. On the history of the women's rights movement, see Ellen Carol DuBois, *Feminism and Suffrage: The Emergence of an Independent Women's Movement in America, 1848 – 1860* (Ithaca, N.Y.: Cornell University Press, 1978); and Eleanor Flexner, *Century of Struggle* (New York: Atheneum, 1970).

12. William O'Neill, ed., *The Woman Movement: Feminism in the United States and England* (Chicago: Quadrangle, 1969), 47 – 54; Gerda Lerner, ed., *Black Women in White America* (New York: Vintage, 1972), chap. 8.

13. DuBois, "Radicalism," 69.

14. On personal networks and loving relationships in the women's colleges, see Judith Schwarz, "Yellow Clover: Katharine Lee Bates and Katharine Coman," *Frontiers* 4, no. 1 (Spring 1979): 59 – 67; and Anna Mary Wells, *Miss Marks and Miss Woolley* (Boston: Houghton Mifflin, 1978).

15. Barbara Welter, "The Cult of True Womanhood, 1820 – 1860," *American Quarterly* 18 (Summer 1966): 150 – 74.

16. Ryan, *Womanhood in America*, 229.

17. For biographical data on these and other reformers, see *Notable American Women, 1607 – 1950*, edited by Edward T. James, Janet Wilson James, and Paul S. Boyer (Cambridge: Harvard University Press, 1971).

18. On women in labor and radical movements, see Nancy Schrom Dye, "Feminism or Unionism?: The New York Women's Trade Union League and the Labor Movement," and Robin Miller Jacoby, "The Women's Trade Union League and American Feminism," both in *Feminist Studies* 3, nos. 1 – 2 (Fall 1975): 111 – 40; Allis Rosenberg Wolfe, "Women, Consumerism, and the National Consumers League in the Progressive Era, 1900 – 1923," *Labor History* 16 (Summer 1975): 378 – 92; Mary Jo Buhle, "Women and the Socialist Party, 1901 – 1914," *Radical America* 4, no. 2 (February 1970): 36 – 55; and Sherna Gluck, "The Changing Nature of Women's Participation in the American Labor Movement, 1900 – 1940s: Case Studies from Oral History," paper presented at the Southwest Labor History Conference, Tempe, Ariz., 5 March 1977.

19. Judith Paine, "The Women's Pavillion of 1876," *Feminist Art Journal* 4, no. 4 (Winter 1975 – 76): 5 – 12; *The Woman's Building, Chicago, 1893/The Woman's Building, Los Angeles, 1973* (Los Angeles, 1975).

20. Bertha Honore Palmer, "The Growth of the Woman's Building," in *Art and Handicraft in the Woman's Building of the World's Columbian Exposition*, edited by

Maud Howe Elliott (New York, 1893), 11–12; Ida B. Wells, ed., *The Reason Why the Colored American Is Not in the World's Columbian Exposition* (Chicago, 1893).

21. See Ryan, *Womanhood in America*, for an exploration of these trends.

22. *The New York World's Fair Bulletin* 1, no. 8 (December 1937): 20–21; *New York City World's Fair Information Manual* (1939), index. Amy Swerdlow kindly shared these references and quotations about the 1939 fair from her own research on women at the world's fairs.

23. Rosalind Rosenberg, "The Academic Prism: The New View of American Women," in *Women of America: A History*, edited by Carol Ruth Berkin and Mary Beth Norton (Boston: Houghton Mifflin, 1979), 318–38.

24. The following account of Blair is drawn from research for a biographical essay that appeared in *The Dictionary of American Biography*, suppl. (New York: Charles Scribner, 1977), 5:61–63. For examples of her writings, see *What Women May Do with the Ballot* (Philadelphia, 1922); "Boring from Within," *Woman Citizen* 12 (July 1927): 49–50; and "Why I Am Discouraged about Women in Politics," *Woman's Journal* 6 (January 1931): 20–22.

25. Radicalesbians, "The Woman-Identified Woman," *Notes from the Third Year: Women's Liberation*, reprinted in *Radical Feminism*, edited by Anne Koedt, Ellen Levine, and Anita Rapone (New York: Quadrangle, 1973), 240–45; Lucia Valeska, "The Future of Female Separatism," *Quest* 2, no. 2 (Fall 1975): 2–16; Charlotte Bunch, "Learning from Lesbian Separatism," in *Lavender Culture*, edited by Karla Jay and Allen Young (New York: Jove Books, 1978), 433–44.

26. A clear example of this contradiction is the contemporary gay subculture, which is both a product of the historical labeling of homosexuality as deviance and a source of both personal affirmation and political consciousness. I am grateful to the San Francisco Gay History Project study group for drawing this parallel between the conflicts in women's and gay politics.

27. Rapp, "Review Essay: Anthropology," 513.

Chapter 2. Separatism Revisited: Women's Institutions, Social Reform, and the Career of Miriam Van Waters

1. Miriam Van Waters Journal, vol. 7, 1 November 1945, Miriam Van Waters Papers, Schlesinger Library, Radcliffe College, Cambridge, Mass. (hereafter cited as MVWP).

2. Lori D. Ginzberg, *Women and the Work of Benevolence: Morality, Politics, and Class in the Nineteenth-Century United States* (New Haven: Yale University Press, 1990); Cynthia Neverdon-Morton, *Afro-American Women of the South and the Advancement of the Race* (Knoxville: University of Tennessee Press, 1989); Paula Baker, "The Domestication of Politics: Women and American Political Society, 1780–1920," *American Historical Review* 89 (June 1984): 620–47; Kathryn Kish Sklar, "The Historical Foundations of Women's Power in the Creation of the American Welfare State, 1830–1930," in *Mothers of a New World: Maternalist Politics and the Origins of Welfare States*, edited by Seth Koven and Sonya Michel (New York:

Routledge, 1993), 43–93; Seth Koven and Sonya Michel, "Womanly Duties: Maternalist Politics and the Origins of Welfare States in France, Germany, Great Britain, and the United States, 1880–1920," *American Historical Review* 95 (October 1990): 1076–1108; Linda Gordon, "The New Feminist Scholarship on the Welfare State," in *Women, the State, and Welfare*, edited by Linda Gordon (Madison: University of Wisconsin Press, 1990), 9–35; Kathleen D. McCarthy, ed., *Lady Bountiful Revisited: Women, Philanthropy, and Power* (New Brunswick, N.J.: Rutgers University Press, 1990).

3. On clubs, see Sheila Rothman, *Woman's Proper Place: A History of Changing Ideals and Practices, 1870 to the Present* (New York: Basic Books, 1978), 186–87; and Karen Blair, "The Limits of Sisterhood: Its Decline among Clubwomen, 1890–1930," paper presented at the annual meeting of the American Historical Association, Los Angeles, December 1981. Peggy Pascoe describes the decline of rescue homes in *Relations of Rescue: The Search for Female Moral Authority in the American West, 1874–1939* (New York: Oxford University Press, 1990). On social workers, see Clarke A. Chambers, "Women in the Creation of the Profession of Social Work," *Social Service Review* 60 (March 1986): 23; and Nancy Cott, *The Grounding of Modern Feminism* (New Haven: Yale University Press, 1987), 224.

4. Robin Muncy, *Creating a Female Dominion in American Reform, 1890–1935* (New York: Oxford University Press, 1991); Paula Baker, "Domestication of Politics," 647. Even historians who stress continuity between progressivism and the New Deal note a contraction of women's authority during the late 1920s: J. Stanley Lemons, in *The Woman Citizen: Social Feminism in the 1920s* (Urbana: University of Illinois Press, 1973), sees an ebb in reform activism between 1925 and 1933, and Muncy states that reform contracted after 1924 (*Creating a Female Dominion*, xvii). Clarke Chambers, in his important early argument for continuity, *Seedtime for Reform: American Social Service and Social Action, 1918–1933* (Minneapolis: University of Minnesota Press, 1963), refers to reform as "quiescent" rather than "dead" (xi). See also Sarah Deutsch, "Learning to Talk More Like a Man: Boston Women's Class-Bridging Organizations, 1870–1940," *American Historical Review* 97 (April 1992): 379–404. For the emergence of historical challenges to the interpretation of a decline in women's politics after suffrage, see my review essay, "The New Woman: Changing Views of Women in the 1920s," *Journal of American History* 61 (September 1974): 372–93.

5. The title of this essay, "Separatism Revisited," refers to my essay "Separatism as Strategy: Female Institution Building and American Feminism, 1870–1930," *Feminist Studies* 5, no. 3 (Fall 1979): 512–29, in which I proposed that "a major strength of American feminism prior to 1920 was the separate female community that helped sustain women's participation in both social reform and political activism." I argued that "the self-consciously female community began to disintegrate in the 1920s" as women attempted to integrate as equals into male politics and social life.

6. Nancy Cott provides a useful summary of the literature that attempts to clarify the definitions of feminism and the women's movement in "What's in a Name?: The Limits of 'Social Feminism'; or, Expanding the Vocabulary of Women's History," *Journal of American History* 76 (December 1989): 809–29.

7. Elsa Barkley Brown, "Womanist Consciousness: Maggie Lena Walker and the

Independent Order of Saint Luke," *Signs: Journal of Women in Culture and Society* 14, no. 3 (Spring 1989): 610–33; Neverdon-Morton, *Afro-American Women of the South*; Darlene Clark Hine, *Black Women in the Middle West: The Michigan Experience* (Ann Arbor: Historical Society of Michigan, 1990), 15–17, 20–23; Darlene Clark Hine, "'We Specialize in the Wholly Impossible': The Philanthropic Work of Black Women," in McCarthy, *Lady Bountiful Revisited*, 70–95; Jacqueline Anne Rouse, *Lugenia Burns Hope: Black Southern Reformer* (Athens: University of Georgia Press, 1989); Kim Philips, "'Heaven Bound': Black Migration, Community, and Working-Class Activism in Cleveland, 1915–1945" (Ph.D. diss., Yale University, 1992), esp. chap. 5; Dorothy Salem, *To Better Our World: Black Women in Organized Reform, 1890–1920* (New York: Carlson Publishing, 1990), chap. 8. On black women who did become more politically active after suffrage, see Evelyn Brooks Higginbotham, "In Politics to Stay: Black Women Leaders and Party Politics in the 1920s," in *Women, Politics, and Change*, edited by Louise Tilly and Patricia Gurin (New York: Russell Sage Foundation, 1990), 199–220. On black women's organizations, see Anne Firor Scott, "Most Invisible of All: Black Women's Voluntary Associations," *Journal of Southern History* 56 (February 1990): 3–22; Paula Giddings, *In Search of Sisterhood: Delta Sigma Theta and the Challenge of the Black Sorority Movement* (New York: William Morrow, 1988); Linda Gordon, "Black and White Visions of Welfare: Women's Welfare Activism, 1890–1945," *Journal of American History* 78 (September 1991): 559–90; and Deborah Gray White, "The Cost of Club Work, the Price of Black Feminism," in *Visible Women: New Essays on American Activism*, edited by Nancy Hewitt and Suzanne Lebsock (Urbana: University of Illinois Press, 1993), 247–70.

8. Felice Gordon distinguishes between two groups of postsuffrage activists: "moral prodders," who sought, for example, goals once labeled "social feminist," such as protective labor legislation and temperance; and "equal righters," who were committed to expanding on the political victory of suffrage through their support of an Equal Rights Amendment. See Felice Gordon, *After Winning: The Legacy of the New Jersey Suffragists, 1920–1947* (New Brunswick, N.J.: Rutgers University Press, 1986). See also Cott, *Grounding of Modern Feminism*, chap. 3.

9. Hine, "'We Specialize in the Wholly Impossible,'" 83–84; Susan Ware, *Beyond Suffrage: Women in the New Deal* (Cambridge: Harvard University Press, 1981); Susan Ware, *Partner and I: Molly Dewson, Feminism, and New Deal Politics* (New Haven: Yale University Press, 1987); Muncy, *Creating a Female Dominion*; Leila J. Rupp, "The Women's Community in the National Woman's Party, 1945 to the 1960s," *Signs: Journal of Women in Culture and Society* 10, no. 4 (Summer 1985): 715–40; Leila J. Rupp and Verta Taylor, *Survival in the Doldrums: The American Women's Rights Movement, 1945 to the 1960s* (New York: Oxford University Press, 1987).

10. Dorothy Sue Cobble, "Rethinking Troubled Relations between Women and Unions: Craft Unionism and Female Activism," *Feminist Studies* 16, no. 3 (Fall 1990): 521, 529; Dorothy Sue Cobble, *Dishing It Out: Waitresses and Their Unions in the Twentieth Century* (Urbana: University of Illinois Press, 1991); Vicki L. Ruiz, *Cannery Women, Cannery Lives: Mexican Women, Unionization, and the California Food Processing Industry, 1930–1950* (Albuquerque: University of New Mexico Press, 1987).

11. Jodi Vandenberg-Daves, "The Manly Pursuit of a Partnership between the Sexes: The Debate over YMCA Programs for Women and Girls, 1914–1933," *Journal of American History* 78 (March 1992): 1324–46; Frances Taylor, "On the Edge of Tomorrow: The Southern Student YWCA and Race, 1920–1944" (Ph.D. diss., Stanford University, 1984); Susan Lynn, *Progressive Women in Conservative Times: Racial Justice, Peace, and Feminism, 1945 to the 1960s* (New Brunswick, N.J.: Rutgers University Press, 1992).

12. Carroll Smith-Rosenberg, "The Female World of Love and Ritual: Relations between Women in Nineteenth-Century America," *Signs: Journal of Women in Culture and Society* 1, no. 1 (Autumn 1975): 1–29; Nancy Sahli, "Smashing: Women's Relationships before the Fall," *Chrysalis* 8 (Summer 1979): 17–27; Lillian Faderman, *Surpassing the Love of Men: Romantic Friendship and Love between Women from the Renaissance to the Present* (New York: William Morrow, 1981).

13. Leila J. Rupp, "'Imagine My Surprise': Women's Relationships in Historical Perspective," *Frontiers* 5, no. 3 (Fall 1980): 61–70; Ware, *Partner and I*; Eric Garber, "'T'Ain't Nobody's Bizness': Homosexuality in 1920s Harlem," in *Black Men/White Men*, edited by Michael J. Smith (San Francisco: Gay Sunshine Press, 1983); Allan Bérubé, *Coming Out under Fire: The History of Gay Men and Women in World War Two* (New York: Free Press, 1990); Madeline Davis and Elizabeth Lapovsky Kennedy, "Oral History and the Study of Sexuality in the Lesbian Community: Buffalo, New York, 1940–1960," *Feminist Studies* 12, no. 1 (Spring 1986): 7–26; Madeline Davis and Elizabeth Lapovsky Kennedy, *Boots of Leather, Slippers of Gold: The History of a Lesbian Community* (New York: Routledge, 1993); Linda Gordon, "Black and White Visions of Welfare," 574–75. See also the essays by Esther Newton, Eric Garber, and John D'Emilio in *Hidden from History: Reclaiming the Gay and Lesbian Past*, edited by Martin Bauml Duberman, Martha Vicinus, and George Chauncey Jr. (New York: New American Library, 1989); and Lillian Faderman, *Odd Girls and Twilight Lovers: A History of Lesbian Life in Twentieth-Century America* (New York: Columbia University Press, 1991).

14. On the women's peace movement, see Barbara Steinson, "'The Mother Half of Humanity': American Women in the Peace and Preparedness Movements in World War I," in *Women, War, and Revolution*, edited by Carol R. Berkin and Clara M. Lovett (New York: Holmes and Meier, 1980), 259–81; and Linda Schott, "The Woman's Peace Party and the Moral Basis for Women's Pacifism," *Frontiers* 8, no. 2 (1985): 18–25. On antilynching, see Jacquelyn Dowd Hall, *Revolt against Chivalry: Jessie Daniel Ames and the Women's Campaign against Lynching* (New York: Columbia University Press, 1979).

15. I am currently writing a biography of Van Waters that uses her life as a window on several themes in U.S. women's history, including women and higher education during the Progressive Era, the politics of the juvenile court movement, Van Waters's complex family and personal relationships, the treatment of women criminals, and the post–World War II reaction to female authority. [Author's note: The book, *Maternal Justice: Miriam Van Waters and the Female Reform Tradition*, was published in 1996 by the University of Chicago Press.]

16. "Coeds and the Franchise," *University of Oregon Monthly* 11 (1907 – 8): 42, Special Collections, University of Oregon Library, Eugene.

17. Henry D. Sheldon, *History of the University of Oregon* (Portland: Binfords and Mort, 1940), 79, 177.

18. On early women social scientists, see Rosalind Rosenberg, *Beyond Separate Spheres: Intellectual Roots of Modern Feminism* (New Haven: Yale University Press, 1982), 239 – 40; and Ellen Fitzpatrick, *Endless Crusade: Women Social Scientists and Progressive Reform* (New York: Oxford University Press, 1990). Van Waters spoke of her quest for constructive work in letters to her parents on 7 February, 15 April 1911, 23 October 1912, MVWP.

19. Mary Ellen Odem, "Delinquent Daughters: The Sexual Regulation of Female Minors in the United States, 1880 – 1920" (Ph.D. diss., University of California, Berkeley, 1989), chap. 1, 2.

20. Miriam Van Waters, "Where Girls Go Right," *Survey Graphic*, 27 May 1922, 361 – 76; Miriam Van Waters, *Youth in Conflict* (New York: Republic Publishing Company, 1925); Miriam Van Waters, *Parents on Probation* (New York: Republic Publishing Company, 1927).

21. Van Waters used the term in a 28 July 1918 letter to her mother to describe the historic step of Orfa Jean Shontz running for political office (MVWP).

22. Miriam Van Waters to her parents, 2 September 1917, 23 March 1919, 8 April 1925, ibid.

23. Miriam Van Waters, untitled and undated memoir, typescript, 14 – 18, ibid.

24. Margaret van Wagenen, interview by author, Ashland, Mass., 31 July 1989.

25. Miriam Van Waters, untitled book proposal, [ca. 1957], MVWP.

26. Journal, vol. 2, 11 August 1934, ibid.

27. Journal, vol. 4, 13 June 1936, ibid.

28. Janis Howe, "Framingham Report," 21 September 1946, 8, ibid.

29. Mrs. Hazel Rubbitt to State Auditor, 21 May 1947, ibid.

30. Report of Mrs. O'Keefe, Massachusetts League of Women Voters, 20 June 1947, ibid.

31. Mrs. M. H. [Willa W.] Brown to Miriam Van Waters, 10 February 1949, ibid.

32. On the Society of the Companions of the Holy Cross, see Mary Sudman Donovan, *A Different Call: Women's Ministries in the Episcopal Church, 1850 – 1920* (Wilton, Conn.: Morehouse-Barlow, 1986); and Vida Scudder, *On Journey* (New York: E. P. Dutton, 1937).

33. Felice Gordon, *After Winning*, 55 – 56, 78, 97; Meline Karakashian, "The Great Lady of Brookdale," in *A Triangle of Land: A History of the Site and the Founding of Brookdale Community College*, by Northern Monmouth Country Branch of the American Association of University Women (Lincroft, N.J.: Brookdale Community College, 1978), 62 – 96.

34. Journal, vol. 2, 11 May 1934, MVWP.

35. Geraldine Thompson to Eleanor Roosevelt, 10 February 1945, ibid.

36. All 11 – 12 March 1949 letters, ibid.

37. *Boston Daily Record*, 29, 31 July 1957; Commonwealth of Massachusetts, *Re-*

port of the Special Committee Authorized to Study the Reorganization of the Correctional System, 19 April 1958, House Document 3015 (Boston, 1958), in "Framingham" file, Human Services, Corrections, Commonwealth of Massachusetts Archives, Boston.

38. Anne Firor Scott, *Natural Allies: Women's Associations in American History* (Urbana: University of Illinois Press, 1993).

39. For capsule biographies of most of these women, see *Notable American Women: The Modern Period*, edited by Barbara Sicherman and Carol Hurd Green (Cambridge: Belknap Press, 1980). On Esther Peterson, see Joan Hoff, *Law, Gender, and Injustice: A Legal History of U.S. Women* (New York: New York University Press, 1991), 231–33; and Mary Q. Hawkes, *Excellent Effect: The Edna Mason Story* (Arlington, Va.: American Correctional Association, 1994).

40. On the persistence of middle-class female "devoted companions," see Faderman, *Odd Girls*, chap. 1. Linda Gordon suggests that such relationships were much rarer among black women reformers ("Black and White Visions of Welfare").

41. Compare the veiled accusations of lesbianism used to discredit Judge Marion Harron, cited by Rupp in "'Imagine My Surprise,'" in Duberman, Vicinus, and Chauncey, *Hidden from History*, 407.

42. *Notable American Women*; Dorothy M. Brown, *Mabel Walker Willebrandt: A Study of Power, Loyalty, and Law* (Knoxville: University of Tennessee Press, 1984).

43. Anne Firor Scott, *Making the Invisible Woman Visible* (Urbana: University of Illinois Press, 1984), xiv. On the League of Women Voters, see Susan Ware, "American Women in the 1950s: Nonpartisan Politics and Women's Politicization," in Tilly and Gurin, *Women, Politics, and Change*, 281–99. For arguments about the persistence of women's reform after 1950, see Lynn, *Progressive Women*; and Joanne Meyerowitz, ed., *Not June Cleaver: Women and Gender in Postwar America, 1945–1960* (Philadelphia: Temple University Press, 1994).

44. Cott, *Grounding of Modern Feminism*, 96, 276–83.

45. Journal, vol. 7, 12 June 1945, and Miriam Van Waters to Hon. Paul Doyle, 20 September 1948, MVWP.

46. Susan Hartmann, *The Home Front and Beyond: American Women in the 1940s* (Boston: Twayne Publishers, 1982), 150–51. These and other women in Congress, Hartmann notes, sponsored legislation to advance women's opportunities. On postwar women's formal politics, see Cynthia Harrison, *On Account of Sex: The Politics of Women's Issues, 1945–1968* (Berkeley: University of California Press, 1988).

47. Sara Evans, *Born for Liberty: A History of Women in America* (New York: Free Press, 1989), 256–60. See also John D'Emilio, *Sexual Politics, Sexual Communities: The Making of a Homosexual Minority in the United States, 1940–1970* (Chicago: University of Chicago Press, 1983); and David J. Garrow, ed., *The Montgomery Bus Boycott and the Women Who Started It: The Memoir of Jo Ann Gibson Robinson* (Knoxville: University of Tennessee Press, 1987).

48. Steinson provides a good example of separate women's organizations taking different political positions, in this case mobilizing for and against World War I, in "Mother Half of Humanity." Conservative women's organizations often began as auxiliaries or adjuncts to right-wing male movements (for example, the Women's

Ku Klux Klan). See Kathleen M. Blee, "Women in the 1920s' Ku Klux Klan Movement," *Feminist Studies* 17, no. 1 (Spring 1991): 57–77.

Chapter 3. Women's Networks and Women's Loyalties: Reflections on a Tenure Case

1. For example, I have learned a good deal about strategies for internal appeals and the literature on sex discrimination cases. The following sources provide initial guides to these subjects: Gloria DeSole and Leonore Hoffmann, eds., *Rocking the Boat: Academic Women and Academic Processes* (New York: Modern Language Association of America, 1981); Emily Abel, "Collective Protest and the Meritocracy: Faculty Women and Sex Discrimination," *Feminist Studies* 7, no. 3 (Fall 1981): 505–38; and *Lynn v. Regents of the University of California*, 656 F.2d 1337 (1981).

2. Mary P. Ryan, "The Power of Women's Networks: A Case Study of Female Moral Reform in Antebellum America," *Feminist Studies* 5, no. 1 (Spring 1979): 66–85.

3. The AAUW has raised funds for the "Cornell Eleven" and Washington State class action suits; it has currently adopted the Nancy Shaw case against the University of California at Santa Cruz. [Author's note: The latter case took over five years in court before the grievant, now Nancy Stoller, won promotion, back pay, and tenure.]

4. Estelle B. Freedman, "Separatism as Strategy: Female Institution Building and American Feminism, 1870–1930," *Feminist Studies* 5, no. 3 (Fall 1979): 512–29.

Chapter 4. Small Group Pedagogy: Consciousness Raising in Conservative Times

1. In planning this course, I benefited especially from the experience of my colleague Jane Collier (Anthropology), who had previously taught FS 101, and from my two graduate teaching assistants, Lisa Hogeland (Modern Thought and Literature) and Kevin Mumford (History). I thank them, along with the following other members of the feminist community at Stanford, for their responses to this essay: Laura Carstensen, John Dupre, Mary Felstiner, Regenia Gagnier, Patricia Gumport, Margo Horn, Susan Krieger, Diane Middlebrook, Adrienne Rich, Alice Supton, and Sylvia Yanagisako.

2. Two experiences outside my own classroom influenced my use of c.r. in FS 101. I learned a great deal from sociologist Susan Krieger's example when she successfully incorporated small groups in a class of conservative prebusiness students. Her students wrote self-reflective papers about small group dynamics, rooted in personal experience. If such groups could work with these students, they seemed to have great potential for feminist studies. Another model was an unlearning-racism workshop I had attended at the Stanford Women's Center some years earlier, facilitated by the late Ricky Sherover-Marcuse. In order to require such a workshop of all FS 101 students, the Feminist Studies Program hired an experienced facilitator to conduct workshops for members of this class.

3. Of the sixty-six students who took this course for credit (not counting auditors), 74 percent were white and 26 percent were black, Asian, or Chicana. Men constituted 17 percent of the entire class, 12 percent of minorities, and 18 percent of whites. Students tended to identify themselves in terms of race and gender. Similarly, in this essay I refer to students by gender and race unless a student has indicated another identity.

4. For earlier resistance to the use of c.r. by women's studies faculty and a review of the theoretical basis for c.r. in the classroom, see Renate D. Klein, "The Dynamics of the Women's Studies Classroom: A Review Essay of the Teaching Practice of Women's Studies in Higher Education," *Women's Studies International Forum* 10, no. 2 (1987): esp. 189–93.

5. I assigned the following readings: Johnetta Cole, ed., *All American Women: Lines That Divide, Ties That Bind* (New York: Free Press, 1986); Emily Honig and Gail Hershatter, eds., *Personal Voices: Chinese Women in the 1980s* (Stanford, Calif.: Stanford University Press, 1988); Buchi Emecheta, *The Joys of Motherhood* (New York: George Braziller, 1979); Virginia Woolf, *Three Guineas* (1938; reprint, New York: Harcourt, Brace, Jovanovich, 1966); Marge Piercy, *Woman on the Edge of Time* (New York: Fawcett Crest, 1976); Alison Jaggar and Paula Rothenberg, eds., *Feminist Frameworks: Alternative Theoretical Accounts of the Relations between Women and Men* (New York: McGraw-Hill, 1984); and a thick course reader.

6. Pamela Allen, "Free Space," in *Radical Feminism*, edited by Anne Koedt, Ellen Levine, and Anita Rapone (New York: Quadrangle, 1973), 271–79; Irene Peslikis, "Resistances to Consciousness," in *Sisterhood Is Powerful*, edited by Robin Morgan (New York: Vintage Books, 1970), 379–81.

7. In this three-hour workshop, an experienced facilitator helped students to explore their personal class, race, and ethnic backgrounds and to dispel unconscious stereotypes about various groups. The workshop attempted to affirm the value of difference, address the costs of discrimination, and create a nonjudgmental space for students to acknowledge the racial fears and misinformation they had acquired in the past. Ideally the students should attend a series of workshops, but because of time and budget limitations, the small group meeting served as a follow-up to reinforce the workshop.

8. Despite my effort to require attendance at the group meetings, several papers complained of members who appeared irregularly because it seemed "almost like a luxury—and when it comes to a clash between 'real' classwork . . . and therapeutic classwork, it's hard to break the Stanford mold and take the ungraded activity seriously." Evaluation papers suggested that attendance would improve if I scheduled group meeting times rather than leaving the meeting times to students. They also complained about the rigid format I outlined and convinced me that in the future the groups should determine their own process and discussion topics. After the second year of teaching this course with c.r. groups, I have decided that it is essential to structure the meeting times in the course schedule in advance. Doing so is especially important at nonresidential schools, where it is even more difficult for students to schedule informal meeting times and places. [Author's note: In subsequent years, I further modified the format in response to student comments, which

included calls for greater, rather than less, direction from me in choosing discussion topics. In response to a suggestion from a visiting colleague, Margaret L. Andersen, I also added an "action project," which culminates in a five-minute group presentation before the entire class. Those projects have included videos, original skits, surveys of student attitudes, feminist analyses of films and pop songs, and reports of field trips to feminist institutions and of public service activities. The students continually impress me with their creativity and capacity to learn from both theory and practice.]

9. John D'Emilio constructed this exercise at the University of North Carolina – Greensboro, and it has been used by several other faculty members around the country. Several students discussed their letters with parents. One of my favorite responses was from the mother of a straight son. The son called to tell her he was writing a coming-out letter to her, "hypothetically real," and wondered what she would say if he sent it. Her reply: "The same thing I said when you went to college: always use a condom." I am grateful to such mothers for sending their daughters and sons to my classes.

10. After the lecture, which did discuss the problem of incest, two other incest survivors identified themselves to me privately, and one suggested readings for the next year. From this experience, I learned about the importance of making sensitive topics visible on the syllabus in advance and not only in the lecture class.

11. In quoting from the student papers, I have corrected typographical errors but have left grammar and punctuation intact. Students did sign the papers, so they may have had an interest in presenting a positive evaluation of the groups in order to please the instructor. The papers, however, did not affect grades, and many students offered criticisms about the structure or timing of groups alongside their reflections on how groups influenced them. [Author's note: In subsequent years, between 60 and 75 percent of the groups fulfilled my expectations for small group learning, around 10 percent utterly failed, and the rest had mixed results.]

12. To my surprise, given my experience of separatism in the 1970s, mixed-gender groups evoked no protest and in fact satisfied almost all students. One all-women's group did report a special openness and a tendency among its members to discuss childhood memories and sexuality more freely. But members of other all-female groups said they missed a "male perspective." In mixed-gender groups, no women complained of male dominance, and many expressed gratitude for the "male insight." Their comments may have been due to the respectful attitude of the men in the class, as well as to women's often-expressed fears of being labeled man-haters.

13. These readings included Pat Mainardi, "The Politics of Housework," in Jaggar and Rothenberg, *Feminist Frameworks*; excerpts from Lenore Weitzman, *The Marriage Contract* (New York: Free Press, 1983); and interviews with domestic workers in Cole, *All American Women*.

14. Another student wrote that when she described her father to the group, she understood why she could not get angry: "I realized that as a child, it seemed to me that my father was constantly yelling. He scared me most of the time with his anger, and for this reason I think that I express my anger quietly and in a somewhat controlled fashion." She did not elaborate on whether she wished to change this

behavior, but she said she felt the insight was "an important step toward an understanding of myself."

15. Bernice Johnson Reagon, "Coalition Politics: Turning the Century," in *Home Girls: A Black Feminist Anthology*, edited by Barbara Smith (New York: Kitchen Table Press, 1983), 356–68.

16. For example, a white woman who missed the meeting on race in her mixed group wrote: "I suppose I could have talked about the white guilt everyone tells me is not healthy to have but that I have anyway. I just don't understand why I can go to Stanford while other people are starving."

Chapter 5. No Turning Back: The Historical Resilience of Feminism

1. Jennifer Pozner, "False Feminist Death Syndrome," *Sojourner* 23, no. 12 (1998): 2. See also Susan Faludi, *Backlash: The Undeclared War against American Women* (New York: Crown Books, 1991).

2. In April 2000, when a Gallup poll asked American adults if they agreed or disagreed with the goals of the women's rights movement, 45 percent strongly agreed and 40 percent somewhat agreed. An NBC News/*Wall Street Journal* poll in June 2000 asked "whether you consider yourself a feminist," and 29 percent responded yes. In 2000–2001, Princeton Survey Research Associates polled adult women in the United States and found that 55 percent gave "mostly positive" responses and 9 percent gave "completely positive" responses when they heard the word "feminist." See Center for the Advancement of Women, *Progress and Perils: How Gender Issues Unite and Divide Women, Part One* (Princeton, N.J.: Princeton Survey Research Associates, 2001), 16 ‹http://advancewomen.org/womens_research/PartOne.pdf›. The European Union data appears in European Commission, EUROBAROMETER 225, Wave 63.1, "Social Values, Science, and Technology," June 2005, 27–31 ‹http://europa.eu.int/comm/public_opinion/archives/ebs/ebs_225_report_en.pdf›. I am grateful to Barnabas Malnay for directing me to this source.

3. In my book, as in this essay, I use "feminism" ahistorically—that is, as an umbrella term for any movement seeking to achieve full economic and political citizenship for women, whether or not the word was used at the time, although at the outset I identify the historical specificity of the term. For my definition of feminism, a well as the data and scholarship on which this essay draws, see my *No Turning Back: The History of Feminism and the Future of Women* (New York: Ballantine Books, 2002). See also the book's web page with links to feminist organizations and documents, ‹http://noturningback.stanford.edu›. For audio lectures based on *No Turning Back*, see "Feminism and the Future of Women" (Recorded Books, 2004) at ‹www.modernscholar.com›.

4. Quoted in Sharon Sievers, *Flowers in Salt: The Beginnings of Feminist Consciousness in Modern Japan* (Stanford, Calif.: Stanford University Press, 1983), 37.

5. Joan Scott, *Only Paradoxes to Offer: French Feminists and the Rights of Man* (Cambridge: Harvard University Press, 1996).

6. Quoted in Corinne A. Pernet, "Chilean Feminists, the International Women's

Movement, and Suffrage, 1915–1950," *Pacific Historical Review* 69, no. 4 (2000): 668–69.

7. Mary Wollstonecraft, *A Vindication of the Rights of Women*, excerpted in *Women, the Family, and Freedom: The Debate in Documents*, vol. 1, *1750–1880*, edited by Susan Groag Bell and Karen M. Offen (Stanford, Calif.: Stanford University Press, 1983), 62; Flora Tristan, *L'Union Ouvrière*, in Bell and Offen, *Women, the Family, and Freedom*, 1:212–15; Francisca Diniz, "Equality of Rights" (1890), in June E. Hahner, *Emancipating the Female Sex: The Struggle for Women's Rights in Brazil, 1850–1940* (Durham: Duke University Press, 1990), appendix B, 214. On Gilman, see Gail Bederman, *Manliness and Civilization: A Cultural History of Gender and Race in the U.S., 1880–1917* (Chicago: University of Chicago Press, 1995).

8. See, for example, Joan Williams, *Unbending Gender: Why Family and Work Conflict and What to Do about It* (New York: Oxford University Press, 2000).

9. Barbara Smith, "Racism and Women's Studies," in *The Truth That Never Hurts: Writings on Race, Gender, and Freedom* (New Brunswick, N.J.: Rutgers University Press, 1998), 96.

10. Audre Lorde, "The Master's Tools Will Never Dismantle the Master's House," in *Sister Outsider* (Freedom, Calif.: Crossing Press, 1984), 112.

11. Quoted in Leila Rupp, *Worlds of Women: The Making of an International Women's Movement* (Princeton, N.J.: Princeton University Press, 1997), 80.

12. Quoted in Charlotte Bunch, *Passionate Politics: Feminist Theory in Action* (New York: St. Martin's Press, 1987), 299.

13. Anne McClintock, *Imperial Leather: Race, Gender, and Sexuality in the Colonial Conquest* (New York: Routledge, 1994), 384; Gwendolyn Mikell, "African Feminism: Toward a New Politics of Representation," *Feminist Studies* 21, no. 2 (Summer 1995): 419.

14. Chetna Gala, "Empowering Women in Villages: All-Women Village Councils in Maharashtra, India," *Bulletin of Concerned Asian Scholars* 29, no. 2 (1997): 35.

15. Quoted in M. G. Fried, "Beyond Abortion: Transforming the Pro-Choice Movement," *Social Policy* 23, no. 4 (1993): 26.

16. Gertrude Mongella, "A Revolution Has Begun" (4 September 1995), excerpted in *Women's Studies Quarterly: Beijing and Beyond, Toward the Twenty-first Century of Women* 24, nos. 1–2 (Spring/Summer 1996): 116.

Chapter 6. The Historical Construction of Homosexuality in the United States

1. On the emergence of modern homosexuality, see Mary McIntosh, "The Homosexual Role," *Social Problems* 16, no. 2 (Fall 1968): 182–92; Jeffrey Weeks, *Sex, Politics, and Society: The Regulation of Sexuality since 1800* (London: Longman, 1981), chap. 6; and Martin Bauml Duberman, Martha Vicinus, and George Chauncey Jr., eds., *Hidden from History: Reclaiming the Gay and Lesbian Past* (New York: New American Library, 1989).

2. John D'Emilio and Estelle B. Freedman, *Intimate Matters: A History of Sexuality in America* (New York: Harper and Row, 1988), chap. 1. This essay summa-

rizes material found in *Intimate Matters*; unless otherwise noted, the sources for all quotations and data cited below can be found in this book. On the *berdache*, see Ramon Gutierrez, "Must We Deracinate Indians to Find Gay Roots?," *Outlook* 1, no. 4 (Winter 1989): 61–67.

3. Sodomy could refer to a variety of nonreproductive acts, including masturbation; buggery meant anal intercourse; and bestiality meant intercourse with an animal.

4. Unless otherwise noted, this essay draws on research about white sexual attitudes and practices. The subject of same-sex love among southern slaves or Asian and Mexican immigrants has yet to be investigated by historians. For free African Americans and immigrants, class could create family and sexual patterns similar to those of whites, though at different historical moments.

5. See Jonathan Ned Katz, *The Invention of Homosexuality* (New York: Dutton, 1995).

6. See George Chauncey, *Gay New York: Gender, Urban Culture, and the Making of the Gay Male World, 1890–1940* (New York: Basic, 1994).

7. See Allan Bérubé, *Coming Out under Fire: The History of Gay Men and Women in World War Two* (New York: Free Press, 1990).

8. On racial integration in the lesbian bars of Buffalo, New York, see Madeline Davis and Elizabeth Lapovsky Kennedy, *Boots of Leather, Slippers of Gold: The History of a Lesbian Community* (New York: Routledge, 1993).

9. For an alternative formulation of same-sex desire in certain Latino cultures, for example, see Tomas Almaguer, "Chicano Men: A Cartography of Homosexual Identity and Behavior," in *The Lesbian and Gay Studies Reader*, edited by Henry Abelove, Michele Aina Barale, and David M. Halperin (New York: Routledge, 1993), 255–73.

Chapter 7. Uncontrolled Desires: The Response to the Sexual Psychopath, 1920–1960

I wish to thank the following scholars for their helpful comments on earlier versions of this essay: Allan Bérubé, John D'Emilio, Barbara Gelpi, Nathan Hale, Elizabeth Lunbeck, Elaine Tyler May, Peggy Pascoe, Elizabeth Pleck, Leila Rupp, Mary Ryan, and Judith Walkowitz.

1. *New York Times*, 3 April 1933, 13; Thea von Harbou, *M*, directed by Fritz Lang, translated by Nicholas Garnham (London, 1968). See also Siegfried Kracauer, *From Caligari to Hitler: A Psychology of the German Film* (Princeton, N.J.: Princeton University Press, 1947), 215–22. The film was based on the actual case of the "Dusseldorf Jack the Ripper," reported in *London Times*, 26 May 1930, 13; *London Daily Express*, 26 May 1930, 1; and *New York Times*, 19 July 1931, sec. 8, 2. On sex crimes, see, for example, Sheldon Glueck, "Sex Crimes and the Law," *Nation*, 25 September 1937, 318–20. The *New York Times Index* and the *Readers' Guide to Periodical Literature* (which created a "Sex Crimes" category for its 1937–39 volume) show parallel fluc-

tuations in newspaper and magazine coverage of sex crimes. The average number of articles per year peaked in 1937–39, 1949–51, and 1957–59.

2. The California, Massachusetts, Nebraska, and Vermont laws used this terminology. Almost every state included the phrase "utter lack of power to control his sexual impulses." For the statutes, see S. J. Brakel and R. S. Rock, *The Mentally Disabled and the Law* (Chicago: University of Chicago Press, 1971), table 10.1, 362–65. For definitions of the term "psychopath," see Alan H. Swanson, "Sexual Psychopath Statutes: Summary and Analysis," *Journal of Criminal Law, Criminology, and Police Science* 51 (July–August 1960): 228–35.

3. Between 1935 and 1956, the number of arrests per 100,000 inhabitants rose from 6.0 to 11.2 for rape and from 24.9 to 48.1 for "other sex offenses," while for prostitution it fell from 108.8 to 35.5. The sharpest increase in arrest rates for rape and other sex offenses occurred in 1936–37, 1942–47, and 1953–56. I calculated all data from a series of annual reports: U.S. Department of Justice, Bureau of Investigation, *Uniform Crime Reports for the United States and Its Possessions* (Washington, D.C., 1932–60), iii–xxx. The one state for which commitment in addition to arrest data are available over time is Michigan. There sex offenders committed to state prisons remained a steady 6–10 percent of all state prison commitments from 1875 to 1935. After the passage of the Michigan psychopath law in 1936, the rate jumped to 12.4 percent; after 1947, it fell below 10 percent again. See Governor's Study Commission, *Report on the Deviated Criminal Sex Offender* (Lansing, Mich., 1951), 21, table 4, 210–11. On the lack of increase in sex offenses, see Ira S. Wile, "Society and Sex Offenders," *Survey Graphic* 36 (November 1937): 569–72; Paul Tappan, *The Habitual Sex Offender: Report and Recommendations of the Commission on the Habitual Sex Offender* (Trenton, N.J., 1950), 19; Edwin Sutherland, "The Sexual Psychopath Laws," *Journal of Criminal Law and Criminology* 40 (January–February 1950): 545–48; California Legislative Assembly, Interim Committee on Judicial System and Judicial Process, *Preliminary Report of the Subcommittee on Sex Crimes* (Sacramento, 8 March 1950), 20; and Karl M. Bowman, *California Sexual Deviation Research Report to the Assembly* (Sacramento, January 1953), 25.

4. For sociological interpretations of the expansion of psychiatric authority through the psychopath laws, see Edwin H. Sutherland, "The Diffusion of Sexual Psychopath Laws," in *The Collective Definition of Deviance*, edited by F. James Davis and Richard Stivers (New York: Free Press, 1975), 281–89; and Nicholas N. Kittrie, *The Right to Be Different: Deviance and Enforced Therapy* (Baltimore: Johns Hopkins University Press, 1971). For general critiques of the "psychiatric state," see Thomas S. Szasz, *The Manufacture of Madness: A Comparative Study of the Inquisition and the Mental Health Movement* (New York: Harper & Row, 1970), 254; Jacques Donzelot, *The Policing of Families* (New York: Pantheon, 1979), esp. 126–50; and Robert Castel, Françoise Castel, and Anne Lovell, *The Psychiatric Society* (New York: Columbia University Press, 1982), esp. 175–213.

5. On the nineteenth century, see Estelle B. Freedman, "Sexuality in Nineteenth-Century America: Behavior, Ideology, and Politics," *Reviews in American History* 10 (December 1982): 196–215. On moral reform and social purity, see Carroll Smith-

Rosenberg, "Beauty, the Beast, and the Militant Woman: A Case Study in Sex Roles and Social Status in Jacksonian America," *American Quarterly* 23 (October 1971): 562–84; Mary P. Ryan, "The Power of Women's Networks: A Case Study of Female Moral Reform in Antebellum America," *Feminist Studies* 5, no. 1 (Spring 1979): 66–85; and David J. Pivar, *Purity Crusade: Sexual Morality and Social Control, 1868–1900* (Westport, Conn.: Greenwood Press, 1973). On prostitution, see Mark Connelly, *The Response to Prostitution in the Progressive Era* (Chapel Hill: University of North Carolina Press, 1980); and Ruth Rosen, *The Lost Sisterhood: Prostitution in America, 1900–1918* (Baltimore: Johns Hopkins University Press, 1982). On World War I and venereal disease, see Allan M. Brandt, *No Magic Bullet: A Social History of Venereal Disease in the United States since 1880* (New York: Oxford University Press, 1985), 52–95; and Estelle B. Freedman, *Their Sisters' Keepers: Women's Prison Reform in America, 1830–1930* (Ann Arbor: University of Michigan Press, 1981), 109–42, 146–48.

6. On changing sexual ideas and practices, see Nathan G. Hale Jr., *Freud and the Americans: The Beginning of Psychoanalysis in the United States, 1876–1917* (New York: Oxford University Press, 1971), 250–73; John C. Burnham, "The Progressive Era Revolution in American Attitudes toward Sex," *Journal of American History* 59 (March 1973): 885–908; Paul Robinson, *The Modernization of Sex* (New York: Harper & Row, 1976); Lewis A. Erenberg, *Steppin' Out: New York Night Life and the Transformation of American Culture, 1890–1930* (Westport, Conn.: Greenwood Press, 1981); Christina Simmons, "Marriage in the Modern Manner: Sexual Radicalism and Reform in America, 1914–1941" (Ph.D. diss., Brown University, 1982); and Paula S. Fass, *The Damned and the Beautiful: American Youth in the 1920's* (New York: Oxford University Press, 1977).

7. Carol Christ, "Victorian Masculinity and the Angel in the House," in *A Widening Sphere: Changing Roles of Victorian Women*, edited by Martha Vicinus (Bloomington: Indiana University Press, 1977), 162; Judith R. Walkowitz, "Jack the Ripper and the Myth of Male Violence," *Feminist Studies* 8, no. 3 (Fall 1982): 546.

8. On moral insanity, see Norman Dain, *Concepts of Insanity in the United States, 1789–1865* (New Brunswick, N.J.: Rutgers University Press, 1964); and Charles E. Rosenberg, *The Trial of the Assassin Guiteau: Psychiatry and Law in the Gilded Age* (Chicago: University of Chicago Press, 1968), esp. 68–70, 247, 254. In this essay, I use the terms "psychopathic," "the psychopath," and "psychopathy." The original term, "constitutional psychopath," reflected the organic explanation of criminal behavior and insanity prevalent in the late nineteenth century. During the 1920s and 1930s, American usage shifted from "constitutional psychopath" to "psychopathic personality." In 1952, the *Diagnostic and Statistical Manual* of the American Psychiatric Association (Washington, D.C., 1952) adopted "sociopathic personality" rather than "psychopathic personality." But some authors continued to refer to "constitutional psychopath" and many to "psychopathic personality." Major texts adopting the "psychopathic" category include Eugen Kahn, *Psychopathic Personalities*, translated by H. Flanders Dunbar (New Haven: Yale University Press, 1931); and Hervey Milton Cleckley, *The Mask of Sanity: An Attempt to Clarify Some Issues about the So-called Psychopathic Personality* (St. Louis: Mosby, 1941). For the best overview of

terminology, see Henry Werlinder, *Psychopathy: A History of the Concepts: Analysis of the Origin and Development of a Family of Concepts in Psychopathology* (Stockholm: Almquist & Wiksell, 1978).

9. The European literature is discussed in Werlinder, *Psychopathy*, esp. 21–51, 86–97; Sidney Maughs, "A Concept of Psychopathy and Psychopathic Personality: Its Evolution and Historical Development, Part I," *Journal of Criminal Psychopathology* 2 (January 1941): 330–31; Sidney Maughs, "A Concept of Psychopathy and Psychopathic Personality: Its Evolution and Historical Development, Part II," *Journal of Criminal Psychopathology* 2 (April 1941): 466, 470–71; and Pierre Pichot, "Psychopathic Behaviour: A Historical Overview," in *Psychopathic Behaviour: Approaches to Research*, edited by R. D. Hare and D. Schalling (London: Wiley, 1978), 62–65. Early treatments of sexual psychopathy appeared in Richard von Krafft-Ebing, *Psychopathia Sexualis, with Especial Reference to Contrary Sexual Instinct: A Medico-Legal Study*, translated by Charles Gilbert Chaddock (Philadelphia: F. A. Davis Company, 1892); and George Frank Lydston, *Diseases of Society and Degeneracy (The Vice and Crime Problem)* (Philadelphia: J. B. Lippincott, 1904), 374–91.

10. William Healy, *The Individual Delinquent* (Boston: Little, Brown, 1915), 132, 575–89, 411. Similarly, Sheldon Glueck, *Mental Disorder and the Criminal Law: A Study in Medico-Sociological Jurisprudence* (Boston: Little, Brown, 1925), does not mention psychopathic sexual behavior. On the association of the psychopath with vagrancy and unemployment in America, see Herman Morris Adler, "Unemployment and Personality: A Study of Psychopathic Cases," *Mental Hygiene* 1 (January 1917): 16–24; and John W. Visher, "A Study in Constitutional Psychopathic Inferiority," *Mental Hygiene* 6 (October 1922): 729–45. On women, see Elizabeth Lunbeck, "'A New Generation of Women': Progressive Psychiatrists and the Hypersexual Female," *Feminist Studies* 13, no. 3 (Fall 1987): 513–43.

11. On the expansion of psychiatry, see Gerald Grob, *Mental Illness and American Society, 1875–1940* (Princeton, N.J.: Princeton University Press, 1983); Ben Karpman, "Milestones in the Advancement of Knowledge of the Psychopathology of Delinquency and Crime," in *Orthopsychiatry, 1923–48: Retrospect and Prospect*, edited by Lawson Gentry Lowry (New York: American Orthopsychiatry Association, 1948); Albert Deutsch, *The Mentally Ill in America: A History of Their Care and Treatment from Colonial Times to the Present* (New York: Columbia University Press, 1949), 405; Walter Bromberg, *Psychiatry between the Wars, 1918–1945: A Recollection* (Westport, Conn.: Greenwood Press, 1982), 102–22; and Janet Ann Tighe, "A Question of Responsibility: The Development of American Forensic Psychiatry, 1838–1930" (Ph.D. diss., University of Pennsylvania, 1983).

12. Peter L. Tyor, "Segregation or Surgery: The Mentally Retarded in America" (Ph.D. diss., Northwestern University, 1972); Aldo Piperno, "A Social-Legal History of the Psychopathic Offender Legislation in the United States" (Ph.D. diss., Ohio State University, 1974), esp. 89, 90; Maughs, "Concept of Psychopathy," 468, 478–79; Deutsch, *Mentally Ill in America*, 369–72; Bernard Glueck, "A Study of 608 Admissions to Sing Sing Prison," *Mental Hygiene* 2 (January 1918): 85, 91–123; Special Committee of the State Commission of Prisons, "The Psychopathic Delinquent," in *31st Annual Report of the State Commissioner of Prisons* (Ossining, N.Y., 1926),

68–96. See also David Rothman, *Conscience and Convenience: The Asylum and Its Alternatives in Progressive America* (Boston: Little, Brown, 1980), 200–201.

13. Edith R. Spaulding, *An Experimental Study of Psychopathic Delinquent Women* (New York: Rand, McNally & Company, 1923), xiii–xvi. On mental defect and female crime, see Freedman, *Their Sisters' Keepers*, 116–21; Glueck, "Admissions to Sing Sing Prison," 93; and Reuben Oppenheimer and Lulu L. Eckman, *Laws Relating to Sex Offenses against Children*, U.S. Department of Labor, Children's Bureau Publication no. 145 (Washington, D.C., 1925). See also Great Britain Home Department, *Committee on Sexual Offenses against Young Persons Report* (London, 1925).

14. Joseph Pleck, "The Theory of Male Sex Role Identity: Its Rise and Fall, 1936 to the Present," in *In the Shadow of the Past: Psychology Portrays the Sexes*, edited by Miriam Lewin (New York: Columbia University Press, 1983), 205–25.

15. For example, in 1936, Random House published an "unexpurgated edition": Havelock Ellis, *Studies in the Psychology of Sex*, 4 vols. (New York: Random House, 1936). This work, originally published in England in 1897, was widely reviewed. See also Magnus Hirschfeld, *Sexual Pathology: A Study of Arrangements of the Sexual Instincts*, translated by Jerome Gibbs (New York: Emerson Books, 1940); Richard von Krafft-Ebing, *Psychopathia Sexualis: A Medico-Forensic Study* (New York: Pioneer Publications, 1939); Katharine Bement Davis, *Studies in the Sex Lives of 2200 Women* (New York, 1928); and Robert Latou Dickinson and Lucy Beam, *The Single Woman: A Medical Study in Sex Education* (London: Williams and Norgate, 1934).

16. For examples of biological and hormonal studies, see Lowell Selling, "The Endocrine Glands and the Sex Offender," *Medical Record*, 18 May 1938, 441–44; and Clifford A. Wright, "The Sex Offenders' Endocrines," *Medical Record*, 21 June 1939, 399–402. For an analysis of sex hormone research, see Diana Long Hall, "Biology, Sex Hormones, and Sexism in the 1920s," *Philosophical Forum* 5 (Fall–Winter 1973–74): 81–97. On both the popularity of biological theories of sexual crime and the use of castration in Europe, see Marie E. Kopp, "Surgical Treatment as Sex Crime Prevention Measure," *Journal of Criminal Law and Criminology* 28 (January–February 1938): 692–706; George Henry, *Sex Variants: A Study of Homosexual Patterns* (New York: P. B. Hoeber, 1941), v–viii; and John Gagnon, "Sex Research and Social Change," *Archives of Sexual Behavior* 4 (March 1975): 124. See also Aron Krich, "Before Kinsey: Continuity in American Sex Research," *Psychoanalytic Review* 53 (Summer 1966): 69–90; and Regina Markell Morantz, "The Scientist as Sex Crusader: Alfred C. Kinsey and American Culture," *American Quarterly* 29 (Winter 1977): 563–89.

17. Eugen Kahn, *Psychopathic Personalities*, esp. 102–13; Franz Alexander and Hugo Staub, *The Criminal, the Judge, and the Public*, translated by Gregory Zilboorg (New York: MacMillan, 1931), x–xi, 109–18; Fritz Wittels, "The Criminal Psychopath in the Psychoanalytic System," *Psychoanalytic Review* 24 (July 1937): 276–91; Walter Bromberg and Charles B. Thompson, "The Relation of Psychoses, Mental Defect, and Personality Types to Crime," *Journal of Criminal Law and Criminology* 28 (May–June 1937): 77–81. For the application of Freud's theories of sexual development to psychopathic behavior, see Werlinder, *Psychopathy*, 154–61; major texts are surveyed there and in Maughs, "Concept of Psychopathy"; and Karpman, "Milestones."

18. Benjamin Karpman's work dominates the American listings on the psycho-path in the *Index of Psychoanalytic Writings*, edited by Alexander Grinstein, 14 vols. (New York, 1957), 2:1066–68. In 1923, Karpman organized a symposium on the psychopath at St. Elizabeth's Hospital, at which William Alanson White made his often-cited comment that the psychopath was the "wastebasket" classification of psychiatry. Nonetheless, Karpman's efforts to define what he called "psychopathol-ogy" as a distinct mental disease persisted through the 1950s. In 1940, in the first volume of a journal on criminal psychopathology, he outlined the principles of the field, and he later called for a national institute to study criminal psychopathol-ogy. See Benjamin Karpman, "The Principles and Aims of Criminal Psychopathol-ogy," *Journal of Criminal Psychopathology* 1 (January 1940): 187–218. For colleagues' perception of Karpman in his later years as an "eccentric, slightly pathetic figure as he honed down year after year on the psychopathic individual," see Bromberg, *Psychiatry between the Wars*, 106. Benjamin Karpman, *The Sexual Offender and His Offenses* (New York: Julian Press, 1954), is both a useful bibliographical guide to research to that date and a testament to Karpman's passion for engaging his op-ponents in debate on the subject of psychopathology. For a bibliography of Karp-man's writings, see ibid., 685–86; for his case study approach, see Ben Karpman, *The Individual Criminal: Studies in the Psychogenetics of Crime* (Washington, D.C.: Nervous and Mental Disease Publishing Company, 1935). For his role in symposia, see Benjamin Karpman et al., "Psychopathic Behavior in Infants and Children: A Critical Survey of the Existing Concepts — Round Table, 1950," *American Journal of Orthopsychiatry* 21 (April 1951): 223–72.

19. Karpman, *Sexual Offender*, 501. See also Karpman, "Principles and Aims of Criminal Psychopathology," 204. For the reversal, see, for example, Cleckley, *Mask of Sanity*, 397.

20. *New York Times Index*, 1936–60. Many urban newspapers expanded coverage of sex crimes. On Detroit, Cleveland, Omaha, and Lincoln, Nebraska, newspapers, see California Legislative Assembly, Interim Committee on Judicial System and Judicial Process, *Final Report of the Subcommittee on Sex Crimes* (Sacramento, 1951), 120; Piperno, "Social-Legal History," 118, 136; and Domenico Caporale and Deryl F. Hamann, "Sexual Psychopathy: A Legal Labyrinth of Medicine, Morals and My-thology," *Nebraska Law Review* 36 (1957): 321n.

21. Howard Whitman, "The City That DOES Something about Sex Crimes," *Col-lier's*, 21 January 1950, 21; "Can We End Sex Crimes?," *Christian Century*, 22 De-cember 1937, 154–55; Michael Brush, "Are Sex Crimes Due to Sex?," *New Masses*, 26 October 1937, 15–16; Glueck, "Sex Crimes and the Law," 318–20; "Queer People," *Newsweek*, 10 October 1949, 52. Not until the 1950s and 1960s did the traditional women's magazines begin to feature articles about sex crimes, usually focusing on protecting children. See, for example, Dorothy Diamond and Frances Tenenbaum, "To Protect Your Child from Sex Offenders," *Better Homes and Gardens* 31 (May 1953): 160–62; and Margaret Hickey, "Protecting Children against Sex Offenders, Omaha, Nebraska," *Ladies' Home Journal* 74 (April 1957): 31–33, 37–38.

22. *New York Times*, 21 March 1937, 24; 23 March 1937, 48; 27 March 1937, 14; 11 April 1937, 40; 6 August 1937, 18; 12 August 1937, 8; 13 August 1937, 19; 15 August 1937,

20; 24 August 1937, 27; 25 August 1937, 3; and 31 August 1937, 11. For the call for action against "suspicious characters," see ibid., 15 August 1937, 20.

23. Ibid., 24 September 1937, 46; 8 September 1937, 16; and 6 November 1937, 18; Wile, "Society and Sex Offenders," 571; *New York Times*, 24 January 1950, 22; and 4 February 1950, 6. For a criminologist's response to public vengefulness, see ibid., 24 October 1951, 26.

24. *New York Herald Tribune*, 26 September 1937, quoted in Jack Frosch and Walter Bromberg, "The Sex Offender: A Psychiatric Study," *American Journal of Orthopsychiatry* 9 (October 1939): 761–67; J. Edgar Hoover, "How Safe Is Your Daughter?," *American Magazine* 144 (July 1947): 32. J. Edgar Hoover's views were quoted to a subcommittee of the U.S. House Judiciary Committee considering a bill making it a federal offense to flee across state borders to escape prosecution for degenerate acts with a minor. See Sheldon S. Levy, "Interactions of Institution and Policy Groups: The Origins of Sex Crime Legislation," *Lawyer and Law Notes* 5 (Spring 1951): 32.

25. "Marty" to "Howard," pseuds., 8 January 1946, in the possession of Allan Bérubé. I am grateful to Allan Bérubé for sharing this and other sources. A burglar confessed to the killing; there was no mention of "degeneracy" in the coverage of his conviction, and the murderer was eventually committed to the penitentiary for the criminally insane. See *Chicago Tribune*, 8 January 1946, 1–2; 9 January 1946, 1–2; 10 January 1946, 1–3; 11 January 1946, 1–2; 12 January 1946, 4; 13 January 1946, 1, 6; and 14 January 1946, 1–2.

26. *New York Times*, 1 October 1937, 46; 14 October 1937, 52; and 15 October 1937, 17; Mayor's Committee for the Study of Sex Offenses in the City of New York, *Report* (New York, 1943), 1–5. The Bellevue program is also discussed in Joseph Wortis, "Sex Taboos, Sex Offenders, and the Law," *American Journal of Orthopsychiatry* 9 (July 1939): 554; and Donald Shaskan, "One Hundred Sex Offenders," *American Journal of Orthopsychiatry* 9 (July 1939): 565–66. In 1937, the Commonwealth of Massachusetts established a Committee of Four to recommend changes in laws relating to sexual delinquency. See *New York Times*, 5 September 1937, 7.

27. Mayor's Committee, *Report*, 5, 11–14; Karl M. Bowman, "The Challenge of Sex Offenders," *Mental Hygiene* 22 (January 1938): 10–24. See also Wile, "Society and Sex Offenders," 571–72. For other criticisms of the expansion of psychiatric authority and of sexual psychopath laws, see Frederick Wertham, "Psychiatry and the Prevention of Sex Crimes," *Journal of Criminal Law and Criminology* 28 (March–April 1938): 848–50; William Scott Stewart, "Concerning Proposed Legislation for the Commitment of Sex Offenders," *John Marshall Law Quarterly* 3 (March 1938): 407–21; Gregory Zilboorg, "The Overestimation of Psychopathology," *American Journal of Orthopsychiatry* 9 (January 1939): 90–91; James E. Hughes, "The Minnesota 'Sexual Irresponsibles' Law," *Mental Hygiene* 25 (January 1941): 76–86; and George H. Dession, "Psychiatry and the Conditioning of Criminal Justice," *Yale Law Journal* 47 (January 1938): 319–40.

28. Piperno, "Social-Legal History," 117–18, 72. Similarly, in 1935, the Michigan state legislature passed the "Goodrich Act" in response to publicity surrounding the mutilation-murder of a young girl by a former mental institution inmate named Goodrich who had a record of sex offenses. Although the original 1935 Michigan

law (rev. 1937) was declared unconstitutional, a 1939 revision remained in force. See ibid., 91–96.

29. Ibid., 118, 134–35.

30. The number of magazine articles about sex crimes dropped from eleven between 1937 and 1939 to three between 1940 and 1947. The number rose to thirty for the decade 1947–57. See *Readers' Guide to Periodical Literature*, 1937–57. For the renewal of antiprostitution campaigns spearheaded by the American Social Hygiene Association, see its publication, the *Journal of Social Hygiene* 29 (1943). See also, for example, Paul Kinsie, "To Combat the Return of Commercialized Prostitution," *American City* 64 (August 1949): 102–3. On World War II, see Francis E. Merrill, *Social Problems on the Homefront* (New York: Harper, 1948), 122–44; and Karen Anderson, *Wartime Women: Sex Roles, Family Relations, and the Status of Women during World War II* (Westport, Conn.: Greenwood Press, 1981), 103–11.

31. Rebecca Green, "The Role of the Psychiatrist in World War II" (Ph.D. diss., Columbia University, 1977); Allan Bérubé, "Coming Out under Fire," book ms., chap. 7, in the possession of Allan Bérubé [author's note: subsequently published as *Coming Out under Fire: The History of Gay Men and Women in World War Two* (New York: Free Press, 1990), chap. 6]; William Chafe, *The American Woman: Her Changing Social, Economic, and Political Roles, 1920–1970* (New York: Oxford University Press, 1972), 174–225; Elaine Tyler May, "Explosive Issues: Sex, Women, and the Bomb in Postwar America," paper presented at the annual meeting of the American Historical Association, Washington, D.C., December 1982, in the possession of Elaine Tyler May. On the relation of the postwar political reaction to strictures against sexual nonconformity, see John D'Emilio, *Sexual Politics, Sexual Communities: The Making of a Homosexual Minority in the United States, 1940–1970* (Chicago: University of Chicago Press, 1983), 40–53. On Kinsey, see Morantz, "Scientist as Sex Crusader."

32. Karl Bowman, "Review of Sex Legislation and Control of Sex Offenders in the United States of America," *International Review of Criminal Policy* 4 (July 1953): 20–39; Swanson, "Sexual Psychopath Statutes," 228–35; Brakel and Rock, *The Mentally Disabled and the Law*, 341–75. The postwar laws, most of which passed between 1949 and 1953, and revisions of older ones remedied some of the most blatant abuses of due process rights by requiring criminal conviction before psychiatric observation and indeterminate sentencing. However, in some states, notably California, released sexual psychopaths were required to register with local police whenever they moved, even if their convictions had been set aside or expunged. Piperno, "Social-Legal History," 94–107, gives an excellent summary of the legal cases concerning the psychopath laws.

33. Bowman, *California . . . Report*, 13; California Assembly, *Final Report*, 43–45; Brakel and Rock, *The Mentally Disabled and the Law*, 348 (n. 59); Kittrie, *Right to Be Different*, 192; Piperno, "Social-Legal History," 181, table 3, 176. On the types of offenses and characteristics of offenders, see Bowman, "Review of Sex Legislation," 22–23, appendix, 33–39; Paul Gebhard et al., *Sex Offenders: An Analysis of Types* (New York: Harper & Row, 1965), 865–66; Governor's Study Commission, *Report on the Deviated Criminal Sex Offender*, 35–36; and California Assembly, *Preliminary*

Report, 30–40. On the race of sex offenders, see A. R. Mangus, "Study of Sex Crimes in California," in Bowman, *California . . . Report*, esp. 28; Leonard D. Savitz and Harold I. Lief, "Negro and White Sex Crime Rates," in *Sexual Behavior and the Law*, edited by Ralph Slovenko (Springfield, Ill.: Thomas, 1965), 210–30; Karl M. Bowman and Bernice Engle, "Review of Scientific Literature on Sexual Deviation: A Review of Recent Medicolegal Opinion regarding Sex Laws," in California Department of Mental Hygiene, *Sexual Deviation Research* (Sacramento, 1953), 115; Piperno, "Social-Legal History," 182; Irwin August Berg, "Mental Deterioration among Sex Offenders," *Journal of Criminal Law* 34 (September 1943): 184; and Frosch and Bromberg, "Sex Offender," 761–76.

34. The concept of sexual identity, as opposed to sexual act, has been influenced by Mary McIntosh, "The Homosexual Role," *Social Problems* 16, no. 2 (Fall 1968): 184. See also Jeffrey Weeks, *Coming Out: Homosexual Politics in Britain, from the Nineteenth Century to the Present* (London: Quartet, 1977), 9–44. In 1931, a Maryland judge explained that he was sentencing a sex offender to death because there was no suitable institution in which this type of criminal could be treated. See Piperno, "Social-Legal History," 72.

35. Commonwealth of Massachusetts, *Final Report of the Special Commission Investigating the Prevalence of Sex Crimes*, House Document 2169 (Boston, 1948); New Hampshire Interim Commission to Study the Cause and Prevention of Serious Sex Crimes, *Report* (Concord, 1949); Tappan, *Habitual Sex Offender*; California Assembly, *Preliminary Report*; Governor's Study Commission, *Report on the Deviated Criminal Sex Offender*; Pennsylvania General Assembly, Joint State Government Commission, *Sex Offenders: A Report to the General Assembly* (Harrisburg, 1951); Virginia Commission to Study Sex Offenses, *The Sex Offender and the Criminal Law: Report to the Governor and the General Assembly* (Richmond, 1951); Illinois Commission on Sex Offenders, *Report to the 68th General Assembly of the State of Illinois* (Springfield, Ill., 1953); Oregon Legislative Assembly, Interim Committee to Study Sex Crime Prevention, *Report Submitted to the 49th Legislative Assembly, 1955* (Portland, 1956); Minnesota Legislature, Interim Commission on Public Welfare Laws, *Sex Psychopath Laws Report* (St. Paul, 1959).

36. State-funded research projects on sex offenders were conducted in New York, California, New Jersey, Nevada, Pennsylvania, and Oregon. Between 1951 and 1954, Bowman's Sexual Deviation Study received almost $200,000 to conduct biochemical research on sexual psychopaths in the state mental hospitals, analyze police statistics on sex crimes, and study the child victims of sexual assault. See California Assembly, *Final Report*, 107–8; Mariana Robinson, *The Coming of Age of the Langley Porter Clinic: The Reorganization of a Mental Health Institute* (Tuscaloosa: University of Alabama Press, 1962), 7; and David Abrahamson, "Study of 102 Sex Offenders at Sing Sing," *Federal Probation* 14 (September 1950): 26–32. Albert Ellis and Ralph Brancale, with Ruth R. Doorbar, *The Psychology of Sex Offenders* (Springfield, Ill.: Thomas, 1956), is based on psychiatric evaluation of 300 men at the New Jersey Diagnostic Center, conducted under the Sex Offender Acts of 1949 and 1950.

37. Bowman, "Review of Sex Legislation," appendix; California Assembly, *Preliminary Report*, 50–55; George N. Thompson, "Electroshock and Other Therapeutic

Considerations in Sexual Psychopathy," *Journal of Nervous and Mental Diseases* 109 (June 1949): 531 – 39. For a critical summary of treatment methods, see Group for the Advancement of Psychiatry, *Psychiatry and Sex Psychopath Legislation: The 30s to the 80s* (New York, 1977).

38. Committee on Forensic Psychiatry, Group for the Advancement of Psychiatry, *Psychiatrically Deviated Sex Offenders* (Topeka, Kans., 1949); Tappan, *Habitual Sex Offender*, 14, 22; Bowman and Engle, "Review of Scientific Literature," 115, 120. See also an influential 1950 essay, Sutherland, "Diffusion of Sexual Psychopath Laws," 281 – 89; Karl M. Bowman and Milton Rose, "A Criticism of Current Usage of the Term 'Sexual Psychopath,'" *American Journal of Psychiatry* 109 (September 1952): 177 – 82; and Manfred S. Guttmacher and Henry Wiehofen, *Psychiatry and the Law* (New York, 1952), 111 – 16.

39. Legal critics include Morris Ploscowe, *Sex and the Law* (New York: Prentice-Hall, 1951); Caporale and Hamann, "Sexual Psychopathy"; Ferd Paul Mihm, "A Re-Examination of the Validity of Our Sex Psychopath Statutes in the Light of Recent Appeal Cases and Experience," *Journal of Criminal Law and Criminology* 44 (March – April 1954): 716 – 36; and Stanton Wheeler, "Sex Offenses: A Sociological Critique," *Law and Contemporary Problems* 25 (Spring 1960): 258 – 78. For a summary, see Kittrie, *Right to Be Different*, 194 – 201. On the "due process revolution" and constitutional challenges to sex-offender laws, see Piperno, "Social-Legal History," 223 – 25, and the following cases: *U.S. ex rel. Gerchman v. Maroney*, 355 F2d 302 (1966); *Specht v. Patterson*, 386 U.S. 605 (1967), 87 S.Ct. 1209 (1967); *Millard v. Cameron*, 125 U.S. App. D.C. 383 (1966), 373 F2d 468 (1966); *Tippett v. State of Maryland*, 436 F2d 1153 (1971); and *Davis v. Sullivan*, 354 F.Supp. 1320 (1973).

40. Mayor's Committee, *Report*, cited in California Assembly, *Preliminary Report*, 34; Karl Bowman, *Sexual Deviation Research*, March 1952 Report to the California Assembly (Sacramento, 1952), 45 – 68; A. R. Mangus, "Child Victims of Adult Sex Offenders," in Bowman, *California . . . Report*, 31 – 34; Estelle Rogers and Joseph Weiss, "Study of Sex Crimes against Children," in Bowman, *California . . . Report*, 47 – 84; and Joseph Weiss, Estelle Rogers, Charles E. Dutton, and Miriam E. Darwin, "Summary of the Study of Child Victims of Adult Sex Offenders," in California Legislative Assembly, *Final Report on California Sexual Deviation Research*, (Sacramento, 1954), 59 – 62. For the feminist critique of the treatment of rape, see Susan Brownmiller, *Against Our Will: Men, Women, and Rape* (New York: Simon and Schuster, 1975), esp. 283 – 404.

41. Commonwealth of Massachusetts, *Final Report*, 7. See also Wini Breines and Linda Gordon, "The New Scholarship on Family Violence," *Signs: Journal of Women in Culture and Society* 8, no. 3 (Spring 1983): 490 – 531; California Assembly, *Preliminary Report*; and Louise V. Frisbie and Ernest H. Dondis, *Recidivism among Treated Sex Offenders*, California Department of Mental Hygiene, Research Monograph no. 5 (Sacramento, 1965), 14. Compare Wheeler on the use of sexual psychopath laws to institutionalize "passive" rather than aggressive offenders: "In a society stressing active mastery of the environment over passive acquiescence, perhaps it is not surprising that the aggressive sex offender who overresponds is judged less disturbed than the passive exhibitionist" ("Sex Offenses," 277). For example, of felons convicted of

sex crimes and diagnosed as sexual psychopaths in New York City between 1932 and 1938, a majority had been accused of pedophilia or homosexuality. See Frosch and Bromberg, "Sex Offender," 762–63. See also Tappan, *Habitual Sex Offender*, 20, 29; Ploscowe, *Sex and the Law*, 216–41; and Mayor's Committee, *Report*, 39, 54–55. Of the men committed to the Nebraska state hospital under the sexual psychopath law between 1949 and 1956, half had been charged with having sexual relations with children (under age thirteen) or sex with force; the other half had engaged in consensual homosexuality (7.3 percent), exhibitionism (19.5 percent), or statutory rape (22 percent). See Caporale and Hamann, "Sexual Psychopathy," 325.

42. D'Emilio, *Sexual Politics*, 23–33; Allan Bérubé, "Coming Out under Fire," *Mother Jones* 8 (February–March 1983): 23–29, 45; Weeks, *Coming Out*, 1–7; Barbara Ehrenreich, *The Hearts of Men: American Dreams and the Flight from Commitment* (Garden City, N.Y.: Anchor Press/Doubleday, 1983), 26.

43. Ronald Bayer, *Homosexuality and American Psychiatry: The Politics of Diagnosis* (New York: Basic Books, 1981), 28–40; D'Emilio, *Sexual Politics*, 40–53. In 1955, when members of the American Law Institute suggested decriminalizing homosexuality in the institute's model penal code, the council rejected the proposal because it claimed homosexuality was "a cause or symptom of moral decay in a society and should be repressed by law" (American Law Institute, *Model Penal Code: Tentative Draft No. 4* [Philadelphia, 1955], 276).

44. William Jaines, H. R. Hoffman, and H. A. Esser, "Commitments under the Criminal Sexual Psychopath Law in the Criminal Court of Cook County, Illinois," *American Journal of Psychiatry* 105 (December 1948): 425. The fear of community-wide sexual corruption — and the exploitation of that fear for political ends — is explored in John Gerassi, *The Boys of Boise* (New York: Collier Books, 1966), a journalist's investigation of the homosexual scandals in Boise, Idaho, in 1955–56. See J. Paul de River, *The Sexual Criminal: A Psychoanalytic Study* (Springfield, Ill.: Thomas, 1951), xii. On the fear of homosexual recruitment, see also Norwood W. East, "Sexual Offenders," *Journal of Nervous and Mental Diseases* 103 (June 1946): 648–49; and Bowman and Engle, "Review of Scientific Literature," 117–19. For the attribution of most perversion to unconscious homosexuality, see Sandor Lorand, "Perverse Tendencies: Their Influence on Personality," *Psychoanalytic Review* 26 (April 1939): 178.

45. The call for greater public discussion of sexuality appeared early and consistently in the psychopath literature. See, for example, Bowman, "Challenge of Sex Offenders"; Guttmacher and Wiehofen, *Psychiatry and the Law*, 136; and Ellis and Brancale, *Psychology of Sex Offenders*, esp. 91–92. Public hearings and attitudinal surveys are described in California Assembly, *Preliminary Report*, 9, 81–223; and Tappan, *Habitual Sex Offender*, 11, 57–67. On the Oregon booklet, see William J. Petrus, "Can We Prevent, Control, and Treat Deviated Sex Offenders?," typescript, [1954 or later], Papers of the American Social Hygiene Association, Social Welfare History Archives, University of Minnesota, Minneapolis. On Long Beach, see Jeree Crowther, "Answer to Sex Fiends," *American City* 119 (April 1950): 65.

46. "Comment: The Spectral Evidence of Sex Offenses," *American Journal of Psychiatry* 108 (February 1952): 629–30. On scapegoating, see Paul Tappan, "Sentences

for Sex Criminals," *Journal of Criminal Law and Criminology* 42 (September – October 1951): 335 – 36. On the importance of Kinsey's work in reassessing "normal" sexuality, see Group for the Advancement of Psychiatry, *Psychiatrically Deviated Sex Offenders*, 2; Bowman, "Review of Sex Legislation," 26 – 28; Bernard C. Glueck Jr., "An Evaluation of the Homosexual Offender," *Minnesota Law Review* 41 (January 1957): 192; Bowman and Engle, "Review of Scientific Literature"; and Bernice Engle, "Sex Offenders and the Law," *Nation*, 4 November 1954, 198. See also Wortis, "Sex Taboos," 563; Guttmacher and Wiehofen, *Psychiatry and the Law*, 136 – 37; and Ellis and Brancale, *Psychology of Sex Offenders*, 93 – 94, 97, 127 – 32.

Chapter 8. The Prison Lesbian: Race, Class, and the Construction of the Aggressive Female Homosexual, 1915 – 1965

I am grateful to Martha Mabie for research assistance and to Allan Bérubé, Susan K. Cahn, John D'Emilio, Sharon Holland, Susan Krieger, Elaine Tyler May, Joanne Meyerowitz, Peggy Pascoe, Leila Rupp, and Nancy Stoller for their extremely useful comments on earlier versions of this essay.

1. Although courts have rarely sentenced women to prison for homosexual acts, lesbianism has long been associated with both crime and insanity. In the nineteenth century, women who passed as men were sometimes arrested and jailed, but it was their defiance of gender roles rather than their sexual acts that labeled them criminals. See San Francisco Lesbian and Gay History Project, "'She Even Chewed Tobacco': A Pictorial Narrative of Passing Women in America," in *Hidden from History: Reclaiming the Gay and Lesbian Past*, edited by Martin Bauml Duberman, Martha Vicinus, and George Chauncey Jr. (New York: New American Library, 1989), 183 – 94. Lesbians have often been institutionalized in mental hospitals and sometimes in reform schools. For an example of a young woman sent to reform school because she was a lesbian, see Madeline Davis and Elizabeth Lapovsky Kennedy, *Boots of Leather, Slippers of Gold: The History of a Lesbian Community* (New York: Routledge, 1993), 59. On the historical association between female criminality, insanity, and lesbianism, see Lynda Hart, *Fatal Women: Lesbian Sexuality and the Mark of Aggression* (Princeton, N.J.: Princeton University Press, 1994), esp. 4 – 28. Hart argues that the incidence of imprisonment for lesbianism has been masked because crimes labeled "lewdness" or prostitution were in fact related to lesbianism. On this point, see Ruthann Robson, *Lesbian (Out)law: Survival under the Rule of Law* (Ithaca, N.Y.: Firebrand Books, 1992). On associations among women criminals, insanity, gender inversion, and lesbianism in specific historical cases, see Lisa Duggan, "The Trials of Alice Mitchell: Sensationalism, Sexology, and the Lesbian Subject in Turn-of-the-Century America," *Signs: Journal of Women in Culture and Society* 18, no. 4 (Summer 1993): 791 – 814; and Claire Bond Potter, "'I'll Go the Limit and Then Some': Gun Molls, Desire, and Danger in the 1930s," *Feminist Studies* 21, no. 1 (Spring 1995): 46.

2. Charles A. Ford, "Homosexual Practices of Institutionalized Females," *Journal of Abnormal Psychology* 23 (January – March 1929): 442; Elizabeth M. Kates, "Sexual

Problems in Women's Institutions," *Journal of Social Therapy* 1 (October 1955): 187. Other later studies include Mary A. Kopp, "A Study of Anomia and Homosexuality in Delinquent Adolescent Girls" (Ph.D. diss., St. Louis University, 1960); James Stephen Howard, "Determinants of Sex-Role Identifications of Homosexual Female Delinquents" (Ph.D. diss., University of Southern California, 1962); Seymour L. Halleck and Marvin Hersko, "Homosexual Behavior in a Correctional Institution for Adolescent Girls," *American Journal of Orthopsychiatry* 32 (October 1962): 911–17; William G. Miller and Thomas E. Hannum, "Characteristics of Homosexuality in Involved Incarcerated Females," *Journal of Consulting Psychology* 27 (June 1963): 277; Max Hammer, "Homosexuality in a Women's Reformatory," *Corrective Psychiatry and Journal of Social Therapy* 4 (May 1965): 168–69; David A. Ward and Gene G. Kassebaum, *Women's Prison: Sex and Social Structure* (Chicago: Aldine Publishing, 1965); and Rose Giallombardo, *Society of Women: A Study of a Women's Prison* (New York: John Wiley, 1966). For a discussion of the criminological literature on race and gender in reform schools for girls, see Kathryn Hinojosa Baker, "Delinquent Desire: Race, Sex, and Ritual in Reform Schools for Girls," *Discourse* 15 (Fall 1992): 41–61.

3. On middle-class lesbian history, see, for example, Lillian Faderman, *Surpassing the Love of Men: Romantic Friendship and Love between Women from the Renaissance to the Present* (New York: William Morrow, 1981); Lillian Faderman, *Odd Girls and Twilight Lovers: A History of Lesbian Life in Twentieth-Century America* (New York: Columbia University Press, 1991); Carroll Smith-Rosenberg, "The Female World of Love and Ritual: Relations between Women in Nineteenth-Century America," *Signs: Journal of Women in Culture and Society* 1, no. 1 (Autumn 1975): 1–29; Nancy Sahli, "Smashing: Women's Relationships before the Fall," *Chrysalis* 8 (Summer 1979): 17–27; and Leila J. Rupp, "'Imagine My Surprise': Women's Relationships in Historical Perspective," *Frontiers* 5, no. 3 (Fall 1980): 61–70. On working-class lesbian history, see, for example, Jonathan Katz, ed., *Gay American History: Lesbians and Gay Men in the U.S.A.* (New York: Thomas Cromwell, 1976), esp. 209–81; San Francisco Lesbian and Gay History Project, "'She Even Chewed Tobacco'"; Eric Garber, "'T'Ain't Nobody's Bizness': Homosexuality in 1920s Harlem," in *Black Men/White Men*, edited by Michael J. Smith (San Francisco: Gay Sunshine Press, 1983); Allan Bérubé, *Coming Out under Fire: The History of Gay Men and Women in World War Two* (New York: Free Press, 1990); Madeline Davis and Elizabeth Lapovsky Kennedy, "Oral History and the Study of Sexuality in the Lesbian Community: Buffalo, New York, 1940–1960," *Feminist Studies* 12, no. 1 (Spring 1986): 7–26; Davis and Kennedy, *Boots of Leather, Slippers of Gold*; and John D'Emilio, *Sexual Politics, Sexual Communities: The Making of a Homosexual Minority in the United States, 1940–1970* (Chicago: University of Chicago Press, 1983). On medicalization, see George Chauncey Jr., "From Sexual Inversion to Homosexuality: Medicine and the Changing Conceptualization of Female Deviance," *Salmagundi* 58–59 (Fall 1982–Winter 1983): 114–46; and Jennifer Terry, "Lesbians under the Medical Gaze: Scientists Search for Remarkable Differences," *Journal of Sex Research* 27, no. 3 (August 1990): 317–39.

4. On the founding, populations, and administrations of reformatory prisons,

see Estelle B. Freedman, *Their Sisters' Keepers: Women's Prison Reform in America, 1830–1930* (Ann Arbor: University of Michigan Press, 1981).

5. More African American women served sentences in state prisons than in reformatory prisons. In 1923, for example, black women constituted 64.5 percent of the women in custodial prisons but only 11.9 percent of the inmates in women's reformatories. See Nicole Hahn Rafter, *Partial Justice: Women in State Prisons, 1800–1935* (Boston: Northeastern University Press, 1985), table 6.5, 146. The overrepresentation of women of color in the prison population is evident from 1950 U.S. Census data on institutional populations. Out of a total of approximately 13,000 adult women prisoners, 56 percent were white and 44 percent were labeled "nonwhite." White women were incarcerated at a rate of 10.8 per 100,000 in the population; "nonwhite" women's rate was 68.8 per 100,000. See *National Institute of Mental Health, Psychiatric Services, and the Changing Institutional Scene, 1950–1985*, DHEW Publication (ADM) 77-433 (Washington, D.C.: Government Printing Office, 1977), 24–25, 60–62, 63–67. For a rare historical analysis of African American women's prison experience, see Anne M. Butler, "Still in Chains: Black Women in Western Prisons, 1865–1910," in *"We Specialize in the Wholly Impossible": A Reader in Black Women's History*, edited by Darlene Clark Hine, Wilma King, and Linda Reed (Brooklyn: Carlson Publishing, 1995), 321–34.

6. On the concerns of male prison administrators, see, for example, Samuel Kahn, *Mentality and Homosexuality* (Boston: Meador Publishing, 1937), a study of New York City penal institutions conducted in the 1920s, and, for Massachusetts, Maurice Winslow, Superintendent, Norfolk Prison Colony, to Arthur T. Lyman, Commissioner of Corrections, 17 August 1939, "Administrative Correspondence" file, Human Services, Corrections, Commonwealth of Massachusetts Archives, Boston.

7. Margaret Otis, "A Perversion Not Commonly Noted," *Journal of Abnormal Psychology* 7 (June–July 1913): 112–16.

8. Freedman, *Their Sisters' Keepers*, 139–40. See also Ruth Alexander's discussion of the Bedford Hills inquiry in *The "Girl Problem": Female Sexual Delinquency in New York, 1920–1930* (Ithaca, N.Y.: Cornell University Press, 1995), 91–92. On the impact of "race suicide" fears on white women, who were urged to bear children, and black women, who were subject to sterilization, see Elaine Tyler May, *Barren in the Promised Land: Childless Americans and the Pursuit of Happiness* (New York: Basic Books, 1995), chaps. 2–3.

9. Ford, "Homosexual Practices," 442–47; Samuel Kahn, *Mentality and Homosexuality*, 123–24; Theodora M. Abel, "Dominant Behavior of Institutionalized Subnormal Negro Girls: An Experimental Study," *American Journal of Mental Deficiency* 67 (April 1943): 429.

10. Felice Swados, *House of Fury* (Garden City, N.Y.: Doubleday, Doran & Company, 1941), 40–41. Swados implicitly criticized her white characters' racist objectification of black women. At the same time, however, the platonic interracial love she favored in the novel served to underscore the pathology of lesbianism.

11. See Chauncey, "From Sexual Inversion to Homosexuality"; and Faderman, *Odd Girls*, chap. 2.

12. Sander Gilman, "Black Bodies, White Bodies: Toward an Iconography of Female Sexuality in Late Nineteenth-Century Art, Medicine, and Literature," in *"Race," Writing, and Difference*, edited by Henry Louis Gates Jr. (Chicago: University of Chicago Press, 1986), 237. On the exclusion of black women from the category "woman," see Evelyn Brooks-Higginbotham, "African-American Women's History and the Meta-language of Race," *Signs: Journal of Women in Culture and Society* 17, no. 2 (Winter 1992): 256–58. On the historical association of blacks with hypersexuality, see Winthrop Jordan, *White over Black: American Attitudes toward the Negro, 1550–1812* (Baltimore: Penguin Books, 1969). A parallel association among nonprison lesbians appears in gynecological literature from the 1930s that described the black lesbian as having a long, erectile clitoris. According to Terry, the description "occupied an analogous position to the common representation of black men as having unusually long penises, signifying an ideological link between blackness and hypersexuality" ("Lesbians under the Medical Gaze," 334).

13. John Holland Cassity, "Socio-Psychiatric Aspects of Female Felons," *Journal of Criminal Psychopathology* 3 (April 1942): 600. Cassity also discussed infanticide and prostitutes who attacked their pimps (ibid., 597–604). See also his "Personality Study of 200 Murders," *Journal of Criminal Psychopathology* 2 (January 1941): esp. 303. On prostitutes, see Margaret Brenman, "Urban Lower-Class Negro Girls," *Psychiatry: Journal of the Biology and Pathology of Interpersonal Relations* 6 (August 1943): 321.

14. Elizabeth Lunbeck, "'A New Generation of Women': Progressive Psychiatrists and the Hypersexual Female," *Feminist Studies* 13, no. 3 (Fall 1987): 538; Elizabeth Lunbeck, *The Psychiatric Persuasion: Knowledge, Gender, and Power in Modern America* (Princeton, N.J.: Princeton University Press, 1994), 194, 204–7, 297–98.

15. Frances Strakosch, *Factors in the Sex Life of Seven Hundred Psychopathic Women* (Utica, N.Y.: State Hospitals Press, 1934), 61–62; Maurice A. R. Hennessy, "Homosexual Charges against Children," *Journal of Criminal Psychopathology* 2 (April 1941): 529. On the middle-class "lesbian taboo," see Christina Simmons, "Marriage in the Modern Manner: Sexual Radicalism and Reform in America, 1914–1941" (Ph.D. diss., Brown University, 1982).

16. Ford, "Homosexual Practices"; Otis, "A Perversion Not Commonly Noted"; Florence Monahan, *Women in Crime* (New York: I. Washburn, 1941), 224–25. On working-class women who first learned about lesbianism while in a girls' reformatory or a women's prison, as well as lesbians who worked as prostitutes and served time in women's prisons, see, for example, the report on "bulldiking" written by Perry M. Lichtenstein, the physician at the New York City Tombs. His "The 'Fairy' and the Lady Lover," *Medical Review of Reviews* 27 (August 1921): 369–74, is extracted in Jonathan Ned Katz, *Gay/Lesbian Almanac: A New Documentary* (New York: Harper Colophon, 1983), 402–3; Rusty Brown, "Always Me," in *Long Time Passing: Lives of Older Lesbians*, edited by Marcy Adelman (Boston: Alyson, 1986), 144–51; Davis and Kennedy, *Boots of Leather, Slippers of Gold*, 60, 96–100, 329; and Joan Nestle, "Lesbians and Prostitutes: An Historical Sisterhood," in *Sex Work: Writings by Women in the Sex Industry*, edited by Frederique Delacoste and Priscilla Alexander (San Francisco: Cleis Press, 1987), 231–47.

17. Samuel Kahn, *Mentality and Homosexuality*, 24; Sheldon Glueck and Eleanor Glueck, *Five Hundred Delinquent Women* (New York: Alfred Knopf, 1934). In a 1932 study of a reformatory for girls, sociologist Lowell Selling labeled the pervasive wife/husband interracial relationships as nonpathological "pseudohomosexuality," in contrast to a mere 2 percent of the inmates characterized by "overt homosexual existence." He recognized, however, that the latter were "usually shrewd enough to conceal this relationship from the authorities." See Lowell S. Selling, "The Pseudo Family," *American Journal of Sociology* 37 (May 1932): 247–53.

18. Women who studied or worked in women's reformatories who had long-term female partners include former Bedford Hills reformatory staff member Jessie Taft, who lived with Virginia Robinson, and Miriam Van Waters, who had a long-term relationship with philanthropist Geraldine Thompson. Democratic Party politician Molly Dewson and social worker Polly Porter met when they both worked at a Massachusetts girls' reformatory. See Estelle B. Freedman, *Maternal Justice: Miriam Van Waters and the Female Reform Tradition* (Chicago: University of Chicago Press, 1996), chap. 9; and Susan Ware, *Partner and I: Molly Dewson, Feminism, and New Deal Politics* (New Haven: Yale University Press, 1987), 55. On reform schools in the 1920s, see Monahan, *Women in Crime*, 223–24. The 1931 case involved the superintendent of the Alabama State Training School for Girls and is detailed in clippings files labeled "Reformatories — Ala. — Girls" in the Southern History Department at the Birmingham, Alabama, library. I am extremely grateful to Susan K. Cahn for sharing this material with me.

19. Minutes of the Conference of Superintendents of Correctional Institutions for Women and Girls, 1944, 21, Miriam Van Waters Papers, Schlesinger Library, Radcliffe College, Cambridge, Mass. (hereafter cited as MVWP). Note that Mead concluded that in the postwar period, "For the first time in our lives, we are going to face society that has more women than men in this generation, and female homosexuality will be a problem, not alone in the institutions but in society at large." In 1942, the women superintendents also heard an address by Caroline Zachery on "Problems of Homosexuality in the Institutions"; in 1943, they invited an Austrian psychoanalyst to discuss "Female Homosexuality in Correctional Institutions" (ibid.).

20. "I Lived in a Hell behind Bars," *True Confessions*, March 1954, 32. Pulp novels include James Harvey, *Degraded Women* (New York: Midwood Tower, 1962); and Ann Aldrich, ed., *Carol in a Thousand Cities* (Greenwich, Conn.: Gold Medal Books, 1960). The 1932 women's prison film *Ladies They Talk About* had a brief scene portraying a comic butch lesbian; in *Caged*, a sinister butch attempted to seduce a young woman played by Eleanor Parker, who was nominated for an Academy Award as best actress for her part. Other 1950s women's prison films include *Girls in Prison* and *Reform School Girl*. (I am grateful to Joanne Meyerowitz for calling to my attention the series of articles in *True Confessions*, to Allan Bérubé for reminding me of the pulp novels, and to Andrea Davies Henderson for providing a tape of *Ladies They Talk About*.) On changing depictions of homosexuality in film, see Vito Russo, *The Celluloid Closet: Homosexuality in the Movies* (New York: Harper & Row, 1981). For an analysis of contemporary films about lesbians in prison, see Kar-

lene Faith, *Unruly Women: The Politics of Confinement and Resistance* (Vancouver: Press Gang Publishers, 1993), 259–62.

21. A. M. Shotwell, "A Study of Psychopathic Delinquency," *American Journal of Mental Deficiency* 51 (July 1946): 57–62; Albertine Winner, "Homosexuality in Women," *Medical Problems* 218 (July–December 1947): 219–20.

22. Donna Penn, "The Sexualized Woman: The Lesbian, the Prostitute, and the Containment of Female Sexuality in Post-War America," in *Not June Cleaver: Women and Gender in Postwar America, 1945–1960*, edited by Joanne Meyerowitz (Philadelphia: Temple University Press, 1994). On a corresponding association of female athletes with aggressive masculinity, see Susan K. Cahn, *Coming on Strong: Gender and Sexuality in Twentieth-Century Women's Sport* (New York: Free Press, 1994), esp. chap. 7.

23. For an inmate's observation of interracial relations in a women's prison, see Elizabeth Gurley Flynn, *The Alderson Story: My Life as a Political Prisoner* (New York: International Publishers, 1963), 178–79. Flynn, like novelist Felice Swados, considered the sexualization of black women by white inmates a form of racism, which she called "'white chauvinism' masquerading as 'love,'" in interracial lesbian relations" (ibid., 178). Interracial lesbian relationships outside prison may have become more common during the 1950s. See Davis and Kennedy, *Boots of Leather, Slippers of Gold*; and Audre Lorde, *Zami: A New Spelling of My Name* (Trumansburg, N.Y.: Crossing Press, 1983). Lorde observed a predominance of black butches and white femmes in 1950s bar culture. On the nexus of race and sexual roles in Lorde's work, see Katie King, "Audre Lorde's Lacquered Layerings: The Lesbian Bar as a Site of Literary Production," in *New Lesbian Criticism: Literary and Cultural Readings*, edited by Sally Munt (New York: Columbia University Press, 1993), 51–74.

24. Kates, "Sexual Problems," 188, 190.

25. Katharine Sullivan, *Girls on Parole* (Boston: Houghton Mifflin/Riverside Press, 1956), 111–19.

26. Ibid., 111–21.

27. Ruth Frankenberg describes a shift from an essentialist race consciousness in early-twentieth-century American society to a "color-blindness" that she labels "color evasiveness" and "power evasiveness." Her categories well describe the social science literature on women's prisons in the 1960s. See Ruth Frankenberg, *The Social Construction of Whiteness: White Women, Race Matters* (Minneapolis: University of Minnesota Press, 1993), 13–15. On shifting racial paradigms in modern America, see also Michael Omi and Howard Winant, *Racial Formation in the United States: From the 1960s to the 1990s*, 2d ed. (New York: Routledge, 1994).

28. Ward and Kassebaum, *Women's Prison*, 136, 197–200; Giallombardo, *Society of Women*, fig. 2, 177, fig. 3, 183. (Six of the ten "marriages" between women diagrammed consisted of interracial couples, three were between white women [two of them "divorced"], and one was between black women.) The only passing reference to race suggested that whites were slightly overrepresented as butches and blacks as femmes, an observation rarely found in this literature. For examples of reform school literature that similarly ignores or evades race, see Halleck and Hersko, "Ho-

mosexual Behavior"; and Sidney Kosofsky and Albert Ellis, "Illegal Communication among Institutionalized Female Delinquents," *Journal of Social Psychology* 48 (August 1958): 155–60.

The absence of any discussion of race in these studies does not reflect the prison population. Giallombardo's figures on prior commitments, broken down by race, reveal that over 40 percent of the Alderson prison population was "Negro" (*Society of Women*). The assumption of a liberal "race-blind" approach during the 1960s may have represented a reaction to earlier social scientific arguments linking biological race and criminality. Ward and Kassebaum, for example, explicitly reject biological explanations of homosexuality, although they tend to substitute psychoanalytic interpretations (*Women's Prison*, esp. 104 [n. 4]). Both studies are sympathetic to their subjects, resisting the demonization of lesbians in popular literature in favor of a functionalist explanation of the sexual and familial roles assumed by women prisoners.

For evidence of the continued eroticization of race in female correctional institutions, see Barbara Lillian Carter, "On the Grounds: Informal Culture in a Girls Reform School" (Ph.D. diss., Brandeis University, 1972), chap. 6. In this study, a black female observer found that "the single most important factor" determining butch/femme roles was race. Disproportionate numbers of blacks became "Butches and high status girls; and whites, equally disproportionately, became Femmes and lower status girls" (ibid., 128).

29. Thus far, I have found only one passing reference to Mexican American lesbians in prison. See Michela Robbins, "The Inside Story of a Girls Reformatory," *Collier's*, 30 October 1953, 74–79, cited in Kathryn Hinojosa Baker, "Delinquent Desire," 59. The juvenile delinquency and post-1945 women's prison literature may provide richer sources for a multiracial account.

30. Hart, *Fatal Women*, 107–9, 117. On postwar sexual regulation, see Estelle B. Freedman, "'Uncontrolled Desires': The Response to the Sexual Psychopath, 1920–1960," *Journal of American History* 74 (June 1987): 83–106; Elaine Tyler May, *Homeward Bound: American Families in the Cold War Era* (New York: Basic Books, 1988), esp. chap. 4; D'Emilio, *Sexual Politics, Sexual Communities*; and Ricki Solinger, *Wake Up Little Susie: Single Pregnancy and Race before Roe v. Wade* (New York: Routledge, 1992).

31. Miriam Van Waters, handwritten notes, 11 April 1938, and Helen Schnefel to Miriam Van Waters, 4 October 1932, MVWP.

32. Dr. Pavenstedt, Report on Student 16590, 1943–47, and Report on Student 18572, 30 March 1948, McDowell Exhibits, 20, 21 February 1949, MVWP; Interview by Mr. Swanson, 19 January 1949, MVWP.

33. All inmate names have been changed.

34. McDowell Exhibits 125, 125A, 18 February 1949, MVWP.

35. MacGregor eventually married a man she had met in a local jail, but she continued to pursue lesbian relationships. McDowell Exhibits 126, 16A, 20 February 1949, MVWP.

36. McDowell Exhibits 125, 125A, 126, 126A, 129, 129A, 18 February 1949, MVWP.

37. Elliot E. McDowell to Miriam Van Waters, 28 July 1948, and Miriam Van

Waters, "Superintendent's Answers," 1 June 1948, MVWP; LoPresti quoted in "Sherborn Probe," *Boston Herald Traveller*, 9 June 1948; "Immorality Charged at Reformatory," *Boston Herald Traveller*, 13, 15 September 1948; *Boston Evening American*, 10 November 1948. On the cultural context for associating homosexuality with communism, see D'Emilio, *Sexual Politics, Sexual Communities*; and May, *Homeward Bound*.

38. Elliot E. McDowell to Miriam Van Waters, 7 January 1949, MVWP.

39. John O'Connor, "Van Waters Rejects Inmate Sex Charge," *Boston Herald*, 1 January 1949, 1.

40. For rumors about Van Waters's sexuality, see Miriam Van Waters to Ethel Sturges Dummer, 26 September 1948, Ethel Sturges Dummer Papers, Schlesinger Library, Radcliffe College, Cambridge, Mass.; and letter from former inmate to Miriam Van Waters, 1 June 1948, and Harry R. Archbald to Miriam Van Waters, 7 February 1949, MVWP.

41. Peg O'Keefe to Miriam Van Waters, 15 June 1949, MVWP.

42. A. Perry Holt Jr., Deputy Commissioner, to Commissioner Reuben L. Lurie, 21 May 1954, in "Escapes" Framingham, Human Services, Corrections, Commonwealth of Massachusetts Archives, Boston.

43. Commonwealth of Massachusetts, *Report of the Special Committee Authorized to Study the Reorganization of the Correctional System*, House Document No. 3015 (Boston, 1958), 12–13, 56–59, 60, in "Framingham" file, ibid.

44. "Remarks Made by Anne L. Clark, M.D., at Hodder Hall, Massachusetts Correctional Institution for Women, Framingham, Massachusetts, on Wednesday, May 13, 1959," 2–7, Massachusetts Society for Social Hygiene Papers, Schlesinger Library, Radcliffe College, Cambridge, Mass. I am grateful to Donna Penn for calling my attention to this document. On the segregation of lesbians in contemporary women's prisons, see Faith, *Unruly Women*, 216; and Robson, *Lesbian (Out)law*, 108.

45. On men's efforts to "reprivatize" women in the 1950s, see Wini Breines, *Young, White, and Miserable: Growing Up Female in the Fifties* (Boston: Beacon Press, 1992), 36. For alternative historical interpretations of women's lives in the 1950s, see Meyerowitz, *Not June Cleaver*.

46. On differential treatment of white and black unwed mothers, see Solinger, *Wake Up Little Susie*; and Regina Kunzel, *Fallen Women, Problem Girls: Unmarried Mothers and the Professionalization of Social Work, 1890–1945* (New Haven: Yale University Press, 1993). On bar dykes, see Davis and Kennedy, *Boots of Leather, Slippers of Gold*. For a discussion of lesbianism and women's sports, see Cahn, *Coming on Strong*, esp. chap. 7. At the same time, sterilization efforts in the South shifted their targets from white to black women. See Rebecca R. Lallier, "'A Place of Beginning Again': The North Carolina Industrial Farm Colony for Women, 1929–1947" (M.A. thesis, University of North Carolina, 1990). I am grateful to Susan K. Cahn for this reference.

47. On the persistence of class divisions among lesbians through the 1970s, see Faderman, *Surpassing the Love of Men*, chap. 7; Davis and Kennedy, *Boots of Leather, Slippers of Gold*, esp. 4, 138–45; Katie Gilmartin, "'The Very House of Difference': Intersections of Identities in the Life Histories of Colorado Lesbians, 1940–1965"

(Ph.D. diss., Yale University, 1995); and Susan Krieger, *The Mirror Dance: Identity in a Women's Community* (Philadelphia: Temple University Press, 1983), chap. 11.

48. Robson, *Lesbian (Out)law*, 109 – 10; Ruthann Robson, "Convictions: Theorizing Lesbians and Criminal Justice," in *Legal Inversions: Lesbians, Gay Men, and the Politics of Law*, edited by Didi Herman and Carol Stychin (Philadelphia: Temple University Press, 1995); Faith, *Unruly Women*, 216.

Chapter 9. The Burning of Letters Continues: Elusive Identities and the Historical Construction of Sexuality

I would like to thank Blanche Wiesen Cook and Darlene Clark Hine for their helpful comments on the original version of this essay, presented at the 1996 Berkshire Conference on the History of Women; the members of the 1996 graduate seminar on interdisciplinary feminist studies at Stanford and the graduate program in women's history at New York University for extremely stimulating discussions of the essay in progress; John D'Emilio, Lori Ginzberg, Susan Krieger, Joanne Meyerowitz, Leila Rupp, and Martha Vicinus for their insightful suggestions for revision; and Martha Mabie Gardner for her exceptional research assistance.

1. Miriam Van Waters Journal, 16, 19, 22 June 1948, Anne Gladding – Miriam Van Waters Papers, Schlesinger Library, Radcliffe College, Cambridge, Mass. (hereafter cited as Gladding-MVWP). A handful of surviving letters were scattered through Van Waters's correspondence in the papers she donated to the Schlesinger Library (Miriam Van Waters Papers, Schlesinger Library, Radcliffe College, Cambridge, Mass. [hereafter cited as MVWP]).

2. For a full account of her life, see Estelle B. Freedman, *Maternal Justice: Miriam Van Waters and the Female Reform Tradition* (Chicago: University of Chicago Press, 1996).

3. On nineteenth-century women's middle-class romantic friendships and their transformation in the twentieth century, see Carroll Smith-Rosenberg, "The Female World of Love and Ritual: Relations between Women in Nineteenth-Century America," *Signs: Journal of Women in Culture and Society* 1, no. 1 (Autumn 1975): 1 – 29; Nancy Sahli, "Smashing: Women's Relationships before the Fall," *Chrysalis* 8 (Summer 1979): 17 – 27; Lillian Faderman, *Surpassing the Love of Men: Romantic Friendship and Love between Women from the Renaissance to the Present* (New York: William Morrow, 1981); Blanche Cook, "Female Support Networks and Political Activism: Lillian Wald, Crystal Eastman, Emma Goldman," in *A Heritage of Her Own*, edited by Nancy F. Cott and Elizabeth H. Pleck (New York: Simon and Schuster, 1979), 412 – 44; Leila J. Rupp, "'Imagine My Surprise': Women's Relationships in Historical Perspective," *Frontiers* 5, no. 3 (1980): 61 – 70; and Lillian Faderman, *Odd Girls and Twilight Lovers: A History of Lesbian Life in Twentieth-Century America* (New York: Columbia University Press, 1991).

4. On the burning of other letters, see, for example, Susan Ware, "Unlocking the Porter-Dewson Partnership: A Challenge for the Feminist Biographer," in *The Challenge of Feminist Biography*, edited by Sara Alpern et al. (Urbana: University of Il-

linois Press, 1992); Annelise Orleck, *Common Sense and a Little Fire: Women and Working-Class Politics in the United States, 1900–1965* (Chapel Hill: University of North Carolina Press, 1995), 300; and Martha Freeman, ed., *Always, Rachel: The Letters of Rachel Carson and Dorothy Freeman, 1952–1964* (Boston: Beacon Press, 1995). The burning of parts of Alice Paul's letters was reported to me by Paul's grandniece, Eloise Lawrence. According to her grandchildren, Geraldine Thompson saved Miriam Van Waters's letters under her bed but destroyed them before her death (Geraldine Boone to author, 1989; Anne Bristow to author, 1989). According to Blanche Cook, all of Eleanor Roosevelt's friends burned their letters (Blanche Cook, comment on earlier version of this essay at the Berkshire Conference on the History of Women, University of North Carolina, Chapel Hill, 7 June 1996). On reading historical silences about sexuality, see Darlene Clark Hine, "Rape and the Inner Lives of Black Women in the Middle West: Preliminary Thoughts on the Culture of Dissemblance: Conference Report," *Signs: Journal of Women in Culture and Society* 14, no. 4 (1989): 912–20; and Elaine Sargent Apthorp, "Speaking of Silence: Willa Cather and the 'Problem' of Feminist Biography," *Women's Studies* 18, no. 1 (1990): 1–11.

5. Blanche Cook, "The Historical Denial of Lesbianism," *Radical History Review* 20 (Spring/Summer 1979): 60–65; Adrienne Rich, "Compulsory Heterosexuality and Lesbian Existence," *Signs: Journal of Women in Culture and Society* 5, no. 4 (1980): 631–60.

6. On the dilemma of resolving versus holding the tension between categories of race, gender, ethnicity, or sexuality—categories that we know to be constructed—without either denying the lived experience of identities or obliterating the political usefulness of these categories, see Stuart Hall, "Ethnicity: Identity and Difference," *Radical America* 23, no. 4 (1989): 9–20; Dana Takagi, "Maiden Voyage: Excursion into Sexuality and Identity Politics in Asian America," *Amerasia Journal* 20, no. 1 (1994): 1–17; and Earl Lewis, "To Turn As on a Pivot: Writing African Americans into a History of Overlapping Diasporas," *American Historical Review* 100, no. 3 (1995): 765–88.

7. See, for example, Joan Scott, "The Evidence of Experience," in *The Lesbian and Gay Studies Reader*, edited by Henry Abelove, Michele Aina Barale, and David M. Halperin (New York: Routledge, 1993), 397–415. For a useful summary and critique of these theories, see Martha Vicinus, "Introduction," in *Lesbian Subjects: A Feminist Studies Reader*, edited by Martha Vicinus (Bloomington: Indiana University Press, 1996), 1–12.

8. Mary McIntosh, "The Homosexual Role," *Social Problems* 16, no. 2 (Fall 1968): 182–92; John D'Emilio and Estelle B. Freedman, *Intimate Matters: A History of Sexuality in America*, rev. ed. (Chicago: University of Chicago Press, 1997). See also Jeffrey Weeks, *Coming Out: Homosexual Politics in Britain, from the Nineteenth Century to the Present* (London: Quartet, 1977); and John D'Emilio, "Capitalism and Gay Identity," in *Making Trouble: Essays on Gay History, Politics, and the University* (New York: Routledge, 1992), 3–16.

9. None of these forms of female relationships were strictly class-bound, for some middle-class women assumed male attire or male/female gender roles, while black

and working-class women also formed romantic friendships and shared households with other women. See, for example, Lisa Duggan, "The Trials of Alice Mitchell: Sensationalism, Sexology, and the Lesbian Subject in Turn-of-the-Century America," *Signs: Journal of Women in Culture and Society* 18, no. 4 (1993): 791–814; Karen V. Hansen, "'No Kisses Like Youres': An Erotic Friendship between Two African-American Women during the Mid-Nineteenth Century," *Gender and History* 7, no. 2 (1995): 153–82; and Joanne Meyerowitz, *Women Adrift: Independent Wage Earners in Chicago, 1880–1930* (Chicago: University of Chicago Press, 1988), 113–14. On the varieties of working-class lesbian history, see Jonathan Katz, ed., *Gay American History: Lesbians and Gay Men in the U.S.A.* (New York: Thomas Crowell, 1976), esp. 209–81; San Francisco Lesbian and Gay History Project, "'She Even Chewed Tobacco': A Pictorial Narrative of Passing Women in America," in *Hidden from History: Reclaiming the Gay and Lesbian Past*, edited by Martin Bauml Duberman, Martha Vicinus, and George Chauncey Jr. (New York: New American Library, 1989), 183–94; Eric Garber, "'T'Ain't Nobody's Bizness': Homosexuality in 1920s Harlem," in *Black Men/White Men*, edited by Michael J. Smith (San Francisco: Gay Sunshine Press, 1983); Allan Bérubé, *Coming Out under Fire: The History of Gay Men and Women in World War Two* (New York: Free Press, 1990); Madeline Davis and Elizabeth Lapovsky Kennedy, "Oral History and the Study of Sexuality in the Lesbian Community: Buffalo, New York, 1940–1960," *Feminist Studies* 12, no. 1 (Spring 1986): 7–26; Madeline Davis and Elizabeth Lapovsky Kennedy, *Boots of Leather, Slippers of Gold: The History of a Lesbian Community* (New York: Routledge, 1993); Katie Gilmartin, "'The Very House of Difference': Intersections of Identities in the Life Histories of Colorado Lesbians, 1940–1965" (Ph.D. diss., Yale University, 1995); and John D'Emilio, *Sexual Politics, Sexual Communities: The Making of a Homosexual Minority in the United States, 1940–1970* (Chicago: University of Chicago Press, 1983).

10. Estelle B. Freedman, "The Prison Lesbian: Race, Class, and the Construction of the Aggressive Female Homosexual, 1915–1965," *Feminist Studies* 22, no. 2 (Summer 1996): 397–423. On medical and psychiatric views of lesbianism, see George Chauncey Jr., "From Sexual Inversion to Homosexuality: Medicine and the Changing Conceptualization of Female Deviance," *Salmagundi* 58–59 (Fall 1982–Winter 1983): 114–46; and Jennifer Terry, "Lesbians under the Medical Gaze: Scientists Search for Remarkable Differences," *Journal of Sex Research* 27, no. 3 (August 1990): 317–39.

11. In this essay, I am concerned with women like Van Waters who rejected lesbian identity rather than with women who understood themselves to be lesbians but discreetly avoided the term. On the latter, see, for example, Elizabeth Lapovsky Kennedy, "'But We Would Never Talk about It': The Structures of Lesbian Discretion in South Dakota, 1928–1933," in *Inventing Lesbian Cultures in America*, edited by Ellen Lewin (Boston: Beacon Press, 1996), 15–39.

12. A notable exception is Helen Lefkowitz Horowitz's masterful treatment of multiple subjectivities in her biography, *The Power and Passion of M. Carey Thomas* (New York: Knopf, 1994).

13. Chauncey, "From Sexual Inversion to Homosexuality"; Carroll Smith-Rosenberg, *Disorderly Conduct: Visions of Gender in Victorian America* (New York: Knopf, 1985), 245–96; Esther Newton, "The Mythic Mannish Lesbian: Radclyffe Hall and the New Woman," *Signs: Journal of Women in Culture and Society* 9, no. 4 (1984): 557–75.

14. Horowitz, *Power and Passion*; Duggan, "Trials of Alice Mitchell."

15. Miriam Van Waters to her parents, 10 October 1911 (misdated, probably 9 October 1911), MVWP; Miriam Van Waters, "Topical Syllabus No. 44 (A) and No. 44 (B) [for teachers], Psychology of Adolescence," 15 November 1911, G. Stanley Hall Papers, Clark University, Worcester, Mass.

16. Miriam Van Waters, "The Adolescent Girl among Primitive People," *Journal of Religious Psychology*, pt. 1, 6, no. 4 (1913): 375–421 (esp. 377–78), and pt. 2, 7, no. 1 (1914): 75–120 (esp. 102–5). Her thesis adviser, Alexander Chamberlain, had been Franz Boas's first doctoral student at Clark.

17. Ibid., pt. 2, 108–12.

18. Miriam Van Waters, *Youth in Conflict* (New York: Republic Publishing Company, 1925), 35–36.

19. Elliot E. McDowell to Miriam Van Waters, 7 January 1949, MVWP.

20. John O'Connor, "Van Waters Rejects Inmate Sex Charge," *Boston Herald*, 1 January 1949, 1.

21. Miriam Van Waters, Boston University lecture transcript, 24 October 1951, in the possession of the author.

22. Rumors about Van Waters's sexuality are discussed in Miriam Van Waters to Ethel Sturges Dummer, 26 September 1948, Ethel Sturges Dummer Papers, Schlesinger Library, Radcliffe College, Cambridge, Mass.; and letter from former inmate to Miriam Van Waters, 1 June 1948, and Harry R. Archbald to Miriam Van Waters, 7 February 1949, MVWP. For a full discussion of Van Waters's interpretation of lesbian identity and the political response to rumors of her own homosexuality, see Freedman, *Maternal Justice*, esp. chaps. 9, 12, 14, 15.

23. Journal, 30 March 1929, Gladding-MVWP. Van Waters's phrasing suggests an ambivalence about the experience of marriage and reproductive, as opposed to social, motherhood: Gordon, she wrote, might have been "anything—everything in fact but a stupid wife and mother—Wife she co[uld] have been and mother too."

24. When I began my research, the Schlesinger Library inventory listed only twelve volumes of these journals, from 1932 to 1959, with several gaps between 1937 and 1938, 1939 and 1941, 1942 and 1945, and 1948 and 1951. Well into my first draft of the biography, a chance comment made by an archivist while I was arranging to deposit newly discovered materials alerted me to the fact that another box of her journals had never been inventoried because of a bureaucratic delay. In addition to the missing years, these journals included material from 1913–16 and 1927–30. I suspect that journals for intermediate years were lost when a fire destroyed Van Waters's residence in 1927.

25. See, for example, Geraldine Thompson to Miriam Van Waters, 31 October, 4, 14 November 1930, Gladding-MVWP.

26. Journal, 28 June 1928, Gladding-MVWP. Compare Hans Weiss's sweet memory of "what you did for me when you had the tremendous courage of giving yourself to me" (Hans Weiss to Miriam Van Waters, 24 July 1930, Gladding-MVWP).

27. Journal, 19 February, 14 June, 23 November 1928, and Hans Weiss to Miriam Van Waters, 7 August 1930, Gladding-MVWP. For complex reasons, Van Waters refused to consider marrying Weiss. Aside from the emotional distance she kept, the formal obstacle to their marriage was his "tremendous longing for a home and for children." He accepted "the cruel reality" that he could not have these with her, for like many professional women, she had chosen career over marriage. Although some women reformers did try to combine the two, having a job and children would have been too physically taxing for her and, given her history of tuberculosis, possibly life-threatening. See Hans Weiss to Van Waters, 19 January 1929, Gladding-MVWP.

28. Miriam Van Waters to Edna Mahan, 20 July 1930, Gladding-MVWP; Katherine B. Davis, *Factors in the Sex Life of Twenty-Two Hundred Women* (New York: Harper and Row, 1929), 312, 295, 280. The data showed that 28 percent of the women's college graduates and 20 percent of those from coeducational schools recognized sexual components in their relations; in addition, almost equal numbers had enjoyed intense emotional attachments that involved kissing and hugging.

29. Geraldine Thompson to Miriam Van Waters, 31 October, 10, 6 November 1930, and Journal, 27 September 1930, 11 June 1931, Gladding-MVWP. On self-discipline in women's erotic relationships, see Martha Vicinus, "Distance and Desire: English Boarding-School Friendships," *Signs: Journal of Women in Culture and Society* 9, no. 4 (1984): 600 – 622. On the erotic content of Van Waters's dreams, see *Maternal Justice*, chap. 12.

30. Journal, 27 September 1930, and Geraldine Thompson to Miriam Van Waters, 13 November 1930, Gladding-MVWP.

31. On Rorschach, see, for example, Inmate record, 21 February 1949, and Journal, 11 June 1938, 213v, Gladding-MVWP; and Journal, vol. 5, 26 June 1938, MVWP.

32. Eleanor Roosevelt letter, 19 December 1948; Geraldine Thompson to Dorothy Kirchwey Brown, 4 January 1949; and Eleanor Roosevelt to Geraldine Thompson, n.d., in response to enclosed letter from Thompson dated 5 January 1949, Eleanor Roosevelt Papers, Franklin D. Roosevelt Presidential Library, Hyde Park, N.Y.; Eleanor Roosevelt to Geraldine Thompson, 13 January 1949; Miriam Clark Nichols to Eleanor Roosevelt, 18 January 1949 (reprinted in *Civil Service Reporter*, 8 February 1949, 5); and George Hooper to Friends of Framingham, 1 January 1949, Friends of Framingham Papers, Schlesinger Library, Radcliffe College, Cambridge, Mass.

33. SAC, Boston (100-15782), to Director, FBI (100-206852), "Office Memorandum," Re: Helen Reid Bryan, 20 January 1954, declassified 12 April 1994 pursuant to Freedom of Information Act Request (emphasis in original).

34. Telephone interview with Geraldine Boone, 17 February 1995; Geraldine Boone to author, 6 March 1995. Although we disagreed on other points of interpretation of her grandmother, I gained invaluable insights from Boone's observations.

Chapter 10. When Historical Interpretation Meets Legal Advocacy: Abortion, Sodomy, and Same-Sex Marriage

1. "Historical Interpretation and Legal Advocacy: Rethinking the Webster Amicus Brief," *Public Historian* 12, no. 3 (Summer 1990): 27–32; "Boston Marriage, Free Love, and Fictive Kin: Historical Alternatives to Mainstream Marriage," *OAH Newsletter* 32 (August 2004): 1, 16.

2. On the role of historians as expert witnesses and amici curiae, on distinctions between "lawyers' history" and the use of historical scholarship, and for a review of the legal scholarship on uses of history, see Laura Kalman, *The Strange Career of Legal Liberalism* (New Haven: Yale University Press, 1996), esp. chaps. 5–7. On testimony by historians in *Brown v. Board of Education*, see Peter Novick, *That Noble Dream: The "Objectivity Question" and the American Historical Profession* (New York: Cambridge University Press, 1988), 507–8. On welfare reform, see Alice Kessler-Harris, Linda Kerber, et al., "Brief of Amici Curiae Women's History Scholars," *Nevada Department of Human Resources v. Hibbs*, 538 U.S. 721 (2003), no. 01-1368.

3. *EEOC v. Sears, Roebuck & Co.*, 628 F.Supp. 1264 (N.D. Ill. 1986), affirmed 839 F.2d 302 (7th Cir. 1988). Discussions of historians' conflicting testimony in the Sears case appear in Ruth Milkman, "Women's History and the Sears Case," *Feminist Studies* 12, no. 2 (Summer 1986): 375–400; Thomas Haskell and Sanford Levinson, "Academic Freedom and Expert Witnessing: Historians and the *Sears* Case," *Texas Law Review* 66 (June 1988): 1629–59; Alice Kessler-Harris, "Academic Freedom and Expert Witnessing: A Response to Haskell and Levinson," *Texas Law Review* 67 (December 1988): 429–40; and Novick, *That Noble Dream*, 502–10. On historians as expert witnesses, see Brian W. Martin, "Working with Lawyers: A Historian's Perspective," *OAH Newsletter* 30, no. 2 (May 2002): 1, 4, 6. For other examples of conflicting historical testimony by expert witnesses, in this case concerning Western cultural attitudes toward homosexuality, see Randall Baldwin Clark, "Platonic Love in a Colorado Courtroom: Martha Nussbaum, John Finnis, and Plato's *Laws* in *Evans v. Romer*," *Yale Journal of Law and the Humanities* 12, no. 1 (Winter 2000): 1–38.

4. Other scholars also contribute these briefs. See, for example, James R. Acker, "Social Science in Supreme Court Criminal Cases and Briefs: The Actual and Potential Contribution of Social Scientists as Amici Curiae," *Law and Human Behavior* 14, no. 1 (February 1990): 25–42. For overviews of the use of amicus briefs, see Samuel Krislov, "The Amicus Curiae Brief: From Friendship to Advocacy," *Yale Law Journal* 72, no. 4 (March 1963): 694–721; and Gregory A. Caldeira and John R. Wright, "Amici Curiae before the Supreme Court: Who Participates, When, and How Much?," *Journal of Politics* 52, no. 3 (August 1990): 782–806. In his book *Public Intellectuals* (Cambridge: Harvard University Press, 2001), Richard A. Posner is skeptical about the impact of scholarly briefs on judicial opinions (see chap. 10).

5. For the role of history in the debates over originalism, see Kalman, *Strange Career*, esp. chap. 5. American historians hold a range of opinions about the use of originalism in legal advocacy. For example, Kalman states elsewhere that "I find it sad to see anyone, especially historians, appealing to the Framers and deplore Americans' obsession with their intent. . . . Historians appreciate the pastness of

the past." In rejecting absolute, or hard, originalism, however, she acknowledges that she is not troubled by what she terms "sometime-originalism." See Laura Kalman, "The (Un?)Bearable Liteness of E-Mail: Historians, Impeachment, and Bush v. Gore," *Theoretical Inquiries in Law* 4 (July 2003): 592–93, 595. Constitutional historian Jack N. Rakove also expresses ambivalence about originalism when he criticizes its limitations but admits that "I happen to like originalist arguments when the weight of the evidence seems to support the constitutional outcomes I favor—and that may be as good a clue to the appeal of originalism as any other" (*Original Meanings: Politics and Ideas in the Making of the Constitution* [New York: Knopf, 1996], xv).

6. *Roe v. Wade*, 410 U.S. 113 (1973), 117.

7. Introduction to "Roundtable: Historians and the Webster Case," *Public Historian* 12, no. 3 (Summer 1990): 9–10; Sylvia Law, "Conversations between Historians and the Constitution," *Public Historian* 12, no. 3 (Summer 1990): 11–17. Law, Larson, and Spillenger later wrote a brief signed by 250 American historians in *Planned Parenthood v. Casey* (1991), another Supreme Court case concerning limitations on abortion rights.

8. "Brief of 281 American Historians As Amici Curiae Supporting Appellees," *Webster v. Reproductive Health Services*, no. 88-605 (1988), 2. Further page references are cited parenthetically in the text.

9. Barbara Babcock et al., *Sex Discrimination and the Law: History, Practice, and Theory*, 2d ed. (Boston: Little, Brown, 1996), 985.

10. Law, "Conversations between Historians and the Constitution," 14.

11. I first voiced these concerns publicly at a panel at the American Historical Association meeting in December 1989, at which James Mohr also commented. His reflections on the brief appear in "Historically Based Legal Briefs: Observations of a Participant in the *Webster* Process," *Public Historian* 12, no. 3 (Summer 1990): 19–26. Subsequent attacks on Mohr by opponents of abortion rights reveal the vulnerability of historians as legal advocates.

12. Meese quoted in Babcock et al., *Sex Discrimination*, 1007.

13. James C. Mohr, *Abortion in America: The Origins and Evolution of National Policy* (New York: Oxford University Press, 1978), chap. 4. For a more recent analysis of white women's desires for autonomy as a motive for limiting family size, see Susan E. Klepp, "Revolutionary Bodies: Women and the Fertility Transition in the Mid-Atlantic Region, 1760–1820," *Journal of American History* 85, no. 3 (December 1998): 910–45.

14. On the symbolic value of motherhood in the abortion debates, see Kristen Luker, *Abortion and the Politics of Motherhood* (Berkeley: University of California Press, 1984); and Faye Ginsburg, *Contested Lives: The Abortion Debate in an American Community* (Berkeley: University of California Press, 1989).

15. See Linda Gordon, "Why Nineteenth-Century Feminists Did Not Support 'Birth Control' and Twentieth-Century Feminists Do," in *Rethinking the Family: Some Feminist Questions*, edited by Barrie Thorne and Marilyn Yalom (New York: Longman, 1982), 40–53. The subsequent historians' brief in support of reproductive rights in *Planned Parenthood of Southeastern Pennsylvania et al. v. Robert P. Casey et*

al., 505 U.S. 833 (1992), did address nineteenth-century feminist opposition to abortion. See "Brief of 250 American Historians as Amici Curiae in Support of Planned Parenthood of Southeastern Pennsylvania" (submitted October 1991), ibid., 19.

16. On the critique of the constitutional and theoretical reliance on rights, see, for example, Kenneth Karst, "Woman's Constitution," *Duke Law Review* (1984): 447–95; Carol Pateman, *The Sexual Contract* (Stanford, Calif.: Stanford University Press, 1988); Rosalind Pollack Petchesky, "Reproductive Freedom: Beyond a Woman's 'Right to Choose,'" *Signs: Journal of Women in Culture and Society* 5, no. 4 (Summer 1980): 661–85; and Dorothy Roberts, *Killing the Black Body: Race, Reproduction, and the Meaning of Liberty* (New York: Pantheon Books, 1997).

17. "Brief of Professors of History George Chauncey et al. as *Amici Curiae* in Support of Petitioners," *Lawrence v. Texas*, 539 U.S. 558 (2003), 4. (The text of the brief can be found at ‹http://hnn.us/articles/1539.html›). The historians who signed the brief were George Chauncey, Nancy F. Cott, John D'Emilio, Estelle B. Freedman, Thomas C. Holt, John Howard, Lynn Hunt, Mark D. Jordan, Elizabeth Lapovsky Kennedy, and Linda Kerber. Further page references are cited parenthetically in the text.

18. George Chauncey to Estelle Freedman, e-mail, 11 January 2003.

19. The Cato Institute amicus brief did raise this line of argument. Historical evidence from New York City reveals that most sodomy charges in the late nineteenth century involved acts with boys less than eighteen years of age. See Stephen Robertson, *Crimes against Children: Sexual Violence and Legal Culture in New York City, 1880–1960* (Chapel Hill: University of North Carolina Press, 2005), 59.

20. For the decision, see ‹http://www.supremecourtus.gov/opinions/02pdf/02-102.pdf›. Page references are cited parenthetically in the text.

21. Nancy Cott, "Constituting Marriage," paper presented at the Thirteenth Berkshire Conference on the History of Women, Scripps College, Claremont, Calif., 3 June 2005. Cott points out that individual historians have testified in opposition to gay marriage. To the best of my knowledge, however, amicus briefs drafted and signed by groups of historians have been filed in support of but not in opposition to the right to same-sex marriage.

22. Evelyn Blackwood, "Sexuality and Gender in Certain Native American Tribes: The Case of Cross-Gender Females," *Signs: Journal of Women in Culture and Society* 10, no. 1 (Autumn 1984): 31–34.

23. Jonathan Katz, ed., *Gay American History: Lesbians and Gay Men in the U.S.A.* (New York: Thomas Crowell, 1976); Diane Wood Middlebrook, *Suits Me: The Double Life of Billy Tipton* (Boston: Houghton Mifflin, 1998). For a visual survey of what Katz termed "passing women," see the video *She Even Chewed Tobacco*, available from Women Make Movies (‹www.wmm.com›); and San Francisco Lesbian and Gay History Project, "'She Even Chewed Tobacco': A Pictorial Narrative of Passing Women in America," in *Hidden from History: Reclaiming the Gay and Lesbian Past*, edited by Martin Bauml Duberman, Martha Vicinus, and George Chauncey Jr. (New York: New American Library, 1989), 183–94.

24. Lillian Faderman, *Surpassing the Love of Men: Romantic Friendship and Love between Women from the Renaissance to the Present* (New York: William Morrow, 1981), 190–203.

25. Jonathan Ned Katz, *Love Stories: Sex between Men before Homosexuality* (Chicago: University of Chicago Press, 2001); Lillian Faderman, *Odd Girls and Twilight Lovers: A History of Lesbian Life in Twentieth-Century America* (New York: Columbia University Press, 1991), 73; The History Project, *Improper Bostonians: Lesbian and Gay History from the Puritans to Playland* (Boston: Beacon Press, 1998).

26. Nancy Cott, *Public Vows: A History of Marriage and the Nation* (Cambridge: Harvard University Press, 2000); Hendrik Hartog, *Man and Wife in America: A History* (Cambridge: Harvard University Press, 2000).

27. John D'Emilio and Estelle B. Freedman, *Intimate Matters: A History of Sexuality in America* (New York: Harper and Row, 1988), chap. 7; Hal Sears, *The Sex Radicals: Free Love in High Victorian America* (Lawrence, Kans.: Regents Press, 1977), 89–96. Walker and Harmon lost their appeal and served six months in jail.

28. Hendrik Hartog, "What Gay Marriage Teaches about the History of Marriage," *History Network News*, 5 April 2004 (‹http://www.hnn.us/articles/4400.html›). On trends toward heterosexual marriages that do not include reproduction, see Elaine Tyler May, *Barren in the Promised Land: Childless Americans and the Pursuit of Happiness* (New York: Basic Books, 1995).

29. "Brief *Amici Curiae* on Behalf of History Scholars," *Heather Andersen et al. v. King County*, Supreme Court of the State of Washington, no. 75934-1, 75956-1 (2005), 1.

30. "Brief of Professors of History and Family Law as *Amici Curiae* in Support of Plaintiffs-Appellants in *Samuels et al. v. New York State Department of Health and the State of New York*," New York Supreme Court, Appellate Division, Third Department, no. 98084 (2005), 1, 3–9, 13–14; "Brief of Professors of History and Family Law as *Amici Curiae* in Support of Plaintiffs-Respondents in *Hernandez et al. v. Robles*," New York Supreme Court, Appellate Division, First Department, no. 103434/04 (2005). These briefs were initially drafted by attorney Suzanne Goldberg and circulated to a dozen history and family law professors whose comments led to revisions and refinements of the arguments. Other examples of changing marital laws in these briefs include interspousal immunity, spousal testimonial privilege, and child custody. Nancy Cott further contends that marriage has been transformed by contemporary gender roles into an institution "in which the gender of the spouses is immaterial to their legal obligations" ("Constituting Marriage," 5).

31. *Goodridge v. Department of Public Health*, 798 N.E.2d 941 (Mass. 2003), 36–37.

32. "Brief of *Amici Curiae* on Behalf of History Scholars, *Heather Andersen et al. v. King County*," Supreme Court of the State of Washington, no. 75934-1, 75956-1 (2005), 17–18.

33. On gay parenting, see Daniel Rivers, "'The Best Interests of the Child': Lesbian and Gay Custody Cases and Parental Rights Activists Organizations, 1967–78," paper presented at the American Historical Association, Washington, D.C., 10 January 2004; Ellen Herman, personal correspondence, 28 April 2004.

34. On early cases, see David L. Chambers, "Couples: Marriage, Civil Union, and Domestic Partnership," in *Creating Change: Sexuality, Public Policy, and Civil Rights*, edited by John D'Emilio, William B. Turner, and Urvashi Vaid (New York: St. Martin's Press, 2000), 281–304.

35. On conflicting views, see Gust A. Yep, Karen E. Lovaas, and John P. Elia, "A Critical Appraisal of Assimilationist and Radical Ideologies Underlying Same-Sex Marriage in LGBT Communities in the United States," *Journal of Homosexuality* 45, no. 1 (2000): 45–64.

36. Lisa Duggan, "Holy Matrimony!," *Nation*, 5 March 2004, 14–19; Lisa Duggan and Richard Kim, "Beyond Gay Marriage," *Nation*, 18 July 2005, 24–27. See also Alexander Cockburn, "Gay Marriage: Sidestep on Freedom's Path," *Nation*, 5 April 2004, 9. A forum of conflicting views appeared in "State of the Union: The Marriage Issue," *Nation*, 5 July 2004, 15–46.

37. On interracial marriage, see Peggy Pascoe, "Why the Ugly Rhetoric against Gay Marriage Is Familiar to This Historian of Miscegenation," *History Network News*, 19 April 2004 (‹http://hnn.us/articles/4708.html›). On civil rights leaders and interracial marriage, see Renee Romano, *Race Mixing: Black-White Marriage in Post War America* (Cambridge: Harvard University Press, 2003).

38. "Brief of Professors of History . . . in *Hernandez et al. v. Robles*," 3 (n. 1).

39. Superior Court of the State of California, County of San Francisco, Coordination Proceeding, Special Title [Rule 1550], Judicial Council Coordination Proceeding no. 4365, Tentative Decision on Applications for Writ of Mandate and Motions for Summary Judgment, 14 March 2005, 6–7.

Index

LaGuardia, Fiorello, 130
Lambda Legal Defense, 183, 193
Lamphere, Louise, 60
Lang, Fritz, 121
Langley Porter Clinic, 135
Larson, Jane, 178
Las Madres del Plaza de Mayo (The Mothers of the Plaza de Mayo), 103
Lathrop, Julia, 28, 37, 38, 50, 51, 53, 55
Law, Sylvia, 177 – 78
Lawrence v. Texas (2003), 18, 183 – 86, 187, 189, 193, 194, 195
Lazarus, Marx Edgeworth, 189
League of Women Voters, 32, 40, 47, 52, 54
Legal arguments: historical interpretations of, 17 – 18, 175 – 77, 194 – 95; and same-sex marriage, 18, 176, 187 – 94, 195, 238 (n. 21); and sodomy, 18, 176, 183 – 86, 187, 189, 193, 194, 195; and reproductive rights, 177 – 83
Leisure culture, 113, 114
LePen, Jean-Marie, 102
Lerner, Gerda, 11
Lesbian feminism, 34, 41
Lesbian history, 15, 16
Lesbian identity: and working-class women, 142, 147, 149, 163, 171, 172; and Van Waters, 159; assumptions about, 161; and African American women, 171, 189
Lesbianism: conscious choice of, 7; criminalization of, 15; racial meanings of, 17; and stigmatization of, 17, 160; defined as sexual perversion, 41; and working women, 50; and McCarthy era, 51, 52; and white middle-class women, 52, 157, 158, 163; and female institution building, 54; students' fear of, 70 – 71, 77; feminism associated with, 77, 80; and right to parent, 100, 192; women's prisons associated with, 141; and Cold War, 148; Van Waters's resistance to lesbian label, 154 – 55, 157,

165, 166, 167, 172, 173, 233 (n. 11); crime and insanity associated with, 164, 223 (n. 1). *See also* Prison lesbians
Lesbian separatism, 11
Lesbian subcultures, 41, 116, 137, 142, 146, 147, 151, 185, 188. *See also* Prison lesbians
Lewis, Earl, 162
Liberal feminism, 93, 94
Lobdell, Joseph, 112, 188
Lobdell, Lucy Ann, 112, 113, 188
LoPresti, Michael, 154
Lorde, Audre, 96, 228 (n. 23)
Lorre, Peter, 121
Los Angeles Business Women's Club, 44
Loving v. Virginia (1967), 191, 193
Lunbeck, Elizabeth, 145
Lyon, Mary, 27
Lyon, Phyllis, 117

Mahon, Edna, 51
Male abolitionists, 25
Male sexual crime: feminist analysis of, 16
Mann Act, 123
Marriage: and reproductive sexuality, 109; Boston marriages, 114, 118, 149, 163, 188; companionate marriage, 123, 191. *See also* Same-sex marriage
Martin, Del, 117
Masculinity, 126
Massachusetts State Reformatory for Women: and Van Waters, 13, 42, 44 – 46, 151, 159, 166; and prison lesbians, 142, 151 – 56
Maternalism, 40, 90, 91, 93, 94, 103
Matthiessen, Francis, 115, 188
May, Elaine Tyler, 9
McCarthyism, 51, 52, 156, 160
McIntosh, Mary, 162
Mead, Margaret, 147, 227 (n. 19)
Meese, Edwin, 179
Melman, Seymour, 197 (n. 4)
Men: and same-gender relationships,

Southern History across the Color Line, by Nell Irvin Painter (2002).

The Artistry of Anger: Black and White Women's Literature in America, 1820–1860, by Linda M. Grasso (2002).

Too Much to Ask: Black Women in the Era of Integration, by Elizabeth Higginbotham (2001).

Imagining Medea: Rhodessa Jones and Theater for Incarcerated Women, by Rena Fraden (2001).

Painting Professionals: Women Artists and the Development of Modern American Art, 1870–1920, by Kirsten Swinth (2001).

Remaking Respectability: African American Women in Interwar Detroit, by Victoria W. Wolcott (2001).

Ida B. Wells-Barnett and American Reform, 1880–1930, by Patricia A. Schechter (2001).

Taking Haiti: Military Occupation and the Culture of U.S. Imperialism, 1915–1940, by Mary A. Renda (2001).

Before Jim Crow: The Politics of Race in Postemancipation Virginia, by Jane Dailey (2000).

Captain Ahab Had a Wife: New England Women and the Whalefishery, 1720–1870, by Lisa Norling (2000).

Civilizing Capitalism: The National Consumers' League, Women's Activism, and Labor Standards in the New Deal Era, by Landon R. Y. Storrs (2000).

Rank Ladies: Gender and Cultural Hierarchy in American Vaudeville, by M. Alison Kibler (1999).

Strangers and Pilgrims: Female Preaching in America, 1740–1845, by Catherine A. Brekus (1998).

Sex and Citizenship in Antebellum America, by Nancy Isenberg (1998).

Yours in Sisterhood: Ms. Magazine and the Promise of Popular Feminism, by Amy Erdman Farrell (1998).

We Mean to Be Counted: White Women and Politics in Antebellum Virginia, by Elizabeth R. Varon (1998).

Women Against the Good War: Conscientious Objection and Gender on the American Home Front, 1941–1947, by Rachel Waltner Goossen (1997).

Toward an Intellectual History of Women: Essays by Linda K. Kerber (1997).

Gender and Jim Crow: Women and the Politics of White Supremacy in North Carolina, 1896–1920, by Glenda Elizabeth Gilmore (1996).

Delinquent Daughters: Protecting and Policing Adolescent Female Sexuality in the United States, 1885–1920, by Mary E. Odem (1995).

U.S. History as Women's History: New Feminist Essays, edited by Linda K. Kerber, Alice Kessler-Harris, and Kathryn Kish Sklar (1995).

Common Sense and a Little Fire: Women and Working-Class Politics in the United States, 1900–1965, by Annelise Orleck (1995).

How Am I to Be Heard?: Letters of Lillian Smith, edited by Margaret Rose Gladney (1993).

Entitled to Power: Farm Women and Technology, 1913–1963, by Katherine Jellison (1993).

Revising Life: Sylvia Plath's Ariel Poems, by Susan R. Van Dyne (1993).

Made from This Earth: American Women and Nature, by Vera Norwood (1993).

Unruly Women: The Politics of Social and Sexual Control in the Old South, by Victoria E. Bynum (1992).

The Work of Self-Representation: Lyric Poetry in Colonial New England, by Ivy Schweitzer (1991).

Labor and Desire: Women's Revolutionary Fiction in Depression America, by Paula Rabinowitz (1991).

Community of Suffering and Struggle: Women, Men, and the Labor Movement in Minneapolis, 1915–1945, by Elizabeth Faue (1991).

All That Hollywood Allows: Re-reading Gender in 1950s Melodrama, by Jackie Byars (1991).

Doing Literary Business: American Women Writers in the Nineteenth Century, by Susan Coultrap-McQuin (1990).

Ladies, Women, and Wenches: Choice and Constraint in Antebellum Charleston and Boston, by Jane H. Pease and William H. Pease (1990).

The Secret Eye: The Journal of Ella Gertrude Clanton Thomas, 1848–1889, edited by Virginia Ingraham Burr, with an introduction by Nell Irvin Painter (1990).

Second Stories: The Politics of Language, Form, and Gender in Early American Fictions, by Cynthia S. Jordan (1989).

Within the Plantation Household: Black and White Women of the Old South, by Elizabeth Fox-Genovese (1988).

The Limits of Sisterhood: The Beecher Sisters on Women's Rights and Woman's Sphere, by Jeanne Boydston, Mary Kelley, and Anne Margolis (1988).